DARK

Love, Murder, and Revenge in 1930s' Kentucky

HIGHWAY

DARK

Love, Murder, and Revenge in 1930s' Kentucky

HIGHWAY

Dear Karen,

Best wishes always!

Ann DAngelo

Aug. 19, 2016

ANN DANGELO

This is a work of nonfiction. It is based on years of meticulous research that includes the close examination of trial transcripts, attorneys' letters, newspaper accounts, and other documentation, as well as interviews with Taylor and Denhardt family members. The observations and conclusions expressed in this volume are the author's alone.

ISBN 978-1-941953-32-7

Printed in the United States of America

Published by:

Butler Books
P.O. Box 7311
Louisville, KY 40257
phone: (502) 897-9393
fax: (502) 897-9797
www.butlerbooks.com

This book is dedicated to Dr. Elissa May Plattner,
and to my daughters Kelly and Linton.

CONTENTS

PART III SHELBYVILLE

INTRODUCTION

In the final months of 1936 and throughout most of 1937, Kentuckians were riveted by a tragic drama playing out in three adjoining Kentucky counties: Henry, Oldham, and Shelby. The death of an Oldham County woman, Verna Garr Taylor, and the subsequent murder trial of her fiancé, Kentucky politician and brigadier general Henry Denhardt, mesmerized the reading public, both locally and on a national scale.

The small-town tale of a mysterious death had all the scandalous and lurid elements needed to capture the imagination of the 1930s' reading public—a beautiful woman brutally shot to death, a powerful politician suspected of her murder, and a sensational trial to determine his guilt or innocence. The story made its debut in the *New York Times* on November 8, 1936, two days after Verna Taylor's death. More coverage quickly appeared in *Time*, *Newsweek*, and *Life* magazines. Daily newspapers from coast to coast reported the latest news on the murder case for nearly a year. For quiet Kentucky, rarely in the spotlight, the continuous national news coverage over such a long time was unprecedented. Not since 1925, when Floyd Collins was trapped in a cave, had a Kentucky story merited such protracted national attention. The attempts to save Collins, a trapped spelunker, captured the nation's imagination for nearly three weeks in 1925. Ironically, General Henry Denhardt was a major player in that tragedy, too.

In 1936, Kentucky was a rural, farming state that depended on growing tobacco, producing excellent bourbon, and breeding a yearly crop of fine thoroughbred racehorses. Its people were grounded in traditional values, strong family ties, and religion. Time generally passed with few sensational events that the world outside the state would consider newsworthy. But the latter part of 1936—and the year 1937—would be different.

During the murder trial of Denhardt and the later trial of the Garr brothers, Kentucky was on center stage, and its rural way of life and its citizens were under intense scrutiny. The often-predatory "big city" reporters, looking for a scandalous and titillating news story, descended on rural Kentucky with the fervor of bloodhounds. The reporters brought with them preconceived ideas of what the state and its citizens were like, and they incorporated those unflattering notions into the articles they wrote. Even the venerable brick courthouse in New Castle received criticism. The *Associated Press* described it as "weather rotted" and "worn," while *Newsweek* reported that chunks of the ceiling fell during Denhardt's trial, but the large crowd in attendance did not move.[1] The locals were widely portrayed as simple country people, farmers and their wives who left the spring plowing and planting to witness the trial of a former lieutenant governor accused of murder. But as it turned out, the stereotypes they published of gun-toting citizens and frontier retribution were not so far removed from the truth. In the case of Henry Denhardt, people eventually discovered that while they outwardly considered themselves law-abiding with a belief in legal justice for the accused, they also quietly supported taking the law into their own hands if they believed it was justified.

On the morning of November 6, 1936—when Brigadier General Henry Denhardt and Verna Garr Taylor left LaGrange on a day trip—Denhardt was a controversial political figure, but his legacy was fairly secure. By the time he closed the door of his home behind him that night, the reputation and persona he had spent a lifetime creating had vanished. After Taylor's death, Denhardt was popularly viewed as a black-hearted villain. If he was ever kind, loving, or considerate, there is no mention of it anywhere. Almost overnight, he had become the man Kentuckians loved to hate, and the newspapers of the time obliged by painting him in the worst possible light. William Shakespeare could have penned his phrase from *Julius Caesar* for Henry Denhardt: "The evil that men do lives after them; the good is oft interred with their bones."[2] If Henry Denhardt had any good deeds associated with his name, they were forgotten after the death of Verna Taylor. Today he is not remembered as a man with serious aspirations to the governorship of Kentucky. If he is remembered at all, it is for the final disastrous year of his life.

I am often asked how I became interested in this tragic story. I remember reading with great interest a local magazine article in 2007 marking the seventieth year of Denhardt's murder. I must have stored it away in my mind because a couple of years later, it came rushing back with a vengeance. In September 2009, another prominent Kentucky politician named Steve Nunn was accused of murdering his ex-fiancée. That tragedy triggered my memory of the previous murder; I suddenly had to know more about what happened in 1936. The story of Verna Garr Taylor and Henry Denhardt gripped me and held me in its clutches as tightly as it did people in the 1930s. I found the story compelling and haunting; its issues of domestic violence, justice, and revenge were universal and just as important today as they were then.

In the past, the focus of the story had been on the downfall of the distinguished General Denhardt. But I discovered that Verna Garr Taylor was just as remarkable a person as Denhardt. She did not run for public office or command troops in a world war as Denhardt had done, but she was a very unusual woman for the 1930s. Her abilities as a businesswoman during the worst economic time in American history have largely been overlooked. At the time, society did not routinely recognize the ability of a woman to operate a successful business, support her household, and raise children by herself as a widow. In news coverage, Verna Taylor became merely the victim whose death led to Denhardt's fall. Yet both Verna Garr Taylor and Henry Denhardt were remarkable, unusual people.

In writing this book, I learned firsthand how violent crime can continue to haunt a family for generations. Some of Verna Taylor's direct descendants were hesitant to speak of their family's tragedy. After meeting them, I recognized in their attitudes my own mother and grandmother, women who did not speak about family problems and took most of their secrets to the grave. Typical Kentuckians—proud and private—Verna's family members remain anonymous sources for this book. There is no doubt that the murder of Verna Garr Taylor and the spectacular fallout from her death changed the dynamic of her family forever.

Descendants of the Denhardt family were more matter-of-fact. Denhardt left no children to contend with his mixed legacy, so there are only collateral descendants. They were delightful to interview, and for them 1937 was a long time ago. While Denhardt's family remains uncertain of his guilt or innocence, the shock waves from his trial and ignominious death were felt throughout his immediate and extended family. Before 1936, Denhardt was a source of family pride, a war hero and successful politician. After his death, he became the relative that no one wanted to discuss. He died a disgraceful death for someone who had once played an important role in Kentucky politics. His final self-destructive year is a tragedy that Aeschylus, Euripides, or Shakespeare would recognize. I have done my best to be fair to the general, even when it was hard.

If the crime had occurred today, the case would probably have been solved using modern forensics and crime scene investigation techniques. The general, of course, would have been referred to as the "alleged murderer." He was at the scene with the victim and had a motive. As attorney Ralph Gilbert said during his defense of the Garr brothers, "Whether or not General Denhardt killed their sister in cold blood, the facts are she was in his presence when she came to a horrible death."[3]

In researching this book, I found that most people accept the prosecution's version of events—Verna spurned Denhardt and he chased her down a dark highway and shot her. For months, I tried to make the facts fit the theory. Denhardt was probably guilty, but I do not think it happened in the way we have been led to believe.

After so many years, the physical evidence and exhibits from Denhardt's April 1937 trial have disappeared. Somewhere out there is a .45 caliber revolver that once belonged to Henry Denhardt. I was able to handle an exact replica of the revolver, thanks to staff at the Kentucky Military History Museum. The 1917 officer's revolver is heavy and unwieldy, measuring a foot in length from the grip to the end of the steel barrel. It is hardly a weapon that a woman could turn on herself with one hand, as Denhardt claimed Verna had done.

The most important items still in existence from 1936 and 1937 are the court transcripts. Without them, I would have been left with only the newspaper accounts, which were sometimes inaccurate and exaggerated.

When I could not locate a transcript from the murder trial of the Garr brothers, I used testimony from their examining trial, along with newspaper accounts to recreate key elements of the murder trial.

When I was very young, my grandmother would turn to me on rainy summer days and ask how I wanted to spend my time. I would invariably reply, "Let's go exploring in the attic." In the attic of the nineteenth-century home where I grew up, there were always undiscovered treasures—yellowed documents, aging clothes from another time, personal items left behind from family members I never knew.

During the years I've spent researching and writing about the tragically intertwined lives of Verna Garr Taylor and Henry Denhardt, I've remembered those rainy summer days many times. Digging into the fact and fiction surrounding this case has been an opportunity to "go exploring in the attic" as an adult. For that reason alone, this story has been an unexpected gift, but it has not been without its challenges.

My manuscript was complete and in the hands of my editor when I located an astonishing document. Henry Denhardt had either dictated or written it a month before his trial, and it revealed what John Berry mysteriously referred to as the "secret angle" or the "dangerous element" of the case. The most daunting challenge as a researcher was attempting to sort truth from fiction in the thirty-three-page document. Some of the accusations made by Denhardt are so detailed and specific that they have the ring of truth, while other allegations make no sense. The document confirmed one of my suspicions in the murder case, but also offered a look into the mind of a once-capable and intelligent man descending into madness.

The memorandum had been stored in Berry's office files for seventy-eight years. At Berry's request, Denhardt's allegations were never revealed in past articles written about the murder case. The document has now been released to the Filson Historical Society in Louisville along with the rest of Berry's files. The time has come to thoroughly examine the case against General Denhardt from all possible angles.

In writing this book, I made a promise to Verna's descendants that I have tried very hard to keep. Much has been written that is exaggerated or blatantly untrue, and I promised to keep as close to the facts as humanly possible. There is no need to sensationalize this story or make it more fantastic. It is one of those stories where the truth is just as amazing as fiction. I have simply been the mechanism by which it has been told.

Like many others who spend untold hours researching and writing about a group of people long dead, I have come to know and appreciate them as more than just names from Kentucky history or players in a tragic drama. I am thankful to each of them for sharing their lives and giving me this story to write.

Part I

LAGRANGE

"Verna Garr Taylor was a woman of unusual ability,
unusual personality; a friendly, vivacious, loveable, and
companionable person . . . and she endeared herself to
everybody who knew her in the community where she
lived and those with whom she came in contact."

—

H. B. Kinsolving
opening argument, April 23, 1937

Chapter 1

A MYSTERIOUS DEATH, NOVEMBER 6, 1936

Funeral director W. S. "Smith" Keightley had just turned on his favorite radio show and settled into a comfortable chair. The evening of November 6, 1936, had been quiet at the McCarty-Ricketts Funeral Home in LaGrange, Kentucky, until the phone rang at about ten o'clock.

Keightley was always on duty and urgent phone calls were part of his job. In a busy town where the trains rolled through the heart of the business district, thirty-eight-year-old Keightley was always prepared for the call that meant someone had died and his services were needed. The passing trains claimed their victims, as did disease, old age, or automobile accidents. Death came for the elderly members of his community as a long-expected visitor, and sometimes it ambushed the young and unsuspecting. But death was Keightley's business, and over the years, he had learned to accept its presence and his role as a funeral director and embalmer.

When the telephone rang that Friday night, it was safe for Keightley to assume that this was an ordinary death call and someone in LaGrange had passed away. But the call was far from ordinary.

Keightley answered the phone. The local barber was on the other end of the line and he sounded excited and nervous.

"Mr. Keightley, this is J. B. Hundley, and you've got to come with me right away. There's a woman dead in a ditch with a bullet wound. She's six miles outside of town just over the Henry County line."

Hundley claimed that the dead woman was LaGrange resident Verna Garr Taylor. Hundley seemed sober and swore he had seen the body, but respectable residents of quiet LaGrange, especially women, did not die from gunshot wounds.

In 1936, the small town of LaGrange in Oldham County, Kentucky, was 109 years old. It was the quintessential small Kentucky town where people sat on their porches on summer nights, watching the lightning bugs and visiting with neighbors.

The town had a hotel, a barbershop, a bank, dry good stores, two undertaking establishments, several physicians and attorneys, and a small group of businesses that were lucky to survive the hardest years of the Depression. The stores on Main Street stayed busy with shoppers and people-watchers on Saturday nights. Local teens congregated downtown at Mary D's, a sweetshop that also served soup and sandwiches. Five cents would buy a ticket to a movie at the Griffith Theater, named for director D. W. Griffith, the town's famous part-time citizen. Horses and buggies shared the dirt streets with automobiles, and the railroad tracks that caused LaGrange to boom in the 1850s divided the heart of downtown like a jagged row of stitches. Trains rumbled past the shoppers and the tall nineteenth- and early twentieth-century brick buildings along Main Street.

In the afternoons, old men sat on wooden benches and gossiped and whittled while children played games after school on the courthouse lawn. In July, the children carried their pails to the large blackberry patches on the Taylor farm, just beyond the home of Verna Garr Taylor on Fourth Avenue. In late October, the whole town turned out for the annual Halloween party at the school. LaGrange was peaceful, and in many ways, idyllic.[4]

All the longtime residents knew one another. Keightley and his wife, Marguerite, had known Verna Taylor for years. She was a devoted member of the LaGrange Methodist Church, a well-liked and beautiful widow with two teenage daughters. She owned and operated the successful Community Laundry. Forty-year-old Verna Garr Taylor was surely one of the least likely people in town to die from a gunshot wound.

If Hundley was telling the truth, this was a coroner's case. Before Keightley left the funeral home, he called Henry County Coroner Dillard "D. L." Ricketts and told him there was a woman's body in the ditch off Highway 22 near George Baker's farm. Keightley did not call Verna Taylor's family before he left LaGrange; he had to see the body for himself before he could believe the story. He started up his funeral ambulance, lights flashing on top, and drove by the garage of a local car company to pick up J. B. Hundley. With Hundley in the passenger seat beside him, Keightley set off to discover what in the world was going on six miles outside of LaGrange.

Two-lane Highway 22 wound east from LaGrange toward Henry County through farm country. Keightley drove on the narrow road through the pitch black of a moonless night, lit by only the ambulance's headlights and light reflecting from kerosene lanterns in the windows of an occasional farmhouse. The temperature was close to freezing, and a rain earlier in the evening had left the roadway wet but not frozen.

Two days earlier, an unseasonable snowstorm of surprising ferocity had swept across Kentucky. In the north central part of the state, the three counties of Oldham, Henry, and Shelby were hit especially hard. The heavy snowfall downed telegraph lines, snapped tree limbs, and toppled large trees, many still bearing the scarlet, orange, and yellow leaves of autumn. Crews of men worked long hours to clear the highways of broken limbs, repair lines, and restore power in the areas where electricity was available. But by Friday, the roads were clear, and the snow had turned to a gray November rain. In the fields beside Highway 22, the remaining patches of snow glowed ghostlike, reflecting the light from Keightley's vehicle.

When Keightley slowed the ambulance as he approached the farm, his headlights illuminated three men standing by a car at the end of a dirt-and-gravel driveway that led to a small white farmhouse. The men were George Baker, the owner of the farm; C. E. "Cuba" Shaver, a LaGrange automobile mechanic; and Brigadier General Henry Denhardt, a prominent state politician who had recently retired from public life and purchased a large Oldham County farm. It was common knowledge around LaGrange that Denhardt had been courting Verna Taylor for several months.

Keightley stopped his ambulance near the men, and Denhardt climbed into the seat beside him while Shaver, Baker, and Hundley rode the short distance on the running board. They signaled for him to stop where the sunken roadbed running parallel to the highway widened at the corner of Baker's property. As Denhardt opened the car door, he abruptly turned to Keightley and said, "You know I couldn't have killed her. I loved her too much."[5]

By the amber glow of the lanterns and flashlights, Keightley could see the body of a woman in the dark void beyond the edge of the highway. Hundley was right, it was Verna Garr Taylor. A single bullet hole had pierced her dress over her left breast, but had not punctured the front of a stylish black coat that lay unbuttoned and thrown open to the cold. Her hips lay in the swag of the muddy ditch with her head facing south and her feet toward the north near the bottom of the old roadbed. One shoe was on her foot, and the other was positioned between her outstretched arm and body. Her left hand tightly clasped one glove; the other glove was discarded in the mud beside her feet. A large army pistol lay approximately four feet away on the side of the embankment. Even for a man who lived daily with death in all its forms, the shattered body—discarded like a child's ragdoll in the snow and mud of the ditch—was a shock.

Saying little to the men, Keightley climbed slowly up the bank and walked over to his vehicle to retrieve a sheet and pillow. He gently placed the pillow under Verna's head and covered her body with the sheet. The general's voice broke the stillness of the eerie scene from where he stood near the ambulance. "Is there a ring on her hand? She had it on this afternoon."

Keightley lifted the limp hand clutching a glove and could see the glitter of an expensive diamond ring. "Yes, it's here," called Keightley, puzzled that Denhardt was interested in a piece of jewelry at such a time.

"Take care of the ring, Keightley," said Denhardt.[6] He explained that the couple had argued during the day and Verna had given the ring back to him. At his insistence, she took the ring back and placed it on her hand. The general also confirmed that the pistol near Verna's body belonged to him. Other than covering the body, Keightley left the scene undisturbed for Coroner Ricketts.

Keightley invited the general to sit with him in his vehicle out of the cold while they waited. Denhardt was tall and broad-shouldered, a heavy man who filled the passenger side of the ambulance with both his physical bulk and imposing presence. He was nervous, but there were none of the usual signs of a man who had just suffered a tremendous loss. There were no exclamations of disbelief—"I can't believe this has happened!"—no signs of grief or remorse—"I don't know how I will go on without her. Why didn't I see this coming?" There were no tears, and Denhardt did not express any regrets for the death of the woman he said was his fiancée. His first concern that night was for Verna's three brothers. Keightley later recalled, "He asked me what attitude would the Garr boys have on finding her dead in his presence, and shot, and asked me if he should go home with the body or go to the farm."[7]

Keightley knew Verna's brothers were going to be very upset, and it was well known that the oldest, Doc, had not been right since he fought in the Great War. He advised Denhardt to go home to his farm and let Coroner Ricketts notify the family. Keightley was not sure what had happened on the dark highway, but it was obvious that the general had failed miserably in the responsibility of a gentleman to protect a lady in his company.

Denhardt calmly explained that Verna had been suicidal in the afternoon during a trip to Louisville. He said that at one point he wrestled the pistol away from her and locked it in the glove box of his car. Keightley cautiously said that if Verna had loved him enough to wear his ring, she had left him in a tough spot by committing suicide.

"Yes, you know she promised me that if she decided to take her life she would leave a note explaining everything."

"Well, we'll probably find a note at the house," suggested Keightley, not quite sure what to say.

"I don't think so," replied Denhardt.[8]

Keightley asked him the most obvious question—why would Verna want to kill herself? Denhardt had a ready answer. Keightley later recalled, "He said that the girls, meaning Mrs. Taylor's daughters, were objecting to his company with Mrs. Taylor, and kept nagging at Mrs. Taylor, and had her worried, and that she had threatened to commit suicide a number of times before this incident."[9]

The lights of Coroner Ricketts's automobile interrupted the conversation and Keightley stepped out of the ambulance to meet him in the roadway. He pointed out the body lying in the old roadbed. Using his flashlight to light the way, Ricketts climbed down the four-foot embankment into the ditch. He pulled back the sheet and could see a gunshot wound in Verna's left breast, but there was no blood on the outside of her dress or on the ground next to her body. He picked up the large pistol lying several feet away and placed it in his car. Denhardt's flashlight and car keys had been found on the road several yards away from Verna's body before Keightley arrived at the scene.

When Ricketts had done his duty as coroner and pronounced Verna dead, the men helped Keightley place her body on a gurney. They made the difficult climb up the slippery embankment and pushed the heavy metal cot into the waiting funeral ambulance. Denhardt looked on silently as the body was loaded, but did not volunteer to help. Ricketts wanted more information, and invited the general and Keightley to sit in his car.

Ricketts recalled, "He and Mr. Keightley and I all got in the car, and I asked Mr. Denhardt what happened. He says, 'Mrs. Taylor killed herself. I didn't kill her. Why would I have killed her? I loved her and was going to marry her. She's one of the most beautiful women I ever knew, and as fine a lady as ever walked.'"[10]

Denhardt said that the two had left LaGrange that morning for a day trip to Louisville. But as the day passed, Verna complained of a headache and became increasingly depressed, talking of death and suicide. It was after dark when they left Louisville and Verna was driving his car. When they reached LaGrange, they drove through town on Highway 22 toward Henry County. Six miles outside of LaGrange, Verna tried to turn around at the Pendleton Schoolhouse and the car stalled; the battery had died. George Baker helped move the car to his driveway, and the couple waited in the dark car for J. B. Hundley to return from LaGrange with a battery. Denhardt claimed that when he walked to Baker's house, Verna disappeared. He heard two shots from the east, one loud and distinct, the other a popping noise. Based on Verna's earlier threats, Denhardt believed the worst had happened when he heard the gunshots. His fears were confirmed when they found her body in the old roadbed.

A day trip to Louisville with a suicidal fiancée, a stalled car, two gunshots in the night, and a dead woman in Keightley's ambulance—the general's story was perhaps the strangest Coroner Ricketts had heard at a death scene. Ricketts did not smell alcohol on Denhardt, and the general appeared to be sober. No one had accused him of murder, but several times during the conversation, Denhardt stated that he did not kill Verna.

This was an unusual case for Coroner Ricketts—a powerful state politician claiming that his fiancée was so distraught over family objections to their relationship that she killed herself with his pistol. The two were on a deserted highway and Ricketts estimated that the general was 400 yards from her when it happened.

Ricketts did not openly dispute the word of General Denhardt, a powerful man, but the whole situation looked peculiar. How did one of Verna's shoes end up lying between her body and an outstretched arm? Why was the pistol four or five feet away on the incline of the bank? The military pistol was long and heavy, a .45 caliber Smith and Wesson, and quite a large weapon for a lady to handle. A glove was clasped tightly in Verna's left hand when Ricketts and Keightley first saw her body. Would it have been possible for her to shoot herself with the heavy gun using only one hand? It was also strange that both Denhardt and George Baker claimed they heard one loud gunshot, then a "pop shot" several minutes later. It prompted Baker to declare to J. B. Hundley, "I don't know this man and I don't know this woman, but General Denhardt couldn't have killed her because I was with him when the second shot was fired."[11]

Baker was excited and nervous at the discovery of the body, but the words would return to haunt him months later.

J. B. Hundley, Cuba Shaver, and George Baker were now unlikely witnesses in a death investigation by the Henry County coroner. The position of the body and gun left a number of mysterious and unanswered questions about what had happened. General Denhardt certainly did not act like a man who had just lost his fiancée, but he claimed to love Verna, and if the two were to be married shortly, as he said, there was no motive for him to kill her.

When there was nothing more that could be said or done that night, it was time for Keightley to begin the drive back to the funeral home with Verna's body. It was also time for the general to return home, and when he requested a driver, Cuba Shaver agreed to chauffer him back to his farm. Ricketts's duty as coroner was to inform Verna Taylor's family of the tragedy.

Denhardt was probably right to worry about the Garr brothers. The Garrs were a tight-knit family, and the three Garr brothers were known to be especially close. Their sister had died a horrible death under strange circumstances, and they would take this news very hard. As he followed the taillights of Keightley's hearse west on the dark highway toward LaGrange, Coroner Ricketts dreaded being the man to deliver the bad news.

Chapter 2

THE MOST BEAUTIFUL WOMAN IN TWO COUNTIES

Edwin Stanton Garr, nicknamed "Doc" or "Stant" by his family and friends, was forty-seven years old in November 1936. He was tall and thin with a gaunt face, sunken cheeks, tousled dark hair, and a small dark mustache in the middle of his upper lip. Doc looked older than his age, and suffered from what the doctors at the veterans' hospital called a nervous condition or shell shock. It was a nagging reminder of his military service in the Great War when he served overseas as a first lieutenant in the Veterinary Corps of the Eighty-First Division. For Doc Garr, the war had never really ended. He had been hospitalized several times since his return from Europe, suffering from what was probably post-traumatic stress disorder. He had struggled with the condition for eighteen years, and it had eventually cost him his marriage and the companionship of his three children.

Doc was the eldest of the six children of Mary Pryor and Edward D. Garr. In order of birth, they were Edwin Stanton, Roy Pryor, Florence Juanita, Verna Elizabeth (born June 17, 1896), Davis Tyler "Jack," and Mary Lillian. They were a close family and, by all appearances, happy. Edward D. Garr made his living as a kennel man, a trainer of fine hunting dogs. Their love of animals and their father's influence helped determine the future professions of the three Garr brothers.

In 1936, Doc was a veterinarian practicing in Oldham, Shelby, and Henry Counties. He was busy and well liked in the community and lived with his widowed mother on the family farm outside LaGrange. His work as a veterinarian paid the bills and put food on the table, but it also gave him a purpose in life that helped occupy his time and thoughts. For Doc, it was easier to spend the night in a barn treating a sick cow or horse than grapple with his private demons.

Forty-five-year-old Roy and his wife, Bettie, lived on a farm close to his mother and Doc. The couple's only child, Edward, died unexpectedly in 1926 when he was five, and they lived alone on the farm. Roy farmed, and raised and trained hunting dogs. The youngest Garr brother, thirty-six-year-old Jack, also raised and trained hunting dogs and lived near Cincinnati, Ohio. Like their father, Roy and Jack achieved national reputations as breeders of bird-hunting dogs. Both men were outdoorsmen and looked every inch the part. They were tanned and broad-shouldered with the same tousled, black hair of their older brother. There was an easy companionship and a strong bond between the brothers, and as time passed, the townspeople of LaGrange came to view them as inseparable.

There were four women in the Garr family in 1936: the mother, Mary Herndon Pryor Garr, was seventy years old; Juanita Garr Holmes was forty-one; Verna Elizabeth Garr Taylor was forty years; and Mary Lillian Garr Williams was the baby of the family at twenty-seven. Mary Pryor Garr, Mary Lillian, and Juanita remained quiet and somewhat forgotten during the sensational events that shook their family in 1936 and 1937. They were eclipsed in life and death by the notoriety of their three brothers, and their middle sister, Verna.

After Verna's tragic death, the press would refer to her as the most beautiful woman in Oldham County, or even the most beautiful woman in two counties (Oldham and Henry). While the reporters may have exaggerated to make the story of her death more sensational, it was true that Verna Garr Taylor was a beautiful woman. She was tall and slender with dark eyes and long black hair that she kept pinned in a knot at the nape of her neck. She was very much a woman of her time, but also a woman ahead of her time. While Verna was kind, elegant, and well spoken, she was also a successful, astute businesswoman who achieved independence at a time when the majority of women were dependent on their husbands and worked only in their homes. She was very much a lady, but not above driving her business's laundry truck around LaGrange.

Verna grew up in the boisterous Garr household and married her high school sweetheart, Rowan Barclay Taylor of LaGrange, when she was eighteen. It was a fine match and appeared to be a solid marriage. Both the Garrs and the Taylors were prominent and respected in the community, and the Taylors boasted ancestors who were original settlers in the area.

Taylor owned and operated the Community Laundry in LaGrange, and life was good for the young couple. Two daughters were born—Mary Pryor in 1915 and Frances "Fannie" in 1920. But life suddenly turned tragic in 1931 when Verna's husband died of complications from acute appendicitis. She found herself at the helm of a small business at the worst possible economic time in American history. For the next five years, Verna worked tirelessly to raise her two daughters and keep the business and its employees afloat through the worst years of the Depression. Her efforts met with success. On the night she died, Verna had no debts and there was a surplus of $3,500 in her bank account. Few businessmen at the time could have done as well.

In 1936, the name "Mrs. R. B. Taylor" appeared often in the "Personal News and Social Events" section of the local newspaper.

Verna was visiting friends, spending weekends at her cousin's home in Louisville—all the everyday events that made it clear that she was actively involved in small-town life. She raised her children as a single mother, ran her household and business, and stayed busy with committees at the LaGrange Methodist Church, where she also served as a Sunday school teacher. Verna was well loved and respected by her family and the townspeople of LaGrange. There is no evidence that anyone disliked her, held a grudge, or wanted to harm her. If sometimes lonely, her life was full and extremely busy without another husband. But in the early summer of 1936, Henry Denhardt entered her life, and the die was cast.

Ironically, it was Doc Garr who set the tragic events in motion. Bertha Denhardt, the general's sister, was tired of living on his remote eight-hundred-acre farm and wanted a house closer to town. In early June, Doc stopped by Denhardt's farm to tell him that his mother had a house for rent. When Denhardt expressed an interest, Doc told him that his sister Verna lived in LaGrange and he was welcome to stop by her home and pick up a key. The general was instantly attracted to the forty-year-old widow who answered the door.

He later recalled, "Well, I went to the door and knocked, and Mrs. Taylor came to the door and very graciously invited me in. We sat and talked for some minutes and then I told her, of course, my business."[12]

He was not handsome, but sixty-year-old Henry Denhardt was distinguished, and could be charming and persuasive. He was tall, balding, and heavy-set, but carried with his extra weight the strength and determination of a man used to having his way. Denhardt was well educated and quite worldly compared to the men Verna knew in Oldham County. He was a man with a reputation as a statesman and war hero. He was different from anyone she had ever met, and he opened up her secluded life in LaGrange to a world of new possibilities. Two days after they met,

Denhardt called Verna to tell her his sister had decided not to take the house. He later recalled the exchange.

"Mrs. Taylor asked me over the phone how I was getting along. I said, 'All right, except that I am pretty lonesome.' I said, 'How are you getting along?'

She said, 'All right, except that I am lonesome too.'

I said, 'Well, two lonesome people ought to get together.'

She said, 'Fine!'

I said, 'Well, may I come to see you?'

She said, 'Yes.'

I said, 'When?'

She said, 'Let me have time to change my dress and you can come over and sit on the front porch with me.'"[13]

After their initial "date," Denhardt became a regular caller, and the infatuated general pursued Verna Taylor with the determination of a man half his age. There were long drives in the countryside, dinners, dances, and movies. He would later say, "The friendship was one of the most wonderful I have ever had, and I became very desperately in love with her . . ."[14]

In late June, Verna and fifteen-year-old Frances took the train for a vacation visit to her sister's home in Alfred, New York. They were gone for three weeks, making stops in Atlantic City and New York City. During this time, Denhardt and Verna exchanged correspondence, and her letters indicate that in the earliest stages of the relationship, she too was interested in seeing where the friendship might lead.

My dear Henry—

Your special came this morning and it was a joy to hear from you. Indeed I shall be very much disappointed if I do not hear from you many times on this trip . . .

Wish I could have kept you company on the journey to Fort Knox. Did you see the Major's wife? Maybe I can run down to see you while you are at camp, at least I hope so.[15]

I must close and get out for a walk with too much food and rest I fear for my figure and consequently your admiration.[16]

Verna signed her letters with affectionate sentiments like "Ever yours," "Always," and "With Love." The letters were good-natured and friendly, full of news from her vacation, but they also encouraged the possibility of something more serious. Verna returned in late July, and Denhardt was absent for two weeks for military maneuvers at Fort Knox. The letters and telephone calls continued. When he was able, he would leave Fort Knox for quick visits with Verna, and she welcomed his company. In a letter addressed to Denhardt at Fort Knox, Verna wrote, "I shall look forward to seeing you at 4 o'clock Saturday afternoon. Always, Verna."[17]

In late August, Denhardt proposed and gave Verna a costly engagement ring of one large diamond surrounded by twenty-six smaller diamonds in a platinum setting. He later claimed that she selected the ring, and it was understood between them to be an engagement ring. "It was definitely so understood. There was no question about it," Denhardt said.[18]

However, Verna's family had doubts that she was really engaged to the general. Mary Pryor said later, "I don't know that they were engaged."[19]

Ultimately, Henry Denhardt was the only person alive who could say whether Verna really accepted his marriage proposal. If she did, the engagement was kept very quiet, and there were no public announcements. Since their initial "date" on June 13, the two had not really spent much time together. There were dinners at the country club in Louisville, or drives in the countryside, but they knew one another best through letters and telephone calls. Verna's final, lighthearted letter was dated August 4, and if Denhardt was telling the truth, they became engaged a few weeks later. If so, something went terribly wrong in the relationship sometime between August 30 and mid-October.

Not everyone was pleased with Denhardt's courtship of Verna. Frances and Mary Pryor were unhappy with the general's continuing presence in their lives. Doc, Roy, and Jack were suspicious of Denhardt and uneasy with his reputation and controversial past.

Henry Denhardt's name had appeared in the newspaper headlines a number of times, sometimes in unflattering circumstances. In 1935, he had been in the headlines again when he was on the run from authorities after illegally leading troops into Harlan County. The fact that he was pardoned by the governor of Kentucky did little to alleviate the concerns of Verna's family. They worried that the courtship was on a fast track to a hasty marriage that Verna might regret.

Denhardt was well aware that the family did not welcome him with open arms. What would later be called the bad blood between the brothers and Denhardt began in the months before Verna's death. As the record-setting heat of summer 1936 gradually drifted into the cooler, shorter days of fall, heated arguments were overheard between the couple when the general called at Verna's house. In late October, her housekeeper, Birdie Bennett, was washing dishes in the kitchen when she overheard an argument between the couple. "I heard Denhardt say, 'You'll be sorry if you don't go out riding with me tonight.' Mrs. Taylor replied that she had a headache and didn't care to go. They were arguing and I heard Denhardt say, 'All your brothers are yellow.' Mrs. Taylor said, 'Please don't make that statement.' He said, 'I'm going to get them all three and especially that big-headed Roy Garr. I will shoot him down like a rat.'"[20]

The general was well known for his blustering and overbearing manner, and Verna evidently did not take him seriously. But Birdie thought that Roy should be warned and let him know what she had overheard. Around the same time in late October, Mary Pryor overheard another argument. "I was in the next room. It was on a Sunday night. I could tell from the voices that there was an argument. In fact, there was a great deal of storming around the room on the part of General Denhardt, which I heard. Then I heard my mother say, 'Well you can leave.'"[21] Denhardt left, but returned several times in the following weeks.

In the days after she received the ring, Verna did not wear it consistently, and by October, she typically kept the ring tied in a handkerchief in the front of her dress. Verna's longtime friend Mildred Connell moved back to LaGrange with her family in October. The two would often spend the cool fall evenings sitting on the front porch steps of the Connell house discussing the situation. Verna told her friend, "Mildred, there are times when I'm tired in the evenings or have a headache. I really don't want to go out with him anymore." As she talked, Verna pulled a handkerchief from the front of her dress and unfolded it to show Connell the ring.[22]

Maude Bell, a Community Laundry employee, was working on November 5, the day before Verna died. She recalled, "Someone said they heard she had a diamond ring and asked her to see it, and she showed us. She took it from the bosom of her dress where she had it tied up in a handkerchief." But Verna did not say whether it was a friendship ring or an engagement ring.[23] She also did not say why she preferred to keep the ring hidden in her dress.

Since her husband's death in 1931, life had been hard for Verna. For five years, she had toiled long hours to keep the laundry and its employees going, and raise her children alone. By 1936, she was exhausted by taking care of everyone else. But there is no indication that Verna ever contemplated an escape into matrimony until Henry Denhardt entered her life. He looked like a golden opportunity for a secure future, but Verna grew increasingly evasive about the marriage.

Perhaps she had begun to see demonstrations of Denhardt's overbearing nature that concerned her. Perhaps she worried about the realities of a future with the aging, red-faced, and overweight general. The glitter of dating an important man and the security offered by a marriage may have begun to tarnish as the realities set in after his proposal. Verna did not approve of drinking alcohol, and it is certainly possible that as time passed she heard more about Denhardt's reputation for heavy drinking. As early as her letter of July 4, she commends him for looking after his farming interests rather than attending parties and drinking "fire water."

Verna had several valid reasons to reconsider a marriage with the controversial general. But it is also possible there was something else that made her hesitate—a secret she kept carefully hidden. In fact, she believed it was so well hidden that only one other living person in LaGrange could possibly know, and he would never tell.

Denhardt would later say during his trial that a date for the wedding had been set for spring 1937, but was later moved to November 1936. If so, it was probably at his insistence. Denhardt had begun to realize that if he did not marry the lovely widow soon, she would not marry him at all. For Henry Denhardt, time was of the essence if there was to be a wedding, and he was not a man who would take no for an answer if there was something he wanted. By early fall, he was desperately in love, obsessed with Verna Garr Taylor, and determined that there would be a wedding. But Verna prevaricated, and Denhardt, always suspicious and alert for plots and conspiracies, wondered why. When he found what he believed to be the answer, there was no safe exit from the relationship for Verna.

On the wintry night of Thursday, November 5, Verna left work in the laundry truck with twenty-six-year-old Chester "Ches" Woolfolk driving. Woolfolk was a trim, dark-haired, strikingly handsome man who worked at the laundry as a truck driver and brought the receipts to Verna's house each evening. It was not unusual for him to drive Verna home from work. Denhardt was aware that Woolfolk was in and out of Verna's house frequently, not just as an employee, but as a friend of the family who gave young Frances music lessons. Verna borrowed Woolfolk's car, and Woolfolk occasionally drove her to Louisville. Verna, youthful and vivacious, enjoyed the young man's presence in her life. As the two drove around the courthouse square that night, Verna was surprised to see Denhardt's car and told Woolfolk to pull alongside so she could roll down her window.

"Henry, what are you doing?"

"I'm coming over to see you after a while."

"Well, that's fine. Come on."[24]

Denhardt and Verna had plans to drive to Louisville the next morning, and he spent the night at a hotel in LaGrange. He would later say, "The weather was bad and it had snowed, so instead of going to the farm I stayed in LaGrange."[25]

If the weather was bad, it is odd that Denhardt would make an additional trip to Louisville on Thursday. It all may have been an innocent coincidence, but the encounter later raised the question whether Denhardt was jealous, suspicious, and quietly keeping an eye on Verna. The ride home from the laundry with Woolfolk that night may have sealed her fate. The next morning, Verna and the general left for Louisville on a day trip from which she did not return alive. But before she left LaGrange on the day she died, Verna removed the elaborate diamond ring from her handkerchief and placed it on her finger. It was still on her hand when Keightley arrived at her death scene.

On the night of November 6, the telephone rang at the house of Doc Garr and his mother. Rather than the usual late call from someone in the county to treat a sick animal, it was his niece, Mary Pryor, and she was very worried. Her mother had called home from a restaurant in Louisville around six o'clock and talked with Frances. Verna said she had a headache and that she and General Denhardt could not chaperone Frances's dance as promised. She planned to be home in an hour and told Frances to wait at the house. By the time Mary Pryor telephoned her uncle, it was far past the time for her mother to have arrived. Doc was calm during the conversation and did not want to upset his niece any further, but it was not like Verna to disappear and not call home. There were the obvious concerns of car problems or an accident. There was no moon that night, making it even harder to see the old road from Louisville after dark. It was also possible that there were slick spots on the road left from the snow two days earlier. If something was wrong, Doc was on his own; Roy was in Indianapolis for the night, and Jack lived hours away in Ohio. Doc did not want to frighten or upset his mother when it might be nothing at all. For all he knew, Verna might be standing in the front parlor when he got to her home. He drove by himself to the house on Fourth Avenue to wait until she arrived, and was waiting with Mary Pryor at 11:45 p.m. when they heard a knock at the front door.

Standing in the doorway looking official, but uncomfortable was the Henry County coroner. Ricketts was no stranger to this kind of situation, but the job never grew easier with time.

"You all better sit down. I'm afraid I have some very bad news."

Doc and Mary Pryor were in complete shock. They could accept that there had been a car accident, or that Verna had suddenly collapsed and died, but they could not comprehend how she could die of a gunshot wound in Henry County. When they heard that Henry Denhardt was at the scene, all the worries and concerns of the past months came flooding back. To Doc and his niece, it was impossible that Verna had taken her life. She had every reason to live, and would never kill herself and leave her two daughters as orphans. She was even making plans to improve the laundry, and had ordered the materials earlier that day. Verna's family believed it was more likely that she had finally called off the shaky relationship and the general killed her in a rage.

On the highway that night, Denhardt had been confident that the two were to be married within days or weeks. There was no mention that Verna had doubts about the relationship. Yet Denhardt claimed that her suicide was caused by family objections to the impending marriage.

The two stories contradicted, and if Doc and Mary Pryor were right, and Verna had spurned the general, Ricketts had a motive for murder. Verna's death required further investigation, and Ricketts was handling a potential bomb. This was not a family squabble that ended in a weekend shooting or a disagreement between two local drunks. This was serious business, and it was going to require a serious investigation. Denhardt was politically powerful with rich, influential friends in the state capital and around Kentucky. He had the money and connections to hire the best lawyers to defend him if he were accused of murder. It was the kind of situation where the wrong decision could cost a coroner his job, and work was hard to find in 1936.

The Garrs might be respected members of the LaGrange community, but if Henry Denhardt had committed murder, it was going to be a real battle to prove it. The fat was in the fire with this one, and no one knew it better than Coroner Ricketts. But no one present at the awful scene on the highway, or sitting in Verna's house as he delivered the bad news could have predicted the firestorm that would erupt from the events of this night.

Ricketts stood to leave and promised Mary Pryor and Doc that he would return to the highway in the morning and begin an investigation. If necessary, he would call a coroner's inquest.

When the coroner left, Doc and Mary Pryor were overwhelmed with grief and the details of what needed to be done. They would have to find Frances at the dance and bring her home immediately.

They would have to telephone Jack in Ohio, Roy in Indianapolis, and Verna's sisters who lived out of state. And somehow, they would have to tell Mrs. Garr the awful news of how her daughter died.

Doc made the funeral arrangements with Keightley that night. Mary Pryor and Frances did not go with him and did not see their mother's body until she was brought home the next morning in a coffin. There were many questions that the family wanted answered, but first they would have to see that the extended family was informed of the tragedy, and that beautiful, vivacious, and independent Verna Garr Taylor was buried.

Chapter 3

THE GENERAL

Brooding, Henry Denhardt rode in silence as his driver, Cuba Shaver, and Shaver's friend Lowell Talbot drove eleven miles from Henry County to the general's farm. It was late at night, and the narrow half-mile road to Denhardt's house, little more than a rutted path through the farm fields, was lighted by only the car's headlights. Shaver slowly slid and bumped his way through the mud and remaining snow. Long before they reached the large white house at the end of the road, the wheels of the automobile mired in the quagmire and could go no further. Shaver and Talbot watched as Denhardt took a woman's purse from the seat and zipped it inside his briefcase. He bid them goodnight and set off on foot down the road that led to his home.

Brigadier General Henry H. Denhardt, usually referred to as General Denhardt, or simply the general, was a man well known to most Kentuckians. During his illustrious career, he had been an attorney, judge, military man and war hero, state lieutenant governor, and adjutant general. Twice, he was a candidate for governor of Kentucky. But for the past thirteen years, Denhardt had also been a consistently stormy figure in Kentucky politics and was often a focus of rumor and controversy. He had a reputation as a politician who carried a big stick, and was widely known as a dangerous man to cross. The general was a man used to being in control. When he decided there was something he wanted, he set out to obtain it with ruthless abandon, and with few exceptions, he got what he wanted. There was little middle ground with Henry Denhardt and he evoked strong emotions in those who knew him. His close, longtime friends supported and admired him, while many other people found him overbearing, egotistical, and officious.

At six feet, two inches, and at least 220 pounds, Henry Denhardt had an oversized physique to match his larger-than-life personality. Bald and red-faced, at the age of sixty he was no longer a strong, physically active man and appeared older than his age. Denhardt had a penchant for two of Kentucky's famous commodities—beautiful women and alcohol. He had a reputation as an expert shot, possessed a large collection of firearms, and was known to carry a gun. As he grew older, he became increasingly paranoid and suspicious, consistently pointing a finger of blame at unnamed political enemies who he believed were busy at work to destroy him.

Denhardt lived with his sixty-five-year-old sister, Bertha, on a remote eight-hundred-acre farm approximately five miles from LaGrange. Bertha took care of her younger brother and the housekeeping. They shared the large house with members of the Cole family who worked and managed the farm for Denhardt. Bertha had lived with her brother for years. She followed him from Bowling Green to Frankfort when he served as lieutenant governor and later as adjutant general. No one in the world loved and believed in Henry Denhardt more than his older sister; she was not just his housekeeper, she was his greatest supporter.

Denhardt purchased the historic house and surrounding acreage at an Oldham County estate sale in May 1935.[26] At the time, he was state adjutant general and living in Frankfort, Kentucky.

The house needed repairs, but it was situated on a beautiful working farm with gently rolling acreage.[27] There was no electricity, and the house was an immense, frigid barn with numerous fireplaces that provided little warmth. But it was a grand and elegant old home that made a definite statement as visitors approached on the half-mile farm road that led to Denhardt's front door. It said that the man who lived here was someone of importance, a man of wealth and influence who appreciated the dignity of a bygone time in Kentucky. Like the general, the house had seen grander days; it had been his ambition with Verna as his wife to return it to some of its previous splendor.

A marriage to Verna Taylor was very important to Henry Denhardt. In fact, the relationship was probably more important to the general than it was to Verna. Verna had an independent life of her own with two children and a business to run. But Denhardt's successful public life was finished, and before he met Verna Taylor, his future looked uncertain and empty. He was a sixty-year-old divorced man with an uncertain political future. The relationship offered a new beginning for Denhardt, an opportunity to resurrect his personal and professional life. Verna was beautiful and accomplished. She would be the perfect wife for a politically connected and distinguished man. But with Verna's death, the door to a new beginning and future slammed shut in Denhardt's face.

When the general told Coroner Ricketts and Smith Keightley that Verna committed suicide, he expected to be believed. He was a convincing, charismatic, and sometimes affable politician. Surely, no one would question the word of a man with his illustrious credentials. Why should there be any further investigation when he had already offered a thorough explanation of Verna's death? He assumed that her family would blame him, and he was immediately concerned about the Garr brothers and what they might think or do. But it was not Denhardt's nature to accept blame, show public remorse, or issue any kind of apology. In the coming weeks and months, the Garr brothers would wait in vain for any indications of remorse. But they could have waited forever, because if there was blame to be assigned, Henry Denhardt typically assigned it elsewhere.

Before he collapsed on his bed for the night, Denhardt checked to be sure a pistol was safely hidden beneath one of his feather pillows. He did not know how the Garr brothers would react to the news of Verna's death, but if they came to the house, he might need his pistol before the night was through. Over the years, the general had increasingly relied on drinking to handle stress, and he picked up a bottle for at least the second time that evening. It had been a very stressful night, one he would rather forget, and Denhardt poured an extra-large drink and proceeded to get very drunk. He would still be under the influence when the sheriff and coroner arrived at his house the next morning.

—

Henry Herman Denhardt was born into humble circumstances in Bowling Green, Kentucky, on March 8, 1876. He was the fifth and youngest child of William and Margaret Geyger or Geiger Denhardt. Both were German immigrants born in the province of Baden, Germany. William and Margaret spoke German exclusively in their home, and the Denhardt children grew up speaking both German and English.

Henry's father, William, had been a soldier in his youth, perhaps inspiring his youngest son to also become a military man. William Denhardt joined the Union Army in 1863 at age eighteen, and participated in engagements at Nashville and Franklin, Tennessee. At the end of the Civil War, he was honorably discharged and moved to Sonora, Kentucky, where he earned his living as a shoemaker. In 1868, William Denhardt moved his growing family to Bowling Green, a thriving town set in the gently rolling hills of southwestern Kentucky. In Bowling Green, he continued to work as a shoemaker for the rest of his life.[28] Three sons and two daughters were born to William and Margaret: Minnie in 1867, William in 1869, Bertha in 1871, Jesse in 1873, and Henry Herman, born the day before his mother's birthday in 1876. The family was solid, respectable, community-minded, and active in the Presbyterian church, where William served as an elder. The Denhardt children were intelligent and ambitious, and attended Bowling Green public schools.

The younger William and his brother Jesse owned and operated the *Bowling Green Times-Journal*, incorporated as the Times-Journal Publishing Company. In the early years, Henry was a vice president of the company and his brothers Jesse and William were president and secretary-treasurer. But Henry was more ambitious, and with his family's help, he attended Cumberland University in Lebanon, Tennessee, and earned a law degree in 1899. In 1900, he was a city attorney and later served as Warren County judge from 1910 to 1920. He purchased his first horse and buggy to drive door to door in the county, working hard to win the confidence and votes of citizens. As a city attorney and judge, he was liked and respected, fair-minded, and had a solid knowledge of the law. He was a young man with a promising future, and there is no indication that he was controversial or plagued with the lapses in judgment common during the last years of his life and political career.

Denhardt was an active member of the local Presbyterian church and superintendent of the Sunday school, a Mason, and a member of the Improved Order of Redmen, a patriotic organization dedicated to promoting America and democracy. An ambitious attorney must also have a worthy wife, and in 1905, he married lovely Elizabeth Glaze.[29]

But even though he was a rising star in the legal community of Bowling Green, Henry Denhardt had other aspirations. Of the three sons of William Denhardt, he was the only one with a passion for the adventurous life offered by the military. Denhardt would be an attorney, judge, and politician during his life, but foremost, he would always consider himself a military man. During the Spanish-American War, he organized a local company but did not see action. By August 1898, he was a first lieutenant. In 1916, he was a major with the Third Kentucky Infantry, and he volunteered for action when General Pershing led an expedition against the elusive Pancho Villa. Denhardt thrived on the hardship of military life in the southwest, and his superior officers praised him as a brave man with a solid future in the military.

Major Denhardt was still on the Mexican border when war was declared against Germany. After nine months of ineffectively chasing Pancho Villa through the deserts of the southwest, Pershing was recalled to command the American operations of the Great War in Europe. As a soldier who had shown promise and potential, Denhardt was detached from his command in the southwest and sent to Fort Sill to receive instructions at the school of heavy artillery. In June 1918, at the age of forty-two, Henry Denhardt left for Europe with the 319th Field Artillery for what would ultimately be the greatest adventure of his life.

He arrived in war-torn France, a decimated no man's-land of trenches, formidable coils of barbed wire, vast shell holes, and deadly chemicals. But ironically, his time as a soldier in active service during the horror and misery of the Great War was a halcyon period for Henry Denhardt. His life as a soldier was uncomplicated, and he excelled at the military tasks assigned to him. In action as an artilleryman during the Grand Offensive, he aided in providing cover for the advance of the infantry at St. Mihiel as the combined French and American troops drove ever forward against the weakened German defenses. In September 1918, Denhardt and the American forces attacked the reformed and strengthened German lines of defense in the Battle of the Argonne-Meuse. Denhardt not only did his duty as a soldier, he excelled.

A local news release issued on November 23, 1918, reported: "Lieutenant Col. Denhardt has been in the thickest of the fighting since August 1. He and the men under him were commended by Major General Liggett following the first battle (St. Mihiel) in which he and his battalion engaged. After the second battle (Argonne-Meuse), Lieutenant Col. Denhardt was cited for bravery under fire and for promotion."[30] Denhardt's performance during the battle was so impressive that he was promoted to lieutenant colonel. A Bowling Green news article reported, "The late Governor McCreary shortly before his death, in speaking of Col. Denhardt, said he considered him 'the most fearless man in Kentucky.'"[31]

Henry Denhardt found his niche in the killing fields of France, and by the time he was discharged in 1919, he was widely heralded as a war hero. Never again would his life be so uncomplicated. Following orders as a wartime soldier, he excelled at aggressively pushing toward the enemy under deadly fire. But as a peacetime National Guard soldier and state politician, life was a challenge for Denhardt. Doc Garr returned from his military service with shell shock or post-traumatic stress disorder. It is likely that Henry Denhardt returned from the war with his own problem, a drinking habit that grew steadily worse as the years passed. It was not until after his wartime service that his name became synonymous with controversy.

Denhardt returned to his family and quiet law practice in Bowling Green, but with a distinguished military record, his ambitions included a future in state politics. Within a month of his return from the war, he formally announced his candidacy for governor of Kentucky. Although he eventually lost, the campaign placed his name at the forefront of rising politicians to watch in the future. Denhardt was not discouraged by the loss and set his sights on the lieutenant governor's race of 1923. However, before he could begin his campaign, labor riots erupted in Newport, Kentucky.

In late 1921 and early 1922, Colonel Denhardt of the Kentucky National Guard was in charge of the troops sent by Governor Morrow to quell the riots stemming from a mill strike. He immediately found himself in the middle of a political firestorm when his soldiers were accused of reacting with unnecessary force against the union workers. Depositions taken during the eventual investigation reported numerous beatings of mill workers and attacks on Newport residents by the National Guardsmen. It was unclear whether they acted on orders from Denhardt, or whether they were acting on their own volition.[32] Regardless, these men were under his watch and command, and Denhardt was ultimately responsible for their actions. His brief time as the head of the National Guardsmen in northern Kentucky would haunt him until his death. It would be used as political fodder against him in his upcoming campaign for lieutenant governor and in his future campaigns.

After the violence in Newport, Henry Denhardt fought an uphill battle in his campaign for lieutenant governor. He was forced to spend much of his time defending his actions and attempting to establish a friendship with organized labor. In April 1923, Denhardt defended himself by saying, "All the daily newspapers of Cincinnati, Covington, and Newport indorsed [*sic*] editorially or otherwise everything that was done by us at that time."[33] He was also quick to point out that the grateful local citizens had given him gifts for suppressing the riots, including an expensive saddle horse and silver tea service. But his political opponents insultingly referred to him as a "czar" and "military dictator." The Kentucky State Federation of Labor issued a damning statement against Denhardt's actions in Newport: "This doughty Colonel holds the record of being the first to use armor tanks in labor disputes, and his record of terrorism and persecution is without parallel or precedent in the history of our nation."[34] It was the first time his name was associated with controversy, and it was a difficult political campaign for Denhardt. He managed to win in 1923, defeating Ellerbe Carter to become Kentucky's thirty-fourth lieutenant governor, serving with newly elected Governor William J. Fields. Denhardt had hit the big time in Kentucky politics. He was a man of importance, a person of power and influence. By winning the office of lieutenant governor in a hard-fought campaign, his ultimate ambition of becoming governor looked to be within his grasp.

On the morning of January 30, 1925, a thirty-seven-year-old cave explorer named Floyd Collins set out from his home in the Mammoth Cave region of Kentucky with a dented kerosene lantern and a seventy-two-foot rope. He was an experienced caver, but known to work alone and take unnecessary risks. That day, as Collins wormed his way upward in complete darkness through a coffin-like tunnel sixty feet below the ground, a boulder dislodged onto his foot and he could not free himself. For days, family, friends, and gathering volunteers worked desperately to rescue him, and by February 3, Collins's plight had become a far-reaching news story. National newspapers, wire services, and radio broadcasts reported continuous updates on the futile efforts to free the trapped man. By February 4, the area around the entrance to the cave had deteriorated into a drunken, lawless carnival, and Cave City's town marshall asked Governor Fields to send the state militia to restore law and order. On February 5, at one fifteen in the morning, Lieutenant Governor Denhardt, newly promoted to Brigadier General Denhardt, received his marching orders by telephone from Governor Fields. Fifteen minutes later, he rushed out of his Bowling Green home in the company of two aides. Denhardt had an important mission to accomplish, a directive by the governor to bring chaos into order, and he was the man in charge.

From the moment he arrived, General Denhardt showed little sensitivity in dealing with the locals, who included Collins's relatives.[35] Engineers supported the challenging idea of digging a shaft through the ground directly to Collins's side. The general was in favor of it too, but the locals who understood the area caves better than the engineers were very unhappy. They insisted that the geologic formation of the hillside was not suited to sinking a shaft, and it would take too long to save Collins. They wanted to continue working within the cave to attempt to free the trapped man. When Homer Collins, Floyd's brother, objected strenuously to sinking the shaft, Denhardt replied, "Practical men have had their way. It's going to take men with brains to get him out. We'll sink a shaft."

The decision sealed Collins's fate. After digging ten feet, the sides caved in and workers had to keep moving the debris they had already cleared. They constantly encountered boulders that took additional precious time to remove. On February 16, the men digging the shaft finally broke through approximately six feet from Collins. General Denhardt dramatically ordered a detail of soldiers with fixed bayonets to the head of the shaft. But the process of digging had taken too long, and it was too late to save Floyd Collins.

Collins's deadly predicament was confounding to all who tried to rescue him even before Denhardt gave his fateful order, and it is possible that he would have died anyway. But when the military closed the cave, and concentrated only on digging the shaft, it prevented volunteers from crawling into the tunnel and attempting to take food and water to Collins. General Denhardt's overbearing manner at the site, and his unrelenting orders to dig the shaft earned him the perpetual enmity of the locals in the Cave City area.

Following the death of Floyd Collins, Denhardt returned to his duties as lieutenant governor. He served as president of the state senate until his term of office ended in 1927 and was praised for his abilities as presiding officer. But as a lieutenant governor, he was outside the circle of the real power brokers in state government. At the end of his term, Denhardt knew it was time to turn his ambitions again toward the office he had coveted for years.

In one of the great ironies of his life, Denhardt began his second campaign for governor in a setting that would become all too familiar to him in 1937—the Henry County Courthouse in New Castle. It was a hotly contested race, and fresh on the heels of his stint as lieutenant governor, Denhardt expected to win the nomination. He suffered a disappointing defeat in the primary to his old opponent and fellow military man, Ellerbe Carter.[36]

Denhardt's political fortunes had reached their zenith and started a gradual decline, probably beginning with his failure to win the nomination in 1928. By that time, Denhardt had gained a reputation for being difficult and controversial. He had burned too many political bridges to become a viable candidate in an election. After the loss, Denhardt returned to his law practice in Bowling Green and continued his service as a brigadier general with the Kentucky National Guard.

Denhardt's troubles continued in 1931 when he was shot in the back in his hometown of Bowling Green during one of the rough-and-tumble statewide elections. On the day of the election, a Republican campaign worker named William K. Dent attacked Judge Henry B. Hines who was working at the precinct for the Democratic nominees. During the melee on a busy street corner, Judge Hines was beaten about the face and head and responded by shooting at Dent. When the judge's bullet missed Dent, Denhardt stepped into the fray to help Judge Hines. Dent pulled his pistol and fired five shots at Denhardt. One of the bullets lodged in Denhardt's back, and he was given a fifty-fifty chance of survival. When he lived, many people were surprised. Dent maintained his innocence, and according to a news article, argued that he fired his pistol because General Denhardt "half-turned toward him and reached for a pocket."[37]

Denhardt's problems continued in 1932 when his wife of twenty-eight years filed for divorce. As her legal grounds for the divorce, Elizabeth Denhardt claimed desertion. Denhardt had not been the easiest of husbands, and during their married life, she had endured the rumors of his infidelities and his growing dependence on alcohol.

It had not been an easy life for Elizabeth Glaze Denhardt, and the couple had no children to occupy her time. At one point in their marriage, Elizabeth suggested adoption, but her husband was not interested. Later, Henry Denhardt noticed a disabled and disadvantaged young boy at the Warren County Courthouse. He wanted to adopt the child and give him a home. But this time, it was Elizabeth who hesitated to adopt and make the commitment.[38] It was certainly not Elizabeth's fault that she did not feel up to the task of raising a disabled child. But Denhardt's actions indicated a nobler, kinder side to his personality that was completely submerged in the poor press he received after the death of Verna Garr Taylor.

The Denhardts eventually divorced, and the agreement with Elizabeth was settled discreetly and to her satisfaction. According to Denhardt, the two remained friends, and on the night he died, a letter from Elizabeth was found in his pocket. However, there is no indication that she attended his 1937 murder trial, or made a recorded statement expressing her belief in his guilt or innocence.

When western Kentuckian Ruby Laffoon was elected governor, he asked his friend and supporter Henry Denhardt to fill the state adjutant general position. Denhardt quickly accepted and moved to Frankfort with his sister, Bertha. With his military background, Denhardt appeared to be a good choice for the position. However, with Denhardt's controversial history, Laffoon might have considered his selection more closely. But as always in Kentucky politics, old alliances prevailed. Denhardt became the state adjutant general in 1931.

As adjutant general, Denhardt made the final blunder that effectively ended his political career. Politics is always a dangerous game, and for a man of action who often exhibited little wisdom, it was especially dangerous. In the summer of 1935, Denhardt very publicly found himself on the wrong side of the law, and on the wrong side of the next governor when he led over seven hundred National Guardsmen into Harlan County, Kentucky, to confront an alleged voting fraud scheme. He claimed that Lieutenant Governor A. B. "Happy" Chandler intended to steal fourteen thousand ballots from the gubernatorial candidate supported by Denhardt and Governor Laffoon. In Denhardt's use of the National Guardsmen, he was undoubtedly following Laffoon's orders, but his actions were foolhardy. As an attorney and former judge, he should have realized that what he was doing would have repercussions.

Denhardt was indicted on a charge of criminal contempt in Harlan, and a bench warrant was issued for his arrest. Accused of unlawfully and forcibly obtaining ballot boxes, and using state troops in a situation that was not an emergency, the defiant general dared the Harlan County judge to put him in jail. The situation became comical when a ninety-eight-cent reward was issued for Denhardt by the Harlan County sheriff. Denhardt countered with a reward of ninety-nine cents for the arrest and conviction of the man who killed another man who helped stuff a ballot box two years earlier.[39]

Denhardt stayed on the run from authorities for days, theatrically claiming he would not surrender because he feared assassination if he went to Harlan County to answer the indictment. Eventually and on his own terms, he surrendered. Governor Laffoon pardoned him before his trial.

The widespread publicity from this escapade was not favorable to Denhardt, and in one newspaper article, he was publicly chastised as Henry "Hitler" Denhardt by the state attorney general.[40] Lieutenant Governor Chandler also disparaged Denhardt "as a 'Hitler' who attempted to influence elections with 'bayonet rule.'"[41] Although the governor sanctioned Denhardt's actions and he received a pardon, his public persona was tarnished by the escapade. Denhardt had fallen out of favor in state politics, and worse, he had backed the wrong candidate for governor. Chandler was elected, and Denhardt had no choice but to retire from public life. However, rather than return to Bowling Green as he had in the past, he moved to the farm he had purchased in Oldham County. It was shortly after his retirement that he met Verna Garr Taylor.

The sixty-year-old man who moved to Oldham County in 1936 was no longer the idealistic young man who served Warren County as a competent, well-liked attorney and judge. He was a completely different man from the forty-two-year-old who served his country so well in the Great War. By 1936, he was aging and quite possibly an alcoholic, suspicious and quick to blame others for his problems. The Harlan County fiasco should have been an embarrassing, humbling experience. Instead, the lesson Denhardt carried with him to Oldham County was that a man with political influence and friends in high places could break the law and defiantly escape the consequences. It was a dangerous concept, and by the time he moved to Oldham County, General Denhardt was a dangerous man. It was simply a matter of time before he was once again embroiled in a controversy, but no one could have predicted that the next one would have such tragic consequences.

In the early morning hours of November 7, 1936, forces were steadily gathering in the investigation of Verna Garr Taylor's death. Denhardt's story of Verna's suicide, and his statements and actions at the death scene raised questions that his explanations failed to answer. Unknown to Henry Denhardt, peaceful in his alcohol-induced slumber, an official death investigation had already begun.

Chapter 4

SUICIDE OR MURDER?

In the pale sunlight of a cold November morning, five somber men walked the pavement of Highway 22 near the farm of George and Nettie Baker. Henry County Sheriff Evan Harrod, Deputy Paul Stivers, Oldham County Sheriff Walter Briggs, and Jack Garr followed Coroner Ricketts as he led them to the place where Verna's body had been found. In the early morning light, everything was hushed and still. It was hard to believe a woman had violently died there only hours earlier. Ricketts pointed out the place beside the highway where the outline of her body remained in the muddy grass at the bottom of the embankment.

The night before, after breaking the news to Verna's family, Ricketts had stopped by the funeral home to help Smith Keightley. Verna's body was on the porcelain table in the center of the embalming room and Keightley was setting up his equipment. In 1936, embalming was tedious and time-consuming, and it typically took eight to ten hours to embalm a body.

When Verna's body was brought to the embalming room, she was dressed entirely in black. She wore a black dress, an elegant black wool coat with a lamb's wool collar, matching black shoes, and a black toque hat that had been found crushed underneath her body in the ditch. The back of her coat was saturated with blood, and was damp from the melted snow.

Ricketts helped Keightley undress Verna, and the first odd thing he noticed was a tear in the hem of her pink slip. The torn undergarment looked out of place with the expensive clothing they removed and laid in a corner of the room. A dark blue bruise between five and six inches in diameter on the inside of her right thigh also caught his attention. If Verna was driving the automobile, her right thigh would be on the same side as her passenger; the torn slip and bruise could indicate a struggle. When Ricketts and Keightley looked closely at the small, ragged hole in her breast, they noticed a slight discoloration the size of a quarter around the perimeter. They gently probed the wound with a steel instrument, but there was no sign of a bullet. It appeared that the bullet passed through the heart and exited the body.

The angle of the wound was peculiar. It was an inch below the left breast in the front, three inches from Verna's breastbone, and exited diagonally to the right of her backbone nearly two inches higher than the wound in front. It was a puzzle to Ricketts. If Verna committed suicide, how could she have handled the heavy army pistol to inflict this kind of wound? Ricketts checked the general's pistol and found that all of the chambers were loaded, but there were two empty shells.

After their examination was completed, Keightley embalmed Verna and then lightly washed her entire body with a formaldehyde-based soap. Marguerite Keightley assisted her husband, and styled Verna's hair and manicured her nails. These were mundane tasks that Ricketts and the Keightleys had done countless times in the past, but never in a case of this importance.

Ricketts knew that the case was either murder or suicide. But after talking with Verna's family, and seeing her body under the lights of the embalming room, there were more questions than answers.

Doc Garr would be coming by to make arrangements. Ricketts gave Keightley instructions not to release Verna's clothes to her family. "Doctor Garr is real sure that Denhardt killed his sister. He'll understand why we need to keep them for now," Ricketts said.

D. L. Ricketts was sixty-three years old and had been a licensed embalmer for thirty-two years. For seven years, he had been the Henry County coroner. On the chilly morning after the embalming, as he walked the highway looking for clues, his additional duties as coroner had suddenly become a heavy burden. He was exhausted, irritable, and overwhelmed with the complexity and enormity of the Taylor-Denhardt case. Ricketts was a man who worked in a small town and rural area. He was not trained to handle a potential murder scene and was in over his head.

On Saturday morning, the situation warranted an inquest, but Ricketts wanted more proof, something definite to use against a powerful man like Denhardt. As he walked the highway with the other men and pondered his dilemma, Sheriff Briggs unexpectedly came to his rescue.

"You know D. L.," drawled Briggs, "there's a man in Louisville who can do a real investigation for you; someone who can tell you more than you will be able to find out on your own."[42]

It was the answer to Ricketts's prayers, and he made a mental note to talk with Sheriff Harrod about hiring an investigator. But for now, they needed to examine the death scene closely. Word of Verna Taylor's death was spreading quickly in LaGrange and the telephones were ringing off their hooks. News reporters on the scent of a promising story involving General Denhardt had begun telephoning the mortuary and sheriff's office looking for any tidbits of information they could publish. Soon, the reporters and the morbidly curious would flock to the old roadbed beside Highway 22. If the men were to accomplish anything, it had to be done early in the morning while the scene was still fresh and relatively undisturbed.

For Jack Garr, the death of his older sister was a horrible

nightmare. After Doc's shocking telephone call, he had driven from Cincinnati and arrived in LaGrange during the early morning hours. Roy was on his way from Indianapolis, and Doc was in such a nervous state that he was scarcely able to function, much less ride with Jack to the place where Verna died. Doc stayed behind at the house on Fourth Avenue with his nieces, waiting for Smith Keightley to bring Verna home in her coffin. But when dawn arrived after a sleepless night, Jack made up his mind to see for himself the place where Verna was found. He also wanted to be able to assure his family that an investigation was really underway. Sheriff Briggs had no jurisdiction in Henry County, but he was a good man to have along for support. Verna's family believed it was a murder scene and it would not hurt to have another pair of eyes there.

Jack and Sheriff Briggs walked slowly up and down the highway, looking back at the increasing distance between George Baker's driveway and the place where Verna's body was found. As their eyes roamed along the side of the road, they spotted punctures in the soft earth next to the pavement. They were the heel marks of a woman's shoes, set within a space of two or three feet, and paired almost side by side in a line parallel to the road. They were pointing west toward the Baker driveway and LaGrange. Jack squatted by the side of the road and placed his finger in one of them. It was a deep hole, and the soles of the shoes had made no prints.

The heel prints were a significant find. It appeared that Verna had been in a defensive position, stepping backward as death approached her in the dark.

Farther up the highway, the men found a dark splotch on the pavement that they immediately assumed was blood. At the time, Ricketts and Harrod were more excited by the discolored pavement than by the heel prints. They hastily dug the piece of paving out of the roadway, and took it with them as evidence, believing that Verna must have been slain on the road and her body carried to the ditch.

That afternoon, Jack drove his brother Roy out to the site to show him Verna's heel prints. Roy later said, "They were right on the bank; like her body was down there and they started right up here parallel with the body and went back that way towards the east . . ."[43] On Sunday, Roy retrieved his sister's shoes from the mortuary basement and noticed that the heels were covered in mud up to the soles. He did an experiment with one of the shoes. "I took it out in the yard and made a print about the same angle that I had saw those tracks and it looked identically the same," he said.[44]

The stained pavement and heel prints were the important finds of the morning and made it all the more compelling that an official inquiry should be held. After conferring with Sheriff Harrod, Coroner Ricketts made two important decisions on Saturday morning. He would call for a coroner's inquest into the death of Verna Taylor, and telephone Police Sergeant John Messmer, the investigator Sheriff Briggs had recommended. Ricketts and Harrod were wise enough to realize they were going to need help.

When he telephoned Messmer, Ricketts introduced himself and briefly reviewed what he knew about the case. He did not need to emphasize the seriousness of the situation. Accusing someone of murder is always serious business, but accusing a former state lieutenant governor and adjutant general of murder could be very dangerous. Such a case had the potential to destroy a career, but Sergeant Messmer did not hesitate, and he volunteered to help without payment. The City of Louisville paid his salary, and that was enough. Ricketts was delighted and relieved. The Henry County authorities would now have the expertise and resources of a larger city to aid in their investigation.

Sergeant John Messmer was in charge of the crime detection

laboratory of the Louisville Police Department. In a case where there was a question of suicide or murder, the department relied on him to perform a paraffin test on the hands of the deceased and the suspect. The test could determine whether nitrates from gunpowder residue remained on the hands of an accused shooter. Messmer suggested that he perform a paraffin test on Verna's hands as soon as possible. The men arranged a meeting for later that day.

"Meet me at six at the McCarty-Ricketts Funeral Home in LaGrange. She's already laid out at her home, and I'll drive you over there," Ricketts said.

John Messmer, born in Louisville in 1897, was a self-made man with a fascination for the use of forensics in crime scene investigation. He had little formal education and was an eighth grade graduate, a shortcoming that would haunt him in the difficult months ahead. The newspapers would later describe Messmer as a "grim, square-jawed, brown-eyed man of German parentage."[45]

Before he became a city patrolman, he worked as a mechanic in Louisville supporting both his mother and father. Somehow, during his early years as a policeman for the city, Messmer became convinced that the use of a microscope could be just as important as a police officer's sidearm. He worked diligently to convince his superiors in the Louisville Police Department that a forensics unit could work hand in hand with an officer's investigation.

In 1930, he was officially listed as a city patrolman, but in that year he finally made his first breakthrough with the murder investigation of an African American barber named Donnie Yates. A suspect had been arrested for the murder of Yates, but the evidence against the man was weak and not likely to produce a conviction. However, Messmer was able to prove that the suspect had been at the scene and the victim had given him a haircut. Messmer analyzed the hair in the clippers with cross sections of the suspect's hair under his microscope and it was a match. The evidence led the man to confess. It was a personal victory for Messmer, and his superiors sent him to St. Louis for instruction in the crime lab. When he returned, he received paid tuition for a physics and chemistry course at the University of Louisville. He was given a laboratory room, four test tubes, a magnifying glass, and some fingerprint powder. It was humble, but it was a beginning for John Messmer's career in forensics. He had a reputation for being thorough and meticulous and was extremely dedicated to his vision of what a laboratory could mean to the investigation of crime scenes.[46] In 1936, he lived in Louisville with his wife and daughter in a quiet, working-class neighborhood of well-kept shotgun-style houses and bungalows.

The Henry County investigation looked like it was made for a man like Messmer. But he would soon find that his involvement in this particular case would present the most difficult personal and professional challenges of his career. There would even come a time when he believed his life was in danger. In the coming months, Police Sergeant John Messmer would learn how treacherous life can become when you challenge a powerful and dangerous man with strong ties to state politics.

Coroner Ricketts set the date of the inquest for Tuesday, November 10, at the Pendleton Schoolhouse in Henry County. The next item on Saturday's agenda was a visit to the general's home to inform him that his presence was required at an official inquiry.

D. F. Lee, the husband of Verna's Louisville cousin, asked Ricketts if he could go with them to talk with Denhardt. The day before, Verna was expected to attend a bridge luncheon at her cousin's house. Denhardt had telephoned and told Bess Lee that Verna had a headache and could not be there. Bess did not speak with Verna when Denhardt called and she was extremely distraught. The two women had been very close, and it was not unusual for Verna and her daughters to make weekend visits to the Lee home, and for Bess to visit Verna in LaGrange. Bess asked her husband to drive to LaGrange, look the general in the eye, and hear his version of Verna's death. D. F. Lee did not look forward to his mission.

Coroner Ricketts, Sheriff Harrod, Deputy Stivers, and D. F. Lee left for the general's farm around ten o'clock in the morning. They did not know what to expect when they arrived, and since they were about to tell Denhardt that he was a murder suspect, they were prepared for a frosty welcome. But the farm and surroundings were peaceful, and Ricketts bravely knocked at the door. Bertha Denhardt opened the door and was obviously surprised when the official group of men asked to see her brother. "He's very sick and not receiving visitors," she said.[47] But Ricketts would not be denied. He insisted that he needed to speak with the general, and Bertha finally opened the door and admitted them.

Denhardt was in bed and obviously drunk, but interested in what Ricketts could tell him about the Garr brothers. "Well, I've had a talk with them and they are very much wrought up, but I think possibly I can handle them," said Ricketts. "For now, I believe you'd better stay out of LaGrange."[48] Denhardt absorbed the news without comment.

Ricketts continued. "General, D. F. Lee is outside and wanting to speak with you about what happened." Denhardt nodded. "Send him back."[49]

Lee walked through the house to the general's bedroom and the other men waited patiently outside. It was not long before they heard Bertha crying, and the general swearing and cursing in a loud voice. Harrod and Stivers ran down the hallway ahead of Ricketts toward the commotion and found the furious, sputtering, and disheveled general sitting on the side of his bed. D. F. Lee stood in the middle of the room, stunned by the general's outburst. Lee had made the mistake of mentioning that the authorities were not going to accept his story of Verna's suicide, and Denhardt erupted in a fury, swearing and protesting.

"I've told Mr. Lee all about it," yelled Denhardt, "and if he's satisfied you should be too!"[50] Fueled by alcohol, he was belligerent, aggressive, and ready to fight. He was completely changed from the cooperative man of the night before.

Sheriff Evan Harrod, known in Henry County for his slow and deliberate manner of speaking, was thirty years old and powerful at six feet, five inches tall. When Henry Denhardt jumped toward him from the side of the bed, Harrod reacted quickly and with force. The younger man easily pinioned the general's arms from behind, and restrained him as he futilely struggled and swore. Harrod told his deputy to search the room for weapons and Stivers soon produced the pistol Denhardt had hidden under his pillow. Denhardt, now disarmed, was in a fury but gradually quieting as he realized his struggles were embarrassing and futile.

Harrod calmly turned to his deputy and said, "Paul, you can go ahead now and read the summons."

"Yes, sir."

As Stivers read the formal legal language summoning him to an inquest into the death of Verna Taylor, Henry Denhardt realized for the first time that he was in real trouble, and for the second time in fifteen months, he was on the wrong side of the law.

Chapter 5

THE PARAFFIN TEST

On Saturday evening, Police Sergeant John Messmer arrived in LaGrange for his first meeting with Coroner Ricketts. For Ricketts, it had been a grueling twenty-four hours since Verna's death. But Verna's funeral was the next day, and Messmer needed to perform a paraffin test on her hands before she was buried. It was very dark and near seven o'clock when Ricketts, Smith Keightley, and John Messmer rode the short distance from the funeral home to the Taylor house on Fourth Avenue. They parked on the curb near a stone Arts and Crafts bungalow with three chimneys, two front doors, and concrete steps that led to a wide, inviting front porch. It was a Sears Modern Home, ordered through the catalog and built around 1918. The house was substantial and solid, but unpretentious, reflecting the character of the family who lived there.

Before her death, Verna, her teenage daughters, and an elderly boarder known only as Mr. Tucker lived comfortably together in the house on Fourth Avenue. Verna's brother-in-law, Reuben "Bookie" Taylor, and her husband's parents lived in a large Victorian home on her right. It was a family enclave next to a wide field called the Taylor farm, which was filled with blackberry brambles that spread into the darkness beyond the lights of the houses.

On that Saturday night, Verna's porch was filled with well-dressed people coming and going, the men and women in hats, gloves, and long coats against the cold of a November evening. Men stood smoking in small groups on the porch or along the front sidewalk, speaking in low respectful voices. They nodded at Smith Keightley and D. L. Ricketts as they passed, but stared curiously at the stranger who walked by them carrying a thick, heavy briefcase.

When John Messmer walked through the doorway into the heavy press of people gathered in the front parlor, he entered a home where the solid foundation had suddenly shifted and cracked, and the woman who was the sole support of her family lay dead. She left behind a myriad of strong emotions—the stunned disbelief that accompanies an unexpected death and the anguish of losing someone who has always been there, but is suddenly gone forever. But Verna also left behind the dilemma of how to prove she did not commit suicide.

Ricketts had called the Garr brothers during the afternoon, and they readily agreed to the paraffin test. The family hoped Messmer's paraffin test would confirm what they already knew: Verna did not commit suicide.

That night John Messmer met the Garr brothers, the three men who would accompany him on one of the strangest journeys of his life. Messmer shook hands with all three: the middle brother Roy, a strong, burly man with a round face; the handsome, youngest brother Jack with his pencil-thin mustache; and Doc Garr, their older brother with the worn, haggard face and a tremor in his handshake. It was obvious that they were protective family men, devoted to their orphaned nieces and dead sister. Messmer was also introduced to Verna's two daughters, sixteen-year-old Frances and twenty-year-old Mary Pryor, both struggling to be brave in front of a houseful of family and friends. The girls were tall and willowy, and bore a resemblance to the woman in the coffin, but while their mother's hair was dark, both daughters had the lighter hair of their father.

In an alcove of the long dining room, a torchiere lamp stood on either side of a bier, throwing soft light over the woman in the coffin. She wore a pink dress. Her dark hair was parted in the middle and pulled back, and her face looked tranquil and serene. Everywhere in the dining room, there were arrangements of flowers that spilled out into the parlor beyond the pocket doors.[51]

When the room was cleared of family and visitors, and the wooden pocket doors closed for privacy, Messmer opened his briefcase and removed the curious tools he would need for the test: a Bunsen burner, brush, a cake of paraffin, an aluminum pan, two cup-shaped watch glasses, and a knife. He took the knife and shaved pieces of the paraffin into the pan to melt, then brushed some of it on the watch glasses as a control. When he was ready, he took Verna's cool, lifeless hands and brushed a warm layer of paraffin over the tops of the index fingers, thumbs, and webs of both hands. Messmer spread several layers of the paraffin and covered it with strips of gauze. He applied several more layers of paraffin over the gauze. Before it could all completely set, he removed what were now molds or casts of Verna's hands. It was obvious from his relaxed, efficient movements that he had performed the test many times. Messmer would later estimate that over the course of his career, he had probably performed a hundred paraffin tests.[52]

When Messmer nodded that he was finished, Keightley carefully wiped and rearranged Verna's hands with a towel and the test was complete. The entire process had taken less than forty minutes, and Messmer had what he needed to determine if Verna had fired a gun. As Messmer replaced the tools in the oversized leather briefcase, Ricketts assured the Garr brothers that he would let them know the results as soon as possible.

Messmer did not wait to complete the test at his Louisville

laboratory. He rode with Keightley and Ricketts to the funeral home where he immediately applied a chemical solution, or reagent, to the molds of Verna's hands. A positive paraffin test relied on the leakage of gases from the gun cylinder; these gases spread in a cloud even before the bullet emerged. The gases contained nitrates and nitrites, and tiny particles from the gases worked their way into the pores of the shooter's hand. The warm paraffin would draw the particles out of the pores of the skin. If the nitrates from gunpowder were present, the particles would turn a deep blue when the reagent was applied. Ordinary wear and tear eventually removed the particles, but Messmer believed they could remain in the pores of the skin for several days.[53]

In 1936, the paraffin test was widely used by law enforcement, but it was subject to controversy. Clever defense attorneys argued that a positive reaction could be caused by other items that contained nitrites and nitrates. The long list included matches, fertilizers, cigarette or pipe tobacco, and even medications used to treat high blood pressure. The accuracy of a paraffin test was always subject to debate in court, and Verna's test would be controversial because her hands had been washed after embalming. Messmer would later admit, "That can be problematical. The liquid soap may take it off and it may not. I've had experience with cases where it has come off and also where it hasn't come off."[54] But on the night he performed Verna's test, he was confident that the tiny particles would be there, still embedded in her hand if she had fired the pistol. Occasionally, Messmer encountered a firearm that was so tightly fitted there was little in the way of gases released. Tests would have to be made on Denhardt's firearm to determine the amount of gases it was capable of producing. But the general's pistol was an older firearm, released as a military pistol for US Army officers in 1917. Messmer was sure that it would have the clearance necessary to release gases when fired.

The men watched closely to see if the characteristic dark blue spots with a comet tail would magically appear on the molds of Verna's hands. But there was nothing, even under a magnifying glass. In Messmer's opinion, the negative test indicated that she had been murdered, and the only suspect with a likely motive present when Verna died was General Denhardt.

As a professional investigator, Messmer probably regretted that they had not done an autopsy. It was only speculation that one bullet from the general's gun killed Verna, and they were unable to say whether she was shot from the front or the back. They did not even have a bullet. Messmer might have regrets, but the gravediggers had been busy on Saturday, and the following day Verna would take her secrets with her to the grave.

Garr and Taylor relatives had been arriving from out of town, and out of state throughout Saturday and into the early hours of Sunday, November 8. They came from the nearby towns of Louisville, Crestwood, Anchorage, and Shelbyville; some drove longer distances from Ohio, New York, and North Carolina. There were immediate and extended family, friends from the LaGrange Methodist Church, the Women's Missionary Society, and employees from Verna's business. Her obituary noted that Verna Taylor was "Well known among her friends for her beauty and kindliness, her willingness to help along all lines."[55] She would be greatly missed by all who had known her.

On Sunday afternoon, the wooden pocket doors stood open, extending the two rooms into one large room to accommodate seating and standing room for the crowd of people. The kitchen in the back of the house was a hub of activity, the table and counters filled with the bounty of food customarily brought by friends to feed a grieving family. Reverend W. B. Garriott, Verna's pastor at the LaGrange Methodist Church, led the service, and the church pianist played softly on Mary Pryor's piano in the front room. The cloying scent of an abundance of flowers filled the house. Those who knew and loved Verna were seated and standing in the parlor and dining room facing the coffin on its bier.

Since Friday night, the general had been in seclusion on his farm. Bertha stayed loyally by his side and spoke to the reporters on his behalf. She described her brother's condition as "broken up and extremely nervous" and the couple as "very much in love," explaining that both her brother and Verna felt badly about her daughters' opposition to their marriage.[56] But on the day of the funeral, neither was missed in the large crowd that came to the Taylor home to say goodbye.

At the end of the service, two hundred mourners made the short journey to the Valley of Rest Cemetery. They followed the hearse from Fourth Avenue through LaGrange, driving horses and buggies, cars, or simply walking to the cemetery where the townspeople had their final resting place. When the hearse reached the gates, it turned into a lane and drove slowly to the family plot where the Taylors and Pryors were buried. The driver stopped next to a freshly dug grave beside the resting place of Rowan Barclay Taylor. As Verna's coffin was unloaded from the hearse, the large crowd of mourners fanned out across the cemetery and into the adjoining field. Reverend Garriott spoke the final words at the short, graveside service.

Just two days before, Frances Taylor had been a carefree teenager attending a dance at the Mary D. Shop. Mary Pryor had been happily planning a wedding with her fiancé, Allen Brown. But on Sunday, Allen was a pallbearer for their mother's coffin. Life had suddenly and irrevocably changed for the two Taylor girls, and it would never be the same again. While they were fortunate to have a large, loving family, both of their parents were gone, and their mother's tragic death would leave a raw wound from which the girls would never entirely recover.

On the day Verna was buried, John Messmer was once again in Oldham and Henry Counties, continuing his investigation and walking the highway near the Baker farm looking for clues. After Verna's negative paraffin test the night before, the objective of Ricketts, Harrod, and Messmer was to convince Denhardt to allow them to perform a paraffin test on his hands. The men dreaded another confrontation with Denhardt, but Messmer believed he would be able to perform the test. If Denhardt was innocent, he had nothing to lose. According to Bertha Denhardt, the general was broken up by Verna's death. The men making plans to visit his farm on Monday hoped that he would be sober, and more broken up than ready to fight.

Chapter 6

THE BLOODSTAINED COAT

On Monday morning, LaGrange was a hotbed of rumor, speculation, and gossip. The death of Verna Garr Taylor was the only topic of conversation at the courthouse, in the stores along Main Street, or on the humming telephone party lines. People were appalled by the callous, brutal death of one of the most respectable women in LaGrange. The newspaper stories and the constant presence of reporters in town ensured that LaGrange stayed in an uproar. No one believed that Verna had committed suicide, and public sentiment against Denhardt was quickly turning ugly. A group of local men were so incensed that they decided to "go get Denhardt" and take justice into their own hands. But Roy Garr discouraged the vigilantes and told them to be patient and let the law take its course.[57]

By Monday, it was common knowledge that Coroner Ricketts was calling for an inquest at the Pendleton Schoolhouse, and as word spread, a large crowd made plans to attend. Hundreds of people also drove out Highway 22 past the Baker farm, looking for the place where Verna's body had been found. George and Nettie Baker had become overnight celebrities, and they were questioned over and over by reporters and curious people who knocked at their door. The Garr and Taylor families remained silent and refused to speak with the reporters who harassed them for a statement or interview. But while they were quiet, the three Garr brothers were active in the investigation of their sister's death. They were resolute in their determination to prove that Denhardt had murdered Verna.

On Monday afternoon, Coroner Ricketts, Sergeant Messmer, Oldham County Deputy Sheriff Clayton Renaker, and Smith Keightley drove to the general's farm. There was strength in numbers, and they were hoping for the best from Denhardt, but prepared for the worst.

The news of Verna's death and Denhardt's involvement had quickly spread beyond Kentucky, and by Sunday, November 8, the Associated Press had picked up the story. The Sunday edition of the *New York Times* featured an article that included comments by Bertha Denhardt. Bertha said that Verna's daughters did not want her to marry. "The sister suggested that distress over this situation may have led Mrs. Taylor to kill herself."[58] The newspapers were fixated on a developing story, and all of the attention placed an added burden on Coroner Ricketts and his investigators. If his small team overlooked something or failed to do their investigation correctly, the entire nation would soon know.

When they reached the farm, the road to Denhardt's house was muddy and impassable, and the men left their car behind and walked the half mile through the farm fields. Ricketts knocked at the door and Denhardt opened it and graciously greeted them. Throughout the weekend, inquisitive reporters had been taking photographs of the outside of his house and asking for interviews. Denhardt was used to dealing with intrusive reporters looking for information or requesting a comment, but it was one thing to challenge a judge in Harlan County, and quite another to be a suspect in a homicide investigation. If Denhardt hoped to return to public office, the continued poor press was damning to his reputation. The embarrassing article about his altercation with the authorities had appeared in the Louisville newspaper on Sunday, and he was not about to let that happen again. Denhardt was clean, sober, and neatly dressed in a blue business suit when he invited them into his home.

It was Messmer's first encounter with Denhardt. The large, heavy-set politician shook his hand courteously but assessed him without a trace of warmth in his pale blue eyes.[59] Denhardt was talkative and quickly introduced comments about Verna into the conversation: "You know I didn't kill her; I loved her" and "We were planning such a fine Christmas this year."[60]

It was an unsettling conversation. At times, he spoke of Verna as though she were still alive and the marriage a possibility. In the same breath, he would shift abruptly back into the dark place where he knew she was dead. When the topic of the upcoming inquest was raised, Denhardt suggested that Ricketts move it to the Henry County Courthouse. It was a good suggestion. The large crowd expected to attend was far beyond the capacity of the old schoolhouse. The crowd could also be hostile; public sentiment against Denhardt was at a fever pitch in Oldham County. The Henry County Courthouse would provide more room for the hearing, and perhaps discourage some of the hotheads from driving the distance to New Castle. Ricketts agreed to speak with Henry County officials and see if they could use the large courtroom on the second floor.

When they finally reached the topic of a paraffin test, Messmer explained that he had performed a test on Verna's hands, and with the general's permission, would like to perform the same test on him. Denhardt agreed with little hesitation. He would later say, "I organized the state police of Kentucky. I knew what it was all about, in a general sort of way."[61] But he also indicated that he did not think the test was necessary because he had not fired a gun in six months.

Messmer opened his crime scene briefcase and removed the articles he had used at Verna's house on Saturday night. He applied the layer of paraffin to both of Denhardt's large hands with his brush and reinforced it with gauze before applying another coat of paraffin over the gauze. When the molds were ready, he removed them from Denhardt's hands and the initial part of the test was complete.

As Messmer was replacing his tools in the briefcase, Ricketts asked the general if he had Verna's purse. When he admitted that he did, Bertha left the room and returned with a woman's purse. As Ricketts took the purse from Bertha, he turned to Denhardt with a question. "I says, 'Did you wear an overcoat that night?' And he says, 'Yes.' He says, 'There it hangs, on the rack. And I says, 'Can we examine that overcoat?' And he says 'Yes.' So he handed it over to me, and I took it, with Mr. Keightley and Mr. Renaker and Mr. Messmer and stayed in the same room where Mr. Denhardt was and examined the overcoat."[62]

The knee-length, wool overcoat was well made and expensive with large fashionable lapels, two-inch cuffs, and a vent or split tail in the back. When Denhardt handed the coat to him, Ricketts held it up and stared long and hard at what he saw. The other men saw it too, but no one spoke as Ricketts reluctantly handed the coat back to the general. Denhardt, however, seemed totally unaware that there were drops of dried blood on his overcoat.

The thought of leaving the overcoat behind nagged at Ricketts as they left. He was in the yard walking away from the house when he decided that he could not leave without it. Everyone came to a stop when he suddenly announced, "Wait a minute. I'm going back and get that overcoat."[63] Ricketts asked Denhardt if he could take his overcoat with him, and he was once again cooperative.

"All right, but I've got to go to Taylorsville in the next day or two, and I'll need my coat to wear."

"If that's the only objection you have, you can have my overcoat and I'll take this one," said Ricketts, pulling off his coat to hand it to Denhardt.

Denhardt initially agreed to take the coroner's coat in exchange, but suddenly remembered his other coat that was not as heavy. "It's a little light one, but I think I can make out with that. Let's go get the coat."[64]

As Denhardt handed him the overcoat, he laid his hand on Rickett's shoulder and said very seriously, "Ricketts, don't let anybody put any blood on this coat. There isn't any on it now."

Ricketts replied, "We're not going to let anybody put anything on this coat that isn't on it now; and since you have mentioned blood, let's go out in the yard and see what's on this coat."[65]

In the afternoon light outside the general's house, Ricketts held up the overcoat and the men gathered around him to see for themselves. Denhardt saw the bloodstains and stared in disbelief, looked puzzled, and scratched at one of them. He started to speak, but caught himself and did not make a comment.

It was not until they had walked the half mile and arrived back at their car that the men thoroughly examined the overcoat. In all, there were fifteen or twenty spots, drops, and trickles of what appeared to be dried blood. The largest spots were the size of a dime, the smallest scarcely the size of a pinhead. They ranged the length of the coat, from the wide lapels to the inside of the vented tails. Clotted blood completely filled an upper front buttonhole.[66] This looked like a significant find, and they immediately assumed that either blood had spurted from Verna's wound onto the coat or that Denhardt had stained his coat while dragging her body to the ditch. The only remaining question for the day was whether his paraffin test would be positive.

By the time they returned to LaGrange, it was late afternoon and Roy and Jack Garr were waiting in the parking lot of the funeral home. If Denhardt agreed to have his hands tested, the brothers wanted to be present to see the results. They watched as Messmer took the chemicals from his briefcase and applied them to Denhardt's casts. A light blue speck quickly appeared and turned to a darker blue on the cast of the right hand.

Messmer later said, "There was one spot that was about the diameter of a pin; and then there were four very much smaller spots. It was necessary to look at them through a magnifying glass to detect them."[67] The spots were embedded between the thumb and index finger and all had a tiny mark that looked like a comet's tail. Messmer had seen similar markings many times before; the small specks indicated the presence of nitrates from gunpowder residue.

No one was surprised at the positive test, especially the Garr brothers who had been certain from the beginning that Denhardt had killed their sister. Ricketts breathed a sigh of relief. The stained overcoat and the positive paraffin test confirmed his decision to call for the inquest. It looked like General Denhardt had some questions to answer about what really happened on Friday night.

Verna's bloody clothes lay untouched in the corner of the embalming room and Messmer examined them carefully. According to Ricketts and Keightley, Verna's bleeding had been more internal than external; however, the back of her crepe dress and wool coat were stiff from saturated blood. Ricketts showed Messmer the torn slip, and he agreed that, with her bruised thigh, it might indicate a struggle before her death. Messmer packed Verna's bloody clothes, Denhardt's overcoat, the paraffin molds, and the piece of road paving to take with him to Louisville for laboratory analysis.

The men were satisfied with the progress of the investigation. They had reached a conclusion that Verna Garr Taylor was murdered, and they had more than circumstantial evidence against Henry Denhardt. His bloody overcoat and positive paraffin test made him their prime suspect. But they never stopped to ask themselves why he had been so cooperative. Denhardt did not have to agree to a paraffin test on his hands; he insisted that he had not fired a gun in six months and barely hesitated before he allowed Messmer to perform the test. He also did not have to cooperate with Ricketts and give him the overcoat. In the investigation against General Denhardt, there were two instances when he was genuinely surprised. The first was when he saw the dried bloodstains on his overcoat, and the second was when he learned his paraffin test was positive. But when he saw the blood and the men left with his overcoat, Denhardt knew he was facing a charge of murder and he would need to hire attorneys to defend himself. Life had suddenly become precarious for Henry Denhardt, and the murder of a woman was not something the governor could pardon.

Chapter 7

IN THE VALLEY OF REST

On Friday afternoon, one week after Verna's death, a mob of people arrived at the Henry County Courthouse and began to fill the seats of the second-story courtroom. The inquest was scheduled for two thirty, but by one fifteen even the standing room was taken and the courtroom was jammed with nearly twelve hundred spectators.[68] The distance had not deterred a large contingent from driving to New Castle to hear what Denhardt would have to say. People who could not find room to sit or stand waited on the courthouse lawn for Denhardt's arrival.

At two thirty, Sheriff Harrod called the inquest to order over the din in the large room. Six men impaneled as a jury sat waiting; a stenographer prepared to take notes. Ten witnesses were present and ready to testify, but the throng of people had come to hear only one—Henry Denhardt.

As the men and women craned their necks for a better view of the doorway, they saw the general square his shoulders and stride into the room. His older siblings Bertha and Jesse, his attorneys, and longtime friend Dr. Arthur T. McCormack followed him. Denhardt walked through the crowded aisles to the table at the front of the courtroom followed by his entourage. He stood perfectly at ease until the seating was rearranged to accommodate his party.

But if the crowd had come to hear the general's version of how Verna Garr Taylor died and decide for themselves if he looked guilty when he told the story, they were sorely disappointed. Denhardt was the first witness called by Ricketts, but when he took his seat in the witness chair, he abruptly announced that although he really wanted to make a statement, his attorneys advised him not to testify.

"You refuse?" said Ricketts incredulously.

Denhardt denied that he was refusing to testify, merely declining on advice from his attorneys. But Ricketts insisted he was refusing. Once again, Denhardt argued he was not refusing. The two went back and forth, and the old courtroom reverberated with the murmuring of hundreds of voices. Ricketts told the stenographer to note that the witness refused to testify and that he was deferring the inquest.

Denhardt's attorneys jumped to their feet objecting and demanded that the inquest continue without the general's testimony. In the confusion and noise, Sheriff Harrod calmly approached Denhardt, who was sitting in the witness chair. He handed him a warrant for his arrest sworn by Doc Garr. Denhardt's face registered surprise, but he was composed as he accepted the official papers from the sheriff.

Fifteen minutes after it began, Coroner Ricketts postponed his inquest indefinitely. He announced that the witness had refused to testify and the examining trial would be held the following week. Ricketts ordered the crowd to stay in their seats or remain standing in place until the sheriff escorted the general out of the courtroom.[69] Denhardt's attorneys and family followed as he was led to the office of County Judge A. S. Morgan. While the arrest warrant was an all-out declaration of war by the Garr brothers, the general would not be going to jail that day. Dr. McCormack quickly furnished bail of $25,000 as surety that his friend would appear at the examining trial.

In the confusion of the crowded hallway outside the courtroom, either the Garr brothers or their attorneys overheard a startling comment. Denhardt and his attorneys were considering an exhumation and autopsy to provide evidence for his defense. Verna's family was horrified at the possibility but quickly weighed their options. If the family authorized the autopsy, they could be certain that it would be done quietly, respectfully, and on their terms. If they waited, they would lose the element of surprise, and the thought of Denhardt requesting the autopsy was intolerable. That afternoon, Roy Garr made the difficult decision and signed the papers authorizing the disinterment and autopsy of his sister's body. Doc might once have led his younger brothers and made the family decisions, but he was no longer in any condition to lead them. Jack had followed his two older brothers his entire life, and went along with the decision. After that day, the family dynamics were clear: where Roy Garr led, the rest of his family would follow. When the issue was settled, the family attorneys made the arrangements to perform the autopsy that night.

Two stone pillars guard the narrow entrance into the Valley of Rest Cemetery in LaGrange. The cemetery was once a large, level pasture lying downhill from the higher plateau of LaGrange. In time, the field became the Valley of Rest Cemetery, and many years before Verna Taylor died, it was designated as a place where the city could bury its dead. Today, a long entrance avenue intersects the heart of the cemetery and leads to an area of older gravesites in the back. Many of these graves are too old for anyone living to remember the faces or voices of the people buried there. Among the graves in this quiet spot are Herndon, Pryor, and Taylor family members, and here Verna Garr Taylor was laid to rest beside her husband.

When Verna's body was carefully lowered into the grave, she took with her some intangible, but important things—the grief and tears of her family and all those who loved her; the best efforts of Marguerite and Smith Keightley to make her as beautiful in death as in life; and the solemn words of Reverend Garriott to speed her on her last journey. When her family said goodbye, and the heavy casket lid was closed, Verna was laid to rest without a thought that her body would ever be disturbed. But shortly after nightfall on November 13, the workers began the grim task of exhuming her by clearing away the flower arrangements that covered the fresh dirt of her grave.

On the night of the inquest, while the unsuspecting people of LaGrange stoked their fireplaces and woodstoves for another fall night, seven men watched the workers in the Valley of Rest Cemetery. Once the bouquets and flowers were carefully set to the side, the workers churned easily through the loose dirt with their shovels, moving ever closer to the buried coffin. The yellow light from the kerosene lanterns and the flicker of flashlights eerily illuminated the nearby gravestones, but the rest of the deserted cemetery remained in heavy darkness.

Coroner Ricketts, Sheriff Harrod, Sheriff Briggs, John Messmer, Coroner Kos Gividen of Oldham County, and Doctors H. B. Blaydes and John T. Walsh stood in the cold November wind watching the grim work of bringing Verna and her coffin to the surface.

Dr. Hubert Blaydes was the quintessential, small-town Kentucky doctor, and by 1936, he had seen nearly everything the medical world could throw his way. He was sixty years old, born in the same year as Henry Denhardt, and for thirty-three years had practiced medicine in Oldham County. Blaydes was the man to call if a child had a fever; if a baby was ready to enter the world; or if a patient had a case of gout or something more serious. He was the doctor Roy and Bettie Garr called in 1926, when their only child was dying, and the treating physician for Verna's husband when he died in 1931. Dr. Blaydes was widely respected and one of the best-known physicians in Oldham, Henry, and Shelby

Counties. He had known "Miss Verna" since she was twelve years old, and the family was comfortable with Blaydes performing her autopsy.[70]

Dr. John Walsh, the young man standing near Blaydes, was the "new" doctor in town. Thirty-seven-year-old Walsh was a graduate of the University of Arkansas School of Medicine and had practiced in LaGrange for six years. He offered the fresh perspective of a younger physician. He was not as seasoned as Dr. Blaydes, but was more knowledgeable in current medical practices.[71] For Dr. Walsh, Verna's exhumation that night was a personal challenge. In January, ten months before Verna's death, his thirteen-month-old son swallowed pills from a bottle of blood-pressure medication. The boy died during a wild ride to Louisville in a futile attempt to save his life.[72] The cold wind of November was a reminder of the bitter January day when they buried his son a short distance from Verna's grave. In December, he would have celebrated his second birthday. But John Thomas Walsh Jr. would always be thirteen months old, and Verna Garr Taylor, who had been Dr. Walsh's patient, would always be forty. That night, Walsh could understand both the anguish of Verna's family and the courage it took for Roy Garr to sign the exhumation papers.

There was a sudden thud when the workers finally reached the depth of the coffin. A draft horse was moved into position and urged slowly forward; pulleys labored to bring the heavy casket to the surface. The ropes strained and creaked as they brought the coffin closer until it finally appeared in the lantern light at the top of the gaping hole. The men carefully lifted the coffin to the side, sat it on the ground, and removed the ropes. Serving as pallbearers, they gently lifted the heavy box and placed it in the hearse. It was a funeral procession in reverse—a cortege of cars that slowly followed the hearse away from the cemetery and through the deserted streets of LaGrange, toward the McCarty-Ricketts Funeral Home.

Like so many other undertaking establishments, the business had begun in a private home where locals could purchase coffins and furniture. As the years passed, it competed for business with the older, established Peak Funeral Home on Main Street. In late 1935 and early 1936, McCarty-Ricketts expanded and moved its business into a beautiful stone building near downtown LaGrange. The new building was built with the funeral business of the future in mind, a place where the dead would lie in state in tastefully decorated individual rooms. The new funeral home offered the perfect option for families who did not have room in their houses for a coffin and mourners. The facility was considered state-of-the-art, and it was a logical choice as the place to perform a secret autopsy.

The hearse entered a basement garage in the rear of the building and a heavy door closed behind it. The casket was removed from the hearse and carried through the short hallway to the basement embalming room. Verna's body was gently removed from her coffin, and placed on the table in the center of the room where she had been embalmed a week earlier. The cold temperatures during the previous days ensured that there had been no decomposition of the body. When Verna's pink dress was removed, the embalming sutures in her torso and the stitches around the front and back gunshot wounds contrasted sharply with her pallid skin. Blaydes and Walsh carefully removed the sutures. For the next two hours, working in a room designed to prepare the dead for burial, they performed a scientific séance to make Verna tell them how she died.

In rural Kentucky in 1936, the possibilities offered by forensic science were little more than a gleam in John Messmer's eyes. Blaydes and Walsh were doctors who operated on the bodies of the living, and forensic pathology was not a regular part of their medical practice. But the Garrs knew and trusted them, and if the autopsy had to be done, they did not want a stranger or out-of-town expert working on their sister's body. The two men were excellent doctors, respected in Oldham County for their abilities, and they did their best to draw medical conclusions from what they observed. They concentrated on the bullet wounds, trying to determine whether Verna had been shot once or twice, and whether she had been shot from the front or the back. Their report was scarcely a page long.

CHEST.

Found a bullet hole in the left chest six (6) centimeters from the mid line between the 6th and 7th ribs, the hole one (1) centimeter in diameter and a powder mark toward the median line.

The flesh had a hardened appearance about the opening and through the fatty tissue. On tracing the path of the bullet we find the 7th rib had been broken and that there was a large hole through the ventricles of the heart and through the aorta, and the 7th vertebrae had been shattered, and another opening between the 5th and 6th ribs in the rear on the right side, fragmenting the 6th rib and fragments of bone found in fat in rear of the ribs near the skin. The opening in the rear five (5) centimeters from the mid line to the right about one (1) centimeter in diameter.

LOWER ABDOMEN.

On opening the lower abdomen we found that the appendix, uterus, left ovary and tubes had been removed some years before, leaving only a normal right ovary and no other abnormalities were present.

LEGS.

A bruise on the right inner thigh about six (6) inches in diameter in between the knee and hip.

Arm length was twenty-six (26) inches, outside length. From shoulder to finger tips.[73]

They also noticed a slight discoloration around the front wound which would later cause a storm of controversy. Denhardt's attorneys would argue that the discoloration was gunpowder or carbon deposits caused by a gun held to Verna's breast during a suicide.

Blaydes and Walsh photographed Verna's wounds, but out of a sense of modesty, the pictures were later cropped so that only the round bullet hole was visible. Two pieces of skin were carefully cut from around the front and back wounds, and placed in a brown bottle containing a preservative solution. John Messmer delivered the bottle to Dr. A. J. Miller, a pathologist and professor at the University of Louisville.

After two hours of meticulously examining the corpse of Verna Garr Taylor, the doctors and investigators reached their conclusions. Verna died from one front gunshot wound through her heart, and the exit wound was almost two inches higher than the entrance wound; her death was probably instantaneous, and she could not have moved on her own to a different location; the hardened appearance of the flesh around the opening of the wound, and a slight powder mark indicated she was shot at close range. They also concluded that with Verna's arm span of twenty-six inches and the trajectory of the front and rear wounds, she would have had to contort herself into an impossible position to commit suicide with a heavy pistol twelve inches long. As for the large bruise on Verna's thigh, Blaydes and Walsh agreed that it had been made recently. Satisfied that they had done their best, the doctors laid their metal instruments on a tray and signaled that they were finished.

Verna was carefully redressed and once more arranged in her coffin for the drive back to the Valley of Rest Cemetery. It had been a challenging but successful night, and the examination had been conducted in absolute secrecy. There was never a question of inviting one of Denhardt's attorneys, and no one present cared whether his legal interests were represented. It was sufficient for the men that the report of the examination was filed at the Henry County Courthouse on Monday, with copies for the court record and Denhardt's attorneys.

When Verna's body was reburied and the flower arrangements carefully replaced, it was impossible to tell that the grave had been opened that night. It was all done so quickly and quietly that neither Denhardt's attorneys, nor the press following the story were aware of an autopsy until it was completed, and Verna was safely reburied.

But news of the report was made public before it was filed in Henry County. As word of the nighttime autopsy spread, it caused a furor in LaGrange and among the newspaper reporters already in a tumult over the case. In a *New York Times* article published on Sunday, November 15, a day before the report was officially filed, John Messmer focused on the section of pavement that had been removed and taken to Louisville for analysis. "If it is proven that this is human blood and the assumption that it came from Mrs. Taylor is established, then from the nature of her wound she could not have walked 410 feet. Somebody carried her body there," he said. Attorneys J. Ballard Clarke of LaGrange and Wirt Turner of New Castle, hired by the Garrs to assist in the case, commented in the same article that the autopsy left the situation unchanged. There was nothing to indicate Verna committed suicide.[74] After Denhardt's refusal to speak at the inquest and the nighttime autopsy, local prosecutor H. B. Kinsolving was prepared to go forward with a case of willful murder against Henry Denhardt.

Attorneys for Denhardt were surprised and furious when they learned about the secret autopsy. They were rightfully incensed that a representative had not been invited to an examination that could produce legal evidence against their client. The attorneys even considered asking for a second autopsy, but after viewing and discussing the report, they decided to live with the findings. A request for a second autopsy would cause a firestorm of sympathetic publicity for the family, and their client did not need more hostile publicity.

Denhardt's attorneys had already advised him that under the circumstances, it was best to remain away from his Oldham County farm. On Friday afternoon after the inquest, Dr. McCormack drove the general and his sister to Louisville for a stay at McCormack's apartment.

It was around the time of the inquest that Denhardt's original version of why Verna committed suicide began to change. At the death scene, he had told Ricketts and Keightley that Verna was distraught and suicidal over her daughters' refusal to accept their engagement. After the inquest, Denhardt was quoted as saying, "If they had let me testify, I'd have told them quick who killed her."[75] Bertha Denhardt reportedly told friends that her brother would tell the story of why Mrs. Taylor killed herself. "It has something to do with a part of her life in which Henry was not concerned."[76]

As the general's story evolved, Chester Woolfolk, the young man riding in the laundry truck with Verna the night before she died, was introduced into the case. In the months ahead, Denhardt's attorneys would attempt to link him romantically with Verna Garr Taylor as they desperately worked to save their client's life.

Chapter 8

THE LAWYERS

From the beginning, people assumed that General Denhardt would have the best attorneys his money and influence could buy. But even Denhardt could not have foreseen how successful his "dream team" of 1936 and 1937 would be. W. Clarke Otte, Rodes Kirby Myers, and John Marshall Berry were the three Kentucky lawyers suddenly thrust into the national spotlight. Otte came from Louisville, Myers from the general's hometown of Bowling Green, and Berry from New Castle. Each member brought his individual abilities to the table, and working together, they were outstanding.

Defending the general was not an easy task. For ten months, his attorneys fought to save a difficult client who spoke to the press against their advice, wrote pages of to-do memorandums for them to follow, and eventually haggled with them over their fees. He questioned their strategy, their ability to defend him, and sometimes even their loyalty. True to his nature, Henry Denhardt worked hard to control everyone around him, even the team of attorneys trying to prove his innocence.

Forty-three-year-old W. Clarke Otte of Louisville brought years of criminal prosecution and defense to the team. As a commonwealth attorney in the 1920s and '30s, he sent forty-three men to their deaths in the electric chair. But after a successful career of prosecuting criminals, he launched into a new career of defending them and was just as successful. He won seventeen consecutive capital murder cases, and had a solid reputation as one of the best criminal attorneys in Louisville. Otte had an uncanny ability to win a case that looked like a certain loser.[77] Before his legal career, Otte was an intern at the old Louisville General Hospital, and the experience gave him an invaluable knowledge of science and medicine. During the Denhardt trial, Clarke Otte was the only attorney on either side able to quickly grasp the complex scientific theories of the expert witnesses.

For Otte, it was all a legal game of strategy. It did not matter whether his client was innocent or guilty; he loved the challenge and he loved to play the game. But despite all his brilliance in the courtroom, Otte suffered from a severe drinking problem that kept him from being one of the most successful attorneys in the country. He was married four times, and divorced from three of his wives as a direct result of his alcoholism.[78] Despite his foibles, Otte was the cornerstone of Denhardt's defense team, and the one attorney Denhardt could not do without. However, both men were headstrong and had aggressive egos that were a barrier to a smooth working relationship; they frequently clashed. As time passed, Clarke Otte often bore the brunt of his client's suspicions and criticisms. Otte was the most valuable man on Denhardt's defense team, but the one least appreciated by his client.

The brilliant orator Rodes Myers was an attorney and politician from the general's home town of Bowling Green. Denhardt and Myers had been friends for twenty-five years, and the general probably turned to Myers for advice in November 1936. Born in 1901, Myers attended the college that later became Western Kentucky University, making a name for himself as a young man with uncanny oratory skills. He attended law school at the University of Cincinnati and won an oratory competition against competitors from the College of William and Mary. He transferred to the University of Kentucky and received his juris doctor from the law school in Lexington in 1925. Myers was sleek and handsome with coal black hair and chiseled features, and all eyes were drawn to him when he took the floor in a courtroom. In 1936, he was a state representative with a law practice; he seemed too busy a man to devote the time and energy to a capital murder case hours away from his home.

Myers eventually served as thirty-eighth lieutenant governor of the state, and was in office from 1939 through 1943. He was a state senator from 1948 to 1950. Like his friend Henry Denhardt, Rodes Myers had a weakness for alcohol and beautiful women. His drinking problem grew steadily worse and his health deteriorated as the years passed, but in 1936, his star was in the ascendant and he stepped forward to help a friend. It was a decision that nearly cost him his life.[79]

Thirty-four-year-old John Marshall Berry was a lawyer and tobacco farmer who lived in Henry County. He had a law office in New Castle, and was acquainted with the local politics involved in trying a case. The Henry County courtroom was a familiar forum to him. He had tried cases in front of Circuit Judge Charles C. Marshall and was familiar with his courtroom etiquette. Berry was a lawyer in a small town, and his cases ran the gamut from domestic issues, wills, and estate work, to personal injury and the occasional criminal case. He was an excellent attorney and a gentleman, respected by those who worked with him. His local experience was invaluable to two out-of-town lawyers that a Henry County jury would quickly size up as "foreigners."

For Clarke Otte, defending the general was a challenge, another chance to defy the odds. For Rodes Myers, it was the need to help an old friend who was in trouble. But for John Berry, it was an opportunity to defend a man he believed was innocent. In 1936, John Berry believed Henry Denhardt did not kill Verna Taylor, and he still believed it when he died in 1991 at age ninety. Berry was a solid attorney, and a loyal friend and supporter of Henry Denhardt and his family. While Berry was often exasperated with Denhardt as a client, his loyalty and friendship never wavered.

For a brief time, Denhardt was also represented by attorney Beckham Overstreet. Overstreet was forty-nine years old, and lived and practiced law in Louisville. He was born in LaGrange, and educated in the Oldham County schools. Overstreet graduated from the Jefferson School of Law in Louisville, and at one point in his legal career had a record of winning thirty-five consecutive cases.[80] Overstreet claimed that the general hired him on November 11, and he was in court for Denhardt at both the inquest and the examining trial. But in February 1937, Overstreet withdrew after only four months of working on the case. When he demanded payment for his legal work, Denhardt claimed that Overstreet was a volunteer. Denhardt had a bad habit of dickering over legal fees as Otte, Myers, and Berry would learn in the future. Overstreet responded by filing suit in Oldham Circuit Court for $2,500, claiming "the conduct of the defendant was degrading and humiliating" to him.[81] The Oldham Circuit Court was not interested in resolving the general's legal disputes with his attorney and promptly dismissed the lawsuit. After his brief time working on the Denhardt case, Overstreet continued his usual law practice. He died in his law office in Louisville in 1942 and is buried near the grave of Verna Garr Taylor in the Valley of Rest Cemetery.[82]

The duty of prosecuting the general fell to Herbert Benton "H. B." Kinsolving, Jr. Kinsolving was a stocky, sandy-haired, commonwealth attorney with law offices on Main Street in Shelbyville. Forty-eight-year-old Kinsolving was the son of a lawyer, and had graduated from the Virginia Military Institute in 1911.[83] After graduation, he stayed on at VMI for a year as an assistant professor of history and tactics. In 1916, Kinsolving was one of the 2,394 Kentucky troops who participated in the Mexican border campaign and the search for Pancho Villa. Captain Herbert B. Kinsolving Jr. was the commander of Company H of Louisville, Kentucky. Ironically, his second lieutenant was W. Clarke Otte. John Messmer served as a sergeant in the Regimental Hospital Corps, and Major Henry H. Denhardt commanded the First Battalion.[84] Whether Kinsolving met or became acquainted with Denhardt or Messmer during the brief campaign or later during his service in the Great War is unknown. But during the Denhardt trial, he was frequently referred to as "Captain" by the other attorneys.

Kentucky law leaves the decision to prosecute a defendant and what charges to file entirely at the discretion of the prosecutor. It was Kinsolving who looked at the mounting evidence against Denhardt and made the decision to prosecute him for murder. He was aided by two attorneys hired by the Garr family to represent their interests, Ballard Clarke and J. Wirt Turner.

In 1936, fifty-five-year-old Ballard Clarke was a seasoned attorney who had practiced law in Oldham County for thirty-three years. Clarke not only assisted in the prosecution against Denhardt, he was one of the witnesses during the trial. On the afternoon of November 6, Clarke was walking to the Pendennis Club in Louisville when he met Verna on the street, who was also walking to the Pendennis Club to meet the general. Clarke was a family friend and had known Verna Garr Taylor for many years. As it turned out, he was one of the last people to have a conversation with her before she died that evening.

Fifty-five-year-old Jonathan Wirt Turner of New Castle was the son of Henry County attorney W. W. Turner. Like Ballard Clarke, Turner was a longtime practitioner with twenty-five years of experience. His law office was located on the town square in New Castle near the courthouse. Turner had an interest in state politics and in 1928, served as a delegate to the Democratic National Convention. In 1939, he challenged Judge Charles

Marshall for circuit judge of the twelfth district, and the returns had Turner in the lead by thirteen votes. When Marshall requested a recount, the two decided amiably to a split term. Turner served as circuit judge of the twelfth district from 1943 to 1951. During the Denhardt trial, he was frequently referred to as a special assistant prosecutor hired by the Garrs to aid the prosecution.[85] His daughter, Elizabeth Turner Rouse, passed her bar exam in 1935 and worked as a lawyer in her father's law office. She also aided the prosecution during the Denhardt trial. Both Turner and Clarke were trusted by the Garr and Taylor families, and Clarke was a longtime family friend. It was logical that they turned to the two attorneys to represent their interests in the murder case against Denhardt.

Henry County attorney James "Jimmy" Thomas, known for his courtroom theatrics and fiery speeches, also assisted the prosecution team. Short in stature, described by the newspapers as plump, Thomas was from a Jewish family in a county that was largely Protestant. He could weep dramatically when it helped his case and kept a handkerchief close to dab his eyes.[86] Thomas was known for his dramatic ability to bring the most sedate crowd to its feet when he took center stage in the courtroom. He was a popular figure around New Castle.

These were the men who squared off in the courtroom in the days following the inquest: one group working diligently to prove Denhardt's innocence, the other group working just as hard to send him to the electric chair. With the entry of the lawyers, the investigation into Verna's death and the prosecution of Denhardt became a desperate legal game of strategy. During the coming months, the lawyers would bicker and squabble, attempt delays, withhold evidence, and file motions in opposition to one another. They were always entertaining to the public avidly following the drama. But in mid-November 1936, the examining trial of November 20 loomed days ahead, and other than the autopsy report, the defense did not know what cards the prosecution was holding against their client. So it came as no surprise that the first legal battle between the general's attorneys and the prosecution was over evidence.

Chapter 9

A PROBLEM WITH EVIDENCE

When Henry Denhardt was agitated or angry, he paced briskly around the room, throwing his hands in the air or hitting the back of chairs in a fury and gesturing wildly.[87] By Monday morning, November 16, he was nearly apoplectic with rage. Rodes Myers, Clarke Otte, John Berry, and Beckham Overstreet watched the display of temper as the general stormed around the front room of Dr. McCormack's apartment, pacing and hitting the backs of chairs. His tantrum was due to the problem with evidence. The general had agreed to the paraffin test, but the prosecution had not shared the results. He had willingly handed over his overcoat and gun, but no one knew where they were or who was conducting tests. There was a piece of pavement missing from Highway 22, but no one knew where that was either. The examining trial, or preliminary hearing was Friday, four days away, and all they had was the report from Verna's secret autopsy. If the court felt there was enough evidence against Denhardt at the examining trial, Dr. McCormack would not have the opportunity to post bond. Denhardt would go to jail until the grand jury met in January. It was an intolerable situation, and they were at a critical impasse. No one could imagine Brigadier General Henry Denhardt, former lieutenant governor and adjutant general, behind bars, but there was a very real possibility that it could happen on Friday.

After considering the options, Denhardt's attorneys decided to file a motion asking the judge to force Kinsolving and his team to share the evidence. If County Judge Morgan denied the motion—and that was a very real possibility—they would appeal to a higher court. But Morgan might also take their motion under consideration and delay the examining trial while he looked over the situation. More than anything else, Denhardt and his team needed a delay. They wanted time to get their defense organized, and time for passions to cool in Oldham and Henry Counties. Many people were ready to turn vigilante and hang their unpopular client. However, before they filed a motion, Denhardt and his attorneys decided to make one more attempt. They would send Beckham Overstreet to reason with Coroner Ricketts, one local man to another. Overstreet saw a golden opportunity to impress his difficult client, and he quickly agreed to see what he could do.

On Monday, Coroner Ricketts was having a quiet day at the funeral home. Of course, the reporters were coming around and pestering him for information, but he had almost gotten used to their constant presence. With Messmer and Kinsolving on the job, his life had become quieter again, a welcome relief from the early days after Verna's death. When he heard the front door open and slam shut, he wearily assumed that it was another reporter arriving to ask more questions. But when he climbed the stairs from the embalming room, he found Beckham Overstreet standing in the front room, paper and pen in hand. Beckham Overstreet irritated Henry Denhardt, and he irritated Coroner Ricketts, too. Overstreet was a LaGrange man who knew the reputation of the Garr and Taylor families. It was appalling that a man from LaGrange had ingratiated himself into the services of someone like Denhardt. When Ricketts bluntly asked him what he wanted, Overstreet did not mince words. He demanded the results of the paraffin tests. "We have a right to know," said Overstreet.[88]

Ricketts did not care for Overstreet's overbearing manner, and the fact that he was a lawyer did not intimidate him. He retorted, "If that's what you want, we'll give it to you. The paraffin tests showed that Mrs. Taylor could not have fired the bullet through her heart. We found no evidence of powder on either of her hands. She did not commit suicide."[89]

Overstreet blinked rapidly and, temporarily at a loss for words, began to take notes. When he recovered, he asked, "What about the general's paraffin tests? We demand that you release those results."[90]

Ricketts was tired of Overstreet's demands and decided to end the confrontation. "We're not going to announce the results right now. We haven't finished our analysis," he said.[91]

Overstreet spun on his heel and left the funeral home. His insolence had ruined Ricketts's peaceful day. But he would have been consoled to know the confrontation had ruined Overstreet's day, too. His mission on behalf of the defense team was a failure. He had learned only that Verna Taylor's paraffin tests were negative.

When he reported the conversation, no one was surprised that he had failed to shake Ricketts. After they spoke with Denhardt, his attorneys decided to release a statement to the press: "We don't regard the test on Mrs. Taylor as a blow to the defense. We don't think the paraffin test is important. Of course, it will be negative for the general, too. We know perfectly well General Denhardt hasn't fired a gun for six months."[92]

While their public response downplayed the results of the paraffin tests, Denhardt's attorneys were very concerned with what cards the prosecution was holding. As planned, they quickly filed a motion in the Henry County Court. They asked the court to impound the evidence, including both sets of paraffin tests, Verna's garments, Denhardt's overcoat, the pistol and cartridges, and the piece of pavement. Their motion read: "The accused states that unless he and his attorneys are accorded this consideration,

and are allowed opportunity to examine and analize [*sic*], or cause
to be examined and analyzed by competent persons, articles and
items of evidence hereinabove referred to, he will be deprived
further of his lawful rights and will be delayed unduly and
injuriously in the investigation of the charge made against him,
and his defense thereto."[93] According to the legal argument made
by his attorneys, Denhardt would be *irreparably harmed* if he could
not defend himself against the unknown evidence. A hearing
on the motion was scheduled at the courthouse for Wednesday,
November 18, and the attorneys prepared for their first legal
battle.

Myers, Otte, and Berry thought they had a solid position.
Their client had been cooperative, and they had a legal right to
know the test results. They also were entitled to conduct their
own tests on Denhardt's coat, Verna's clothes, and the highway
pavement. The secretive nighttime autopsy still rankled, and
they knew they were correct in arguing that one of them should
have been present. On November 18, the teams of lawyers argued
for and against the motion as Judge Morgan patiently listened.
At the end of the oral arguments, he immediately ruled against
Denhardt. The examining trial would go forward as planned, and
the prosecution did not have to share their evidence. Morgan's
ruling was a blow, but not unexpected, and the defense still had
one option remaining. That afternoon, Rodes Myers jumped in
his car and sped to the state capital in Frankfort with an appeal on
the seat beside him. They would appeal Judge Morgan's ruling to
a higher court, the Kentucky Court of Appeals.

The Court of Appeals did not waste time in hearing their
appeal. Late on Thursday, November 19, they overruled the writ
of prohibition, Denhardt's last chance to delay the examining trial.
But it was a partial victory for the defense team. The *Louisville
Courier-Journal* reported, "In handing down its decision, the
Court of Appeals added a ruling that, if any articles of evidence

sought in the motion are introduced by the Commonwealth on Friday, County Judge A. S. Morgan should grant a delay sufficient to let the defense run tests on them."[94]

Wirt Turner commented to the press on behalf of the prosecution team. He explained that they had no objections to sharing any of the items requested, but did not want them to be used as an excuse to delay the examining trial.[95]

Expectation was high that Denhardt would testify at the examining trial, but the reporter for the *Shelby Sentinel*, in nearby Shelbyville, was doubtful. "The curious not to say maudlin people who crowded New Castle last Friday to see and hear the Henry County coroner's inquest into the Oldham County tragedy will be again disappointed, in the opinion of many, if they go back there today, to hear testimony in General Denhardt's examining trial." The reporter predicted that Denhardt's lawyers would advise him not to testify, and would let the case go forward to the grand jury "so that he and his attorneys will know what sort of case is being made against him, before he undertakes to prove his innocence, in what his best friends will admit is a serious situation."[96]

Henry Denhardt was in the most "serious situation" of his life, and during the days before the examining trial, his physical and emotional condition had deteriorated. He stayed in seclusion at Dr. McCormack's apartment with his sister, Bertha. He was confined to bed and under the care of a personal nurse who had difficulty restraining him during several violent episodes that week. On Tuesday, Denhardt was seen outside the hotel in downtown Louisville walking slowly with the nurse. He was reportedly receiving liberal doses of paraldehyde, a sedative and hypnotic used to induce sleep in patients suffering from delirium tremens related to alcohol withdrawal.[97]

Bertha was staying at the apartment with him and was reportedly near collapse from mental strain. She was under the care of the same personal nurse as her brother. On Thursday night, a reporter called the apartment. When Bertha answered, he asked to speak with Denhardt. She told him that her brother was asleep, and she refused to disturb him because he needed his rest; questions should be directed to his attorneys. When asked to supply the name of her brother's physician so that the paper could get a statement on his condition, Bertha replied that it would not be necessary. She said, "He hasn't a physician now."[98] Dr. McCormack had been Henry Denhardt's personal physician for many years, and he undoubtedly wrote the prescriptions for his friend. By the end of the week, there was widespread speculation that Denhardt would send a doctor's note excusing him from the examining trial for medical reasons.

On Friday morning, November 20, the question of whether he would attend was answered when the general and Bertha, with their nurse, Jesse Denhardt, Dr. McCormack, and Rodes Myers, arrived at the chaotic scene in front of the Henry County Courthouse. A mob had gathered on the courthouse lawn, and the Ladies Missionary Society of the New Castle Baptist Church was doing a steady business selling sandwiches. Reporters surged toward the Denhardt car with their cameras held high and bulbs flashing. State police officers and a dozen sheriff's deputies stood guard around the courthouse. It looked like the small town of New Castle had prepared for the arrival of public enemy number one.

Henry Denhardt was completely changed from the confident man who had entered the same second-floor courtroom a week earlier. He was pale and visibly agitated as he walked into the room and found a chair at the table with his back to the hostile crowd.[99] Several state troopers stood guard behind him near the defense table. The three Garr brothers and their nieces sat on the opposite side of the courtroom near the table designated for the prosecution.

Six witnesses waited outside the courtroom to testify: George and Nettie Baker, Smith Keightley, Barney Browning, J. B. Hundley, and Dr. H. B. Blaydes. But there would be no witnesses for the defense that day, and the spectators were disappointed when word spread that the general would not testify. Once Denhardt had taken his seat, and all the attorneys were in place, Judge A. S. Morgan rapped his gavel and called the packed courtroom to order. When the noise subsided, he asked County Attorney Jimmy Thomas to call his first witness in the examining trial of General Denhardt.

Chapter 10

THE EXAMINING TRIAL

On the day of the examining trial, Henry County Attorney Jimmy Thomas was calm and confident, as comfortable in the New Castle courtroom as in the rooms of his home. This was his theater, his stage, and he had paced the cracks of the old wooden floor before the judge's bench countless times. On that Friday morning, two weeks after Verna's death, Thomas was a man on a mission. He was determined that before the day ended, he would send the pompous general to jail where he belonged. But he would have to be cautious in his questioning of witnesses. If he introduced the paraffin tests or any of the physical evidence Denhardt's attorneys demanded, Judge Morgan would have to stop and delay the examining trial. Instead, Thomas intended to focus on the suspicious behavior of Denhardt before and after Verna's body was found. Today there would be no repeat of what happened on the day of the inquest. The examining trial would go forward as planned with or without Denhardt's testimony.

Jimmy Thomas began by asking Judge Morgan to call Barney Browning as his first witness. Browning nervously walked into the courtroom, placed his hand on a Bible to take his oath, and took his seat in the witness chair. The packed courtroom listened spellbound as the first witness of the day began to speak.

Barney Browning owned and operated the Browning Service Station at the Pendleton-Sligo crossroads. On the cold, rainy night of November 6, just before closing time, Verna Taylor had appeared at his door asking for help with a stalled car. George Baker and his wife, Nettie, were visiting that night, and George followed Browning and Verna next door to the Pendleton Schoolhouse where the car was parked. Although Verna appeared to be in a hurry, she took the time to introduce herself to Browning as they walked.

"Mr. Browning, I don't believe you know me."

"I don't."

"Well, I'm Mrs. Taylor from LaGrange and I operate the Community Laundry there."[100]

Browning and Baker followed her and saw the car sitting in the darkness of the schoolyard. There was a large man inside who did not step out to introduce himself, but waited in the car while they attempted to push it to the station. The stalled car was heavy, the ground muddy and slippery, and Browning and Baker were unable to push it very far.

"I asked her what was wrong with this fellow that he couldn't help push the car off the driveway," recalled Browning.

Verna replied, "He's sick," and offered no further explanation.[101]

Verna was behind the steering wheel guiding the car, and George Baker used his vehicle to shove it into the road, hoping the car would restart. Nettie Baker then left the service station with her husband, and Browning returned inside and watched from the doorway. He saw the Denhardt car slowly round the corner at the intersection, and the momentum of the hill sent it a short way down the highway until it stopped again. Browning heard another car approaching and he feared it might collide with the unlighted car in the road. He watched as Verna stepped into the road and flagged down the car, and a few minutes later, it began to push the Denhardt vehicle. The cars were still on the highway when he closed his door. Browning went to bed and did not hear anything unusual that night. He did not know Verna Taylor was dead until the next morning when his early customers told him what had happened.

Thomas dismissed Browning and asked for his next witness, farmer George Baker to come into court. On the night of November 6, 1936, George R. Baker was just one more dirt-poor, Kentucky farmer like so many others in the state—a man with little education and limited opportunities. He was honest and hardworking, and survived from one lean season to the next as he scratched out a living on his farm. He was forty-nine years old, but looked sixty. His face was lined and worn from too many days spent working his farm in the hot Kentucky sun and too many cold winters in the bitter winds. His children had married and moved away, leaving George and his wife to work the acreage that surrounded their white farmhouse.

But since the night he had assumed the role of Good Samaritan, the Bakers' lives had changed as dramatically as those of the Garr, Taylor, and Denhardt families. Their daily routine of milking, canning, quilting, and tending their farm had been turned upside down. The Bakers were besieged by reporters and curiosity seekers looking at landmarks and asking questions. Their photographs appeared in the newspapers reliving their role in the events of November 6. There were pictures of George Baker holding a lantern over a female model lying in a ditch. Another of George and Nettie debating what they should do after hearing a gunshot. The photographers even took pictures of Trixie, the Bakers' mixed shepherd dog who barked furiously at something on the night Verna died.[102] But the Bakers did not mind the hubbub. For them, a new and exciting life had begun on November 6, and while they were kind people and sympathetic to the tragedy that had unfolded on their property, they were quietly enjoying the publicity and attention.

On the day of the examining trial, the Bakers waited anxiously outside the courtroom dressed in their best clothes—Nettie in a simple dress and hat, and George in his good suit. He did not know what to expect, had never been a witness in a trial, and had never seen this many people jammed into such a small space. But he was the key witness for the prosecution, and when he heard his name called, he walked slowly into the courtroom. Baker was amazed at all the faces that looked toward him as he entered. Many he recognized as local people, but there were also strangers, sitting and standing against the walls, in the aisles, and on the iron radiators. It was overwhelming, but he trusted Jimmy Thomas as another Henry County man, and he took his oath. When Thomas began his questions and asked him to return in his mind to the night of November 6, Baker lost his nervousness and began to tell the story of the strangest night of his life.

Baker recalled that he stopped in front of the service station to pick up his wife, and watched the Denhardt car round the intersection ahead of him with Verna at the steering wheel. It drifted downhill on Highway 22, but finally came to a stop in the road. Before he could get his car in gear, he heard the roar of another automobile coming through the intersection and watched as it drove straight toward the unlighted car on the highway. Verna flagged down the approaching car, and when the Bakers arrived, J. B. Hundley had stopped to help. Hundley examined the battery and borrowed a screwdriver from George to check the connections for a loose wire. He remembered that Denhardt got out of the car to watch.

"Mr. Hundley, can you push this car to LaGrange?" asked Verna.

"I could, but I'm afraid to; you can't see how to guide it. I'll take you all over to LaGrange and you can get a garage man there."[103]

Denhardt spoke for the first time. "We don't want to leave the car here with no lights or no one around it."[104]

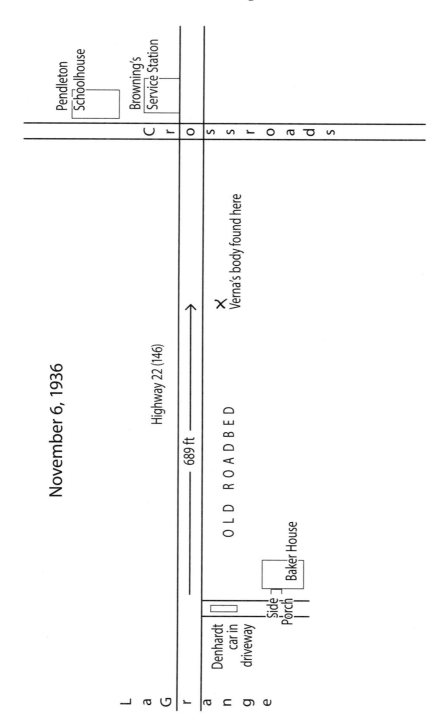

November 6, 1936

Pendleton Schoolhouse

Browning's Service Station

Crossroads

Highway 22 (146)

✕ Verna's body found here

OLD ROADBED

689 ft

Baker House

Side Porch

Denhardt car in driveway

L a G r a n g e

Baker offered a solution to the general's concerns. "Mr. Hundley," said Baker, "I will tell you what we will do. If you will drive in front of this car, I will take my car and push it down the road to my entrance, and you all can leave it off the road and then get a garage man."[105]

It seemed like a logical solution, but before they started pushing, Hundley spotted Verna's glove on the road and handed it to her. Baker saw her pick up her other glove before she slid into the driver's seat. With Verna once again behind the steering wheel guiding the car, Hundley in front lighting the way, and Baker behind pushing with his vehicle, they moved the stalled car to his driveway. He drove around the car, dropped off his wife at the side porch, and parked in his shed. Baker drained his car radiator and checked a short in the lights. When he was finished, he walked into the house and pulled his chair close to the warmth of the fireplace. He assumed Verna and the general had ridden to LaGrange with Hundley.

Baker estimated that twenty minutes after he came into the house, he heard Trixie begin to bark in the front yard. He walked to the door and stepped out on the side porch to calm the dog and see if anything was wrong. He saw Denhardt "walking very fastly, going back this way past the light of my window, out my drive that goes down by the yard . . ."[106]

Denhardt stopped when he saw Baker and asked if there was a telephone in the house. He wanted to call LaGrange and check on delivery of the battery. Baker told him he did not have a telephone, but that the couple was welcome to come inside and stay warm by the fire while they waited. Denhardt said, "I guess not," and Baker watched him walk back toward his car.[107]

Baker closed the door and returned to his chair by the fire. He had been sitting several minutes when he saw the headlights of a car that appeared to be slowing as it approached his driveway. The Bakers thought it might be Hundley returning with the battery.

George walked to the front room and peered out a window into the darkness. He looked at the highway just beyond his gate and could see the taillights of a car receding in the distance toward Browning's Service Station. He watched it turn left at the crossroads in front of the service station and disappear. Baker was still in the front room when he heard the loud explosion of a gunshot. The sound came from the east, the same direction the car had just traveled, but it came from somewhere between his house and the crossroads.

"What was that?" exclaimed Nettie. "It was a gun!" he exclaimed. "I'm afeard something serious has happened—it was so close."[108]

Baker estimated that, when he heard the gunshot, ten or fifteen minutes had passed since he had spoken with Denhardt at the side porch.[109]

The Bakers were startled and afraid. They lived in a rural area, had no telephone, and were not certain what to do. George hesitated and discussed the situation with Nettie, but four or five minutes later, he walked outside to see what had happened. It was very dark and cold that night and there was no moon. There was partially melted snow on the ground and water standing in his yard. As he approached the stalled car, he heard a noise that sounded like "a popgun" or something that sounded like a twenty-two rifle.[110] In the darkness, he could see Denhardt's head and shoulders, and it looked like he was turning around or stepping up to his car. When Denhardt saw Baker approaching, the general walked toward him and they met in the yard.

"Did you hear that gun?" asked Baker.

"Yes, I did. Did you?" asked Denhardt.

"Yes sir, and the second one, too."

Denhardt took a step toward him and asked, "Wasn't that second shot fearful?"

"Yes it was, and the first one, too, Baker agreed, but he

wondered how the general could believe the pop shot was 'fearful' after hearing the first loud report.[111]

"The lady that was with me went up the road to pick up her glove," Denhardt said. He turned and opened his glove box. "I had a gun in here, but it's gone. Have you a flashlight?"[112]

"Yes, sir," replied Baker, and he walked back to his house to get a lantern. When he returned, Hundley was arriving with C. E. "Cuba" Shaver, a LaGrange mechanic, and he pulled his car to a stop beside Denhardt. Baker heard Denhardt say, "Boys, drive up the road and look for her," and the three men got into the car and drove to the intersection and back while Baker stood in his driveway and watched. When they returned, Hundley quietly asked Baker, "What do you think of that? We never saw anything of that lady."[113]

Two gunshots in the night and a missing woman. No one knew whether she was alive or dead. Verna could have been injured and waiting for help, but Baker testified that the general stood and watched as the men started to work on the battery. Removing it was harder than they expected, and it took additional time to install the new one. Baker recalled that Denhardt waited by the car and repeated several times, "She was the finest woman I ever knew."

Denhardt seemed very nervous to Baker, and George could smell whiskey on the general's breath. His first impression was that Denhardt was drunk, but he later changed his mind when he "saw him walking around so fast."[114]

When the battery was finally installed, Hundley said, "Let's go see about the lady."[115] Baker handed him his lantern, but hesitated to leave Nettie alone. He told Hundley to begin the search without him while he checked on his wife.

When Baker caught up with the men, they were walking the highway, Hundley on the right and Shaver on the left with a flashlight. Denhardt lagged behind approximately thirty feet, keeping to the middle of the road as they searched. Hundley spotted Verna's body near the corner of Baker's property line, in the ditch next to the old roadbed. Verna was dead and lying on her back in the water and snow, a glove clasped in her left hand, another by her feet. One shoe was on her foot. Baker testified that the other glove "was setting right in between her arm and body, right by her hip."[116] A large pistol lay nearby. When Denhardt caught up with them and saw Verna's body, Baker heard him say, "Ain't that awful!" but did not hear him say anything else. Baker testified that the general stood and watched the men from the side of the highway, but made no move toward Verna's body.[117]

J. B. Hundley volunteered to go to LaGrange for help, and as he sped away, he yelled out his car window for them to stay with the body until he got back. Baker waited with Denhardt and Cuba Shaver for several minutes, but he was worried about leaving Nettie alone in the house and walked ahead, leaving the two men on the road. Denhardt and Shaver trailed behind Baker, leaving Verna's body alone in the ditch. As they walked, Shaver spotted a flashlight and keys lying on the edge of the road. Baker heard Denhardt confirm that they were his, and the two men continued walking to the car in the driveway.

When Hundley returned from LaGrange with Smith Keightley, Baker was standing at his gate with Denhardt and Shaver. Denhardt climbed in beside Keightley, and Baker rode the running board with the other men. He heard Denhardt ask Keightley to see if Verna was wearing a diamond ring. "I wish you would take care of it for me," he heard Denhardt say.[118] Baker never saw Denhardt leave the highway or approach Verna's body that night. He stood in the road and watched as the other men loaded her in the ambulance.

George Baker's testimony was simply spoken, but believable and compelling. While he often struggled with remembering time and distance, his memory of what he heard on the highway was excellent. It was the first time he told his entire story in a courtroom, and the large crowd was mesmerized. He left them with several important points to consider.

Verna seemed perfectly normal and was the person driving and guiding the vehicle. She led the efforts to get help while Denhardt waited in the car. Denhardt seemed to know Verna was dead before her body was found. He kept a physical distance from the body, lagging behind in the search efforts and never bothered to check for a sign of life. Worst of all, he walked away and left her body alone and unguarded in the dark. His actions at the scene were cold and callous, and it was hard to comprehend that anyone in love would act that way on finding their beloved dead.

Thomas was finished with his witness, and turned to the defense table to see if anyone would ask questions. But there were none, and George Baker's day in court was finished. Thomas called Nettie Baker as his next witness.

Nettie recalled that they arrived home around ten minutes after nine. Perhaps thirty or thirty-five minutes later she was sitting in her dining room and heard a loud gunshot. She believed it was four or five minutes after the shot that her husband stepped outside to see what had happened. It was cold that night, and all of the windows were closed. She heard the first loud shot, but did not hear a second gunshot. Once again, there were no questions from the defense table. Thomas dismissed Nettie and called for J. B. Hundley, the LaGrange barber, to be sent into the courtroom.

Juett "J. B." Hundley was a handsome man in his late twenties or early thirties. He too, was enjoying his new life as a celebrity. But unlike the Bakers, he was an opportunist, and in late November, he was considering a plan to make extra money out of his role in the tragedy and leave LaGrange. But on November 20, Thomas only knew him as the witness who overheard Baker's unfortunate remark at the death scene. On the night of November 6, Hundley was driving home to LaGrange from a visit with his sister. As he came over the hill at the intersection by the Browning Service Station, he could see a green car sitting in the highway ahead of him. A lady ran out from behind it and flagged him down. Hundley had patronized the Community Laundry for several years and recognized Verna Garr Taylor.

Verna explained that the car had stalled and Hundley agreed to help. He pulled up behind Denhardt's car and started pushing, but his bumper slipped over the bumper guard of the other car. Hundley recalled that Baker arrived on the scene in his car and helped unlock the two bumpers.

On the highway, Hundley tested the battery and found that "it was flat, no juice there at all." He noticed Verna's glove lying on the running board. "I picked it up and handed it to her, and told her to be sure she had the other one. She looked in between her and Denhardt, and said, 'I think it is in here.'"[119]

Verna asked Hundley if he would push the car into LaGrange, but he thought it would be too dangerous to try to push the car six miles on a dark road without lights. He volunteered instead to drive to LaGrange and bring back a battery from a garage. When Baker suggested they push the car to his driveway until Hundley returned with the battery, everyone agreed to the plan. Baker drove in front, lighting the way. Verna guided Denhardt's car with the steering wheel, and Hundley pushed from behind as they eased the car safely into Baker's driveway.

Before Hundley left for LaGrange, he hollered back from the highway asking if the couple wanted to ride to LaGrange with him. Someone said, "No, we'll just wait."[120] Hundley was unable to tell who declined his offer because of the noise from his car's motor. As he left, he saw Baker pulling into his driveway past the Denhardt car.

Hundley returned from LaGrange with a new battery and mechanic Cuba Shaver. Denhardt was standing in front of his car alone and Hundley assumed Verna was in the Bakers' house waiting and staying warm. But as they focused the lights to install the battery, he heard Denhardt say, "I heard two shots up the road."

Hundley testified, "I didn't know what he was talking about. Said, 'Come on; let's go see about it.' Shaver said, 'You want to go now?' He said, 'Yes.' I thought Mrs. Taylor was in Bakers' house waiting for the battery, and we got in the car, we drove—Shaver was driving—and I got in the front and Denhardt in the back seat, and we drove up the road." Hundley heard Denhardt say that Verna had walked up the highway to hunt for her glove.[121] But they did not see her on the road and returned to the driveway where they continued working on the battery.

When they were finished, they took lanterns and flashlights, and started a search on foot. Hundley took the right side of the road and Shaver the left. Hundley was the first to spot Verna's body lying beside the road in the ditch. He yelled, "Here she is!" and climbed down into the ditch with Shaver to check her pulse.

Verna was dead, and Hundley could see a bullet hole in the front of her dress. Hundley's description of the body matched Baker's, and he confirmed the odd location of one of Verna's shoes between her left arm and shoulder. He recalled that Denhardt stood near the center of the road and did not approach Verna's body.[122]

After Keightley arrived on the scene, Hundley overheard Denhardt protest his innocence: "You know I couldn't have killed her. I was too crazy about her." He also heard Baker remark, "Mr. Denhardt couldn't have killed that woman, because I was with him when the last shot was fired . . ."[123]

Thomas was finished with Hundley, and the defense asked no questions. Baker's comment at the scene that night was a landmine, an obvious basis for Denhardt's attorneys to ask for a dismissal of the charges against him. On the day of the examining trial, Thomas went forward as though there were no reason to avoid George Baker's statement. There was no way to disguise what was said, and it was better to get everything out in the open and see what would happen. When Hundley was dismissed, he asked for Smith Keightley to be called as his next witness.

Thomas deftly led Keightley through his story of the night he became involved in the Taylor-Denhardt case. Keightley's testimony was limited to what he saw on the highway on the night of November 6. He could not testify about the day he went to Denhardt's house and took his overcoat, and not a word could be spoken about the paraffin tests he witnessed. Things were going well until Keightley described the general's gun as a .45 pistol. Rodes Myers immediately demanded that the gun be admitted as evidence. When Judge Morgan agreed, John Messmer brought the gun into the courtroom, and Keightley identified it as the weapon he saw lying near Verna's body.

The final witness of the day was Dr. Blaydes. As the sheriff called his name, he walked into the courtroom dressed in suit and tie, looking distinguished and respectable. He placed his hand on the Bible, took his oath to tell the truth, and settled into the witness chair. Dr. Blaydes described the autopsy he performed on Verna and his findings based on the short report. He gave his opinion that he believed Verna's death was instantaneous, but there was a loud "Objection!" when Thomas asked him whether the wound was self-inflicted. Thomas withdrew the question and finished with the witness.

For the first time that day, John Berry rose to his feet to question a witness. He peppered Dr. Blaydes with questions on the discoloration around the front gunshot wound. Dr. Blaydes fell into Berry's trap by saying that he initially attributed the discoloration to burned gunpowder. Although he made no microscopic examination of the walls of the hole through the breast, he "was sure the powder marks extended past the skin into the bullet hole."[124]

It was exactly what Berry wanted to hear, and his questions about the discoloration marked the beginning of his efforts to prove that Verna died from a self-inflicted contact wound. Berry thanked the witness and took his seat.[125]

During the short recess, few of the spectators in the courtroom left their seats. The "speeches" of the lawyers were always the dramatic highlight of a trial; no one wanted to miss a minute of the courtroom fireworks that were sure to follow. The six witnesses came back into court to listen, and the crowd pushed closer to make room for them. When Judge Morgan had taken his seat, Rodes Myers walked to the front of the room to make his argument for the defense.

"May it please the court. Your Honor, before an examining trial court can hold a person to answer to charges before the Grand Jury, two things are essential. First, that an offense has been committed in Henry County, and second that there are reasonable grounds to believe the defendant has committed that offense. Let's review the evidence witness by witness and see if there's any evidence by which Your Honor can deduce that an offense has been committed. Browning's testimony did nothing but explain the movements of Mrs. Taylor and the witnesses up to the time Hundley stopped his car on the highway. He said nothing that would tell the court that any offense was committed.

"George Baker's story of the night of November 6 is clear and has been corroborated by every other witness in this case. He said that he heard two shots, one loud and one muffled, and there were two empty shells in the general's gun. He also said that the general could not have killed Mrs. Taylor because he was with him when the second shot was fired. Consider this, if the first shot killed Verna Taylor, then how could she have fired a second shot minutes later? And Mrs. Taylor showed no fear when she stopped by the service station to ask for help that night. She had the opportunity, but she never asked for anyone to take her home.

"Dr. Blaydes testified that there was a powder burn inside Mrs. Taylor's gunshot wound. That says to a layman that the gun was pressed against her body when it was fired. A powder burn going through her dress, slip, and other underclothes, through her skin and down into the wound, paired with what Mr. Baker said, "I know Mr. Denhardt didn't kill her because I was with him when the second shot was fired," gives the answer to who fired the gun.

There's not a shred of evidence that shows that any human being had that gun except Mrs. Taylor. Nor can they place any person within two hundred yards of where her body was found. General Denhardt simply did not have a motive for killing her. No motive, no malice, no premeditation. If this had happened in Henry County under the same circumstances with people of no prominence, and if it had not been played up, people would have looked at it fairly, and there would never have been any further step taken. If the defendant were anyone other than General Denhardt, this case would already have been dismissed as a suicide. The testimony of these witnesses today is just not sufficient to hold General Denhardt to the grand jury."[126]

With a thank-you to the judge, Myers returned to his chair, confident that the judge would be reasonable, and see that the state simply had not shown his client committed a crime.

Jimmy Thomas rose from the table to make his argument, and the spectators from Henry County sat up straighter, waiting expectantly. Rodes Myers was an out-of-town lawyer who knew nothing about Henry County. His comment implying that justice was tainted in their county did not sit well with the locals. They knew Thomas and his reputation for courtroom theatrics, and with a crowd this large, he wouldn't disappoint them.

"May it please Your Honor. Now, let's see what we can deduce from this case, from the physical evidence, the statements of the witnesses, and the attitude of this man charged with murder. The first thing this man said to Baker when he came out of the house

was that 'she was a fine lady.' Before they even found her body—
'she *was* a fine lady.' General Denhardt is an educated man and he
knows the difference between *is* and *was*. From his statement, for
all he knew, she was up the road searching for her glove. So why
did an educated man use the past tense if didn't know Mrs. Taylor
was dead?"

Thomas paced slowly and dramatically back and forth in front
of the judge and packed courtroom, occasionally stabbing his
finger at Denhardt for emphasis.

"Verna Taylor could not have killed herself. Witnesses who
were at the scene that night, and saw her body all testified that
there was a glove in her left hand. The course of the bullet from
the left breast diagonally through her body to the right showed she
could not have shot herself with her right hand. She would have
been in an impossible position to shoot herself with that gun."

He emphasized the point by dramatically twisting his body
to the left, demonstrating how Verna would have had to contort
herself to commit suicide with her right hand.

"Yet, they come in here and told you that woman committed
suicide. Yes, there were two spent shells in Denhardt's pistol, but
why assume there were two shots fired just because two shots were
in the chamber? Maybe he carried that gun on a blank cartridge.
A lot of people who know something about firearms carry a gun
on an empty chamber or a blank cartridge to prevent an accidental
discharge. This man has been in the army and knows all about
firearms."

Thomas turned to Denhardt, who stared back at him from the
defense table with cold eyes, but without a hint of emotion on his
face. Thomas continued his argument and slow pacing across the
front of the courtroom.

"If you were out with a woman and going to marry her, and she
went up the road, and you heard a pistol shot, would you wait for
somebody to come with a battery before you searched? Denhardt

didn't go *because he knew what he was going to find!*" Thomas shouted. "Several times he made the statement, 'I couldn't have killed her because I was in love with her.' Do his actions prove he was in love with her? A woman four hundred yards up the road, a pistol shot, and he doesn't budge from in front of his car! Was he afraid?"

Thomas shook his head and said, "No, I don't believe he is afraid of anything, but he knew what was up there and he didn't have to investigate. And another thing, they tell you that General Denhardt was in love with Mrs. Taylor, was going to marry her. The first thing he said when they found her dead body was '*take care of my ring!*' Jesus Christ, Judge, a man in love with a woman would have rushed down and taken her in his arms, he wouldn't have cared anything about a diamond ring or ten diamond rings!"

Thomas' words rang out over the courtroom, and people in the hallway downstairs could hear him shouting. He finished by returning to Myers's comment about justice in Henry County, and prejudice against the general.

"In Henry County, if some man had a wife, and that wife was found dead with his gun, regardless of the circumstances, since last Saturday morning he would have been in the Henry County Jail."

Thomas, his voice now at the pitch of a fervid preacher at a local revival, yelled, "I have been county attorney for seven years and no man has ever been charged with murder that didn't go to jail—except Denhardt!"[127]

Throughout the afternoon, the large crowd had been quiet and attentive, but Thomas's fiery delivery whipped them into action. The applause started slowly, and built into a crescendo until the whole courthouse resounded with the sound of clapping, stamping, whistling, and cheering people. Even with the windows closed against the cold, the tumult could be heard outside on the narrow streets around the courthouse. People standing on the courthouse lawn looked up at the second-story windows wondering what had happened.

Judge Morgan was furious and jumped to his feet, banging his gavel loudly on the bench for order. But his voice could hardly be heard over the din in the room. "One more outburst like this and I will clear the courtroom! I won't have that in my court!" he declared.[128]

The noise gradually subsided with the judge's fury, but public opinion was clear. Denhardt, his family members, and his attorneys had stared in shock as the courtroom exploded around them.

Once the judge had restored order, Kinsolving took the floor to speak briefly and ask the judge to overrule Myers's motion to dismiss the case. But he did not need to add anything to Jimmy Thomas's rousing speech. Judge Morgan had made up his mind before Thomas sat down at the prosecution's table.

He overruled Rodes Myers's motion to dismiss, and held the case to the January grand jury for Denhardt to answer to a charge of murder. He asked all the lawyers to follow him into the jury room for a closed session. Morgan immediately refused to renew Denhardt's $25,000 bond over the objections of his attorneys. Denhardt was now officially a defendant in a capital murder case, and he would be held in jail until the grand jury met in January. But the question for all was which jail? Berry and Myers argued that their client's health was delicate and he was receiving medical treatment in Louisville. After the raucous demonstration in court, they feared for his health and safety if he was jailed in Henry County. Kinsolving protested any court order moving Denhardt to Louisville. "All they want it for, Your Honor, is to be able to produce it when they ask for a change of venue."[129]

Judge Morgan listened to both sides, but finally made the decision to send Denhardt to the Jefferson County Jail in Louisville. "I've heard some talk and rumors that there might be a little chance of violence if we jail him here," he said.[130] Morgan also ordered Kinsolving to hand over the articles of evidence the defense had requested earlier in the week. They should be allowed to hire their own experts and conduct tests. "But," he said sternly to John Berry, "don't wait thirty days to hire an expert."

"Of course not," replied Berry quickly.[131]

Kinsolving and his team knew all along that it was only a matter of time before they would have to share the evidence. They had waited as long as possible because of what was certain to follow.

"Your Honor, we have not yet had time to find an expert to perform the tests."

"But judge, our expert hasn't had time to finish his analysis."

"Your Honor, we need more time."

Time could extend to three months, six months, or God knows how long for the attorneys to finish their examination of the evidence. But if Kinsolving were in their shoes, he would have tried to delay as long as possible, too.

In November, the public outcry against Denhardt was loud and impassioned, and the majority of people following the case believed he had murdered an innocent woman. Kinsolving would have to share the bloody clothes, paraffin tests, and pavement, but the prosecution could keep the scientific tests by John Messmer for themselves.

General Denhardt barely listened to the arguments of the attorneys and Judge Morgan's order. He was hardly aware that the judge had ordered Kinsolving to share the evidence he wanted so badly earlier in the week. Denhardt only knew that the day had ended badly and he was going to jail. He showed no reaction when Judge Morgan decided to send him from Henry County to the Jefferson County Jail. He was led to the grand jury room, and sat waiting tiredly as hundreds of people lingered in the courtroom and the downstairs hallway of the courthouse.

When the crowd finally thinned and they felt it was safe,

Sheriff Harrod and several officers led General Denhardt, once a distinguished state political figure and now a prisoner, downstairs and out a side door of the courthouse where an automobile waited to drive him to Louisville. The popping of the photographers' flashbulbs lit up the dark November evening and the sound followed his footsteps as he walked to the waiting car. Bertha sobbed as she hugged and kissed him goodbye, then turned and left with her older brother, Jesse. Denhardt's attorneys shook hands with him and said goodbye. They promised to work on a way to get him out of jail, and he was able to muster a weak smile as he climbed into the car with the officers. But it was the lowest point in Henry Denhardt's sixty years when the car left New Castle and headed toward Louisville and jail.[132]

Chapter 11

HABEAS CORPUS

As Sheriff Harrod and his deputies escorted Denhardt from New Castle to Louisville, they were followed by armed state troopers in a second automobile. The authorities were taking no chances with their extremely unpopular prisoner.

Denhardt was talkative during the long drive. He entertained Harrod and his men with war stories from his glory days and tales of leading the National Guard into Harlan and Clay Counties. He chatted pleasantly about farming, crops, and the weather, talking incessantly of anything that would take his mind off where he was going and why. But when the car pulled to the curb in front of the Jefferson County Jail, the general finally grew quiet. His door was opened, and a deputy helped him to his feet on the sidewalk.

Denhardt appeared tired, downcast, and worried as he was led inside. The Jefferson County Jail was a brick and stone fortress with long, narrow rectangular windows. It had imprisoned many inmates since it was built in 1905, but none with the credentials of the prisoner who arrived from Henry County on the night of November 20. When General Denhardt arrived, the facility was as secure as any jail in Kentucky; there was no risk that he would be taken by force in the middle of the night.

Denhardt walked slowly to the office wall and studied the calendar while Deputy Jailer E. J. Columbus inspected his commitment papers. "Everything appears to be in order," he said with a nod. After the routine search and surrender of the contents of his pockets, Denhardt turned to the men who had driven him to Louisville and politely shook their hands. "Goodnight gentlemen," he said, and he walked with the guard through the inner barred doors to his temporary home in the Jefferson County Jail.[133] He was escorted down the bare hallways to cell block 1-B, where he would be allowed to mingle with other prisoners awaiting trial or serving sentences. Outwardly, he was to be treated no differently than any other prisoner. But the difference between General Denhardt and the other prisoners on cell block 1-B soon became apparent when he started issuing statements to the press.

The reporters were delighted when the general consented to interviews, and he quickly began to use the press to defend himself.

"I am not a killer. I didn't fire the shot that killed her. I couldn't have done such a thing. I loved her too much. We were happy together until this dreadful thing happened."[134]

"I have been a soldier and they made much of my record with firearms. The truth is that during the war I never wounded a person. I never shot anybody in my life."[135]

"In the first place, the evidence given in court at New Castle proved that I could not have fired the death shot. Mr. Baker is an honest and truthful man, and he testified that I was with him when we heard the second shot, the one that killed her."[136]

"She told me she was happier in my company than any time since her husband died. The engagement had not been broken. We were to be married early next year. She was wearing my engagement ring when she died. The reason I asked about it that night was because I thought she might have been robbed."[137]

"The people of Henry and Oldham Counties have believed the lies built up so that when they heard the truth they preferred not to believe it."[138]

"I was thoroughly vindicated by every bit of evidence at the trial. I believe if it had been anyone else brought to court under the same circumstances they would have been discharged from custody."[139]

Denhardt claimed that the murder charge "was due mainly to two things—prejudice against me in the vicinity of New Castle and LaGrange, and purely circumstantial evidence."[140]

Denhardt's attorneys winced with each self-serving attempt of their client to proclaim his innocence in the newspapers. By November 25, John Berry was so concerned that he wrote a letter to Rodes Myers.

"He persists in making statements, or in authorizing persons to issue denials for him, and of course he would not do so were he not continuing to take the medicine," Berry wrote. "He has been under the influence of it ever [*sic*] time we have seen him. The conditions there at the jail, I think, are everything but conducive to his proper behavior, and I doubt if you and I, or anybody can regulate them."[141]

Something had to be done to control their headstrong client while they worked on a plan to get him released. Berry asked Myers to use his influence as an old friend and urge Denhardt to pull himself together before he damaged his case. He also asked him to see what he could do to change Denhardt's attitude toward Beckham Overstreet. The rift between the two was becoming a distraction. Defending the general was a full-time job, and they could not afford to lose Overstreet when they needed his help more than ever.

While General Denhardt issued statements to the press—allegedly under the influence of his medication—the Garr and Taylor families remained very quiet. Reporters asking for interviews hounded the families, but they refused to talk. The continuing publicity was embarrassing and a daily reminder of their loss. But the reporters watched closely for anything newsworthy that they could print about the family. On November 21, Mary Pryor made national news when she quietly married her fiancée in a simple ceremony in Shelbyville. "The marriage was revealed by Mrs. Smith Keightley, friend of the Taylor family, who said the couple had been engaged for three years," the *New York Times* reported.[142]

Denhardt's attorneys were committed to the task of getting him released from prison, and they needed to do it quickly. They had a plan that they hoped would work. Denhardt was being held on a charge of capital murder, and Kentucky law required him to remain in jail without bond unless he could show that he was illegally confined. In late November, Denhardt's attorneys decided to file a motion for a writ of habeas corpus. It did not matter whether he was guilty or innocent. Their motion would test the legality of jailing Denhardt, whether the proof against him was evident and the presumption of his guilt was great."[143] They asked the court to release him and requested bond for him to appear at the session of the grand jury in January. But they went one step further and used a clever ploy that they felt certain would ensure his release.

The case against the general was in circuit court in Henry County. Judge Charles Marshall, the short-tempered, irascible judge for Kentucky's Twelfth Judicial District, would hear the motion. When he received their paperwork, Judge Marshall ordered the Jefferson County jailer to bring Denhardt to Henry County on December 9 for the hearing on his motion for a writ of habeas corpus. As soon as the date was set, Denhardt's attorneys immediately issued a subpoena for Sergeant John Messmer to appear for questioning at the hearing. Kinsolving's team was taken by surprise. They expected the writ of habeas corpus, but the subpoena for Messmer effectively forced them into a legal corner. They could agree to Denhardt's release on bond until the grand jury met in January, or they could produce Messmer's scientific evidence for them to see.

It was a difficult situation for Kinsolving. Verna's family and many other people were going to be disappointed if Denhardt left the jail so soon. Kinsolving and his team weighed the options, but ultimately made the painful decision not to contest the motion. They would hold onto the results of Messmer's scientific tests, and let Denhardt go free until the grand jury met in January. It was also around this time that Kinsolving, Clarke, and Turner formulated a theory to account for the second gunshot heard by George Baker. He was their cornerstone witness. If they relied on the rest of his testimony as the truth, it was obvious from the examining trial that they had to account for the second shot. But Kinsolving's investigation turned up no one else who heard this mysterious "pop shot."

On the night of November 6, George and Preston Carpenter, two brothers who lived near the Pendleton crossroads, were trying out a new hunting dog. At approximately nine-thirty, they heard one loud gunshot, and the sound of it was startling across the farm fields a half mile away. At the time, they believed it was a "torpedo" on the railroad—a detonator attached to the rails that served as a warning or signal. But after hearing the one explosive gunshot, they heard nothing else.[144]

George Baker said that Denhardt immediately drew his attention to the second gunshot, calling it "fearful." His focus on the second shot was odd considering that the first was much louder and more distinct.

Kinsolving was aware that Denhardt had a collection of firearms. Robert Jones, a LaGrange banker, said, "General Denhardt told me he carried a gun at all times and had various guns of many calibers."[145] One of the guns in his collection was a fountain pen pistol Denhardt had received as a gift from a military associate. Kinsolving's team decided to use the theory that Denhardt had the fountain pen pistol with him on November 6 and fired it to distract George Baker. Their investigation turned up several witnesses who claimed to have seen the pistol.

One spring day, Clarence Roberts was visiting his friend Carl Cole who lived on the Denhardt farm. The two boys were in the Denhardt house and Carl showed him the fountain pen pistol. Clarence described it as "greenish brown" and a little larger than the average fountain pen. Clarence claimed that he saw Denhardt carrying the pistol shortly before Verna's death. "Well, I would be safe in saying eight or ten days before the death of Mrs. Taylor," he said.[146]

His brother Emmett saw the fountain pen pistol on Denhardt's dresser. He also claimed that Carl Cole showed the pistol to him one day in the spring. "It was a little longer and the same on top as the ordinary fountain pen; but it had a blunt end where the bullet came out," he said.[147] Emmett never saw Denhardt carrying the pistol, but recalled that it was a light red color.

A third brother, sixteen-year-old Gilbert, also said that Carl Cole showed him the pistol. He remembered seeing it one time, but never on Denhardt.

Clarence was the most important witness of the three brothers because he claimed to have seen the fountain pen pistol on Denhardt just days before Verna's death.

Kinsolving placed Clarence on his witness list for the January meeting of the grand jury. Kinsolving and his team resolutely pursued the theory that Denhardt was carrying the pistol on the night Verna died and used it to distract George Baker. With a single-minded determination, they disregarded the conflicting statements given by teenage witnesses who couldn't even agree on the color of the pen. In the upcoming trial, the fountain pen pistol and the piece of stained road paving from Highway 22 would both prove to be red herrings in the case against Denhardt.

On December 9, the Jefferson County jailer brought his prisoner to Henry County for a hearing on the motion for habeas corpus. The crowd in the courtroom was small that day in comparison with the examining trial, but the ever-present reporters were there with pencils, paper, and cameras ready. Judge Marshall tapped his gavel and called the motion, and John Berry approached the bench. But as he began to argue why the writ of habeas corpus should be granted, and why the general should be released from prison on bond, Kinsolving interrupted him with an air of resignation. "Your Honor, we will accede to the petitioner's motion and ask the court to grant him bail."[148] The ploy had worked, and from where they sat at the defense table, Denhardt and his attorneys smiled their satisfaction at the victory.

Remembering the public demonstration in court at the examining trial, Kinsolving issued a lengthy statement to the press explaining why he agreed with Denhardt's release on bond. He was well aware that he was an elected official, and Denhardt's early release from prison would not be popular.

"The way this case has developed" he explained, "made it more desirable at this time to let the general have bond than to expose the Commonwealth case. We thought it proper strategy not to disclose our evidence. Some of our tests are incomplete and we could not present all our scientific evidence now, even if we desired to do so. We decided to keep more or less inviolate the evidence we have gathered because we thought it would be improper to divulge it to the defendant, or to the public at this time."[149]

Once again, Dr. McCormack supplied his $25,000 bond, and General Denhardt was free from his temporary imprisonment.

A local reporter wrote, "The object of the writ of habeas corpus, Denhardt's four lawyers retorted from a Louisville hotel room where they conferred with him all afternoon, was only to secure bail. This was accomplished. The result justified our belief that General Denhardt has been unjustly confined in jail."[150]

When a reporter asked Denhardt where he would stay until the grand jury met in January, he replied testily, "I'll go where I want to."[151]

But privately, his attorneys were very concerned with where he would stay for the next month, and what he might say to damage his case.

On December 18, an exasperated Berry wrote to Myers complaining of Denhardt's behavior. "Last night General Denhardt was in Shelbyville at a restaurant eating a lunch and drinking some beer. He was engaged in conversation and made a dam (sic) fool of himself. Not only must his mouth be stopped, but he must be removed from this locality if you and Judge Milligan (sic) can devise any way to do it."[152]

One possibility was to encourage Denhardt to sell his farm, and a generous offer was currently on the table. William Wight, a Louisville real estate agent had approached Denhardt and his attorneys with a plan to develop the farm as a site for the proposed Kentucky State Reformatory. Wight wrote to Denhardt: "It was suggested to me by your attorneys, that the Secretary to the Governor had told me that after consulting with him on the subject, he felt it impossible to touch the matter because of present attending circumstances." Wight suggested, with the blessings of Denhardt's attorneys, for Denhardt to transfer the ownership of his farm to a third party. The third party would offer it for sale to the state. Wight considered the scheme both fair and just, and urged Denhardt to transfer his title immediately.[153]

Wight also wrote to Berry: "At private sale, 840 acres located in the particular neighborhood, could not be expected to bring $30,000 of the price at which the state would, I think, pay cash for it. It would bring Oldham County considerable business and make a city out of the town of Ballardsville."[154]

Regardless of the outcome of the January grand jury, Denhardt's safe return to his quiet life on the farm in Oldham County was impossible. But the general hesitated to transfer the title to a third party, even for a profit. On December 19, the day after Berry's letter reported Denhartdt's foolishness in Shelbyville, Myers wrote to Denhardt.

Dear General,

Mr. William A. Wight called on Mr. Milliken and me yesterday relative to the fact that he had a purchaser for your 800-acre farm at $110 per acre or $88,000. The reason he discussed the matter with us is because you had an idea that the sale of the property at this time might have some bearing on the outcome of the case. I am sure it would not were it a bona fide sale, and if this is the only thing that is prevent [*sic*] you from selling it, I think if I were in your place, I would proceed to sell it.[155]

The scheme would benefit everyone involved—the small community of Ballardsville would prosper, Wight would make a tidy commission, Denhardt's attorneys could breathe a sigh of relief with him removed from the farm, and the general would make a profit from the sale. Denhardt had purchased the farm for $31,265 eighteen months earlier, and if he accepted the offer, he would make an astounding $57,000 profit. But the general refused to sell his farm, concerned that it might appear he was preparing for a civil suit for wrongful death and a judgment against him by Verna's family.

Months later, Bertha Denhardt sold the farm as part of his estate. By that time, the general was no longer worried whether Verna's family would sue him for wrongful death or whether he received a good price for the property. By then, he was past the point of caring.

Chapter 12

A FLOOD AND AN INDICTMENT

As Henry Denhardt considered whether to sell his farm, the final days of December 1936 moved ever closer to a fateful January. On Thursday, December 31, as the hours and minutes ticked steadily toward a new year, people celebrating in the city of Louisville attended the usual dinners and parties, unaware that within days they would be facing a weather catastrophe. As the partiers spilled out the doors from downtown hotels and restaurants, there was nothing to warn them that the heart of the city with its gaily lighted marquees would soon be pitch dark, and the streets and sidewalks covered with muddy water. On New Year's Eve 1936, they would never have imagined that instead of taxis, cars, and the downtown trolley, boats would soon become the only means of travel in the city. The Great Flood of 1937 was only days away.

The first indication of trouble began with a cold rain that fell steadily over most of the state on January 6. While two cold fronts in the country stood still, tropical air masses laden with moisture barreled northward between them. When the cold air met the warm, the heavens opened and it began to rain in torrents. By January 14, a deluge of 2.7 inches brought the Ohio River in Louisville up to twenty-three feet, only five feet below flood stage. On January 15, the river reached flood stage and continued to rise. As the rain continued day after day, flood warnings were issued for areas close to the river, and people desperately began to move from their homes to escape the floodwaters.[156]

In New Castle, the docket for January 18 went forward as scheduled, and Kinsolving prepared his witnesses for the grand jury hearing. As the rain fell steadily outside the Henry County Courthouse on Monday morning, witnesses and prospective grand jury members began to arrive in New Castle. General Denhardt arrived looking dapper and rested, and sloshed his way through the rain to John Berry's law office across the street from the courthouse. He was unable to resist making a statement to reporters. "I can explain away this charge if the grand jury will hear me. I am ready and willing to answer any and all questions."[157] No one asked him why he was ready to make a statement then when he had chosen not to do so during his inquest or examining trial.

Judge Marshall called the court to order, and work began immediately on selection of a grand jury from the list of white men on the voting list and property tax rolls in Henry County. African Americans would not be selected and neither would women. Marshall did not express a sentiment about African Americans as jurors; it was taken for granted that none could serve on a jury that might condemn a white defendant. However, he did offer a public opinion that female jurors could not be trusted to give an impartial judgment. "You know, women may know more than you do in ascertaining the guilt of a person, but they certainly cannot solve this case with an impartial mind."[158]

The work of the grand jury would take place behind closed doors. Nine jury members would have to agree for an indictment to be returned against Denhardt. Finally, the pool was whittled down to twelve men. Before they left the room to begin work, Judge Marshall agreed to hear a defense motion from John Berry. Berry approached the bench as the judge frowned over his glasses at the paperwork on his desk.

Berry launched into his argument, working hard to make it

compelling. General Denhardt was an innocent man who had "taken the tough end of this and been subjected to humiliation and unjust imprisonment."[159] He attacked the validity of the paraffin test and argued that the blood on Denhardt's overcoat was the general's own blood. Berry also noted that Dr. Alexander Wiener, a renowned blood expert, had tested the pavement taken from Highway 22. The stain on the pavement was only two or three inches in diameter and was not human blood. The defense was willing to bring crime experts who would testify on Denhardt's behalf. Further, the general was present and willing to speak privately to the grand jury without Kinsolving or a stenographer present.

It did not take long for the judge to make his decision. After thirty years on the bench, Marshall was used to all the games attorneys attempted in his courtroom. Turning to the grand jury members who stood listening intently, he said, "This attorney said he had a motion. It now appears he wants to try the case before the grand jury. You are an investigating body and have no right to pass on the guilt or innocence of a person. It is your duty to determine whether the persons being investigated by you should be brought to trial or not. After that, your duty is ended. You are not members of the trial jury.[160] He ended his speech firmly. "Mr. Berry, your motion is denied."

It was a foregone conclusion that the judge would dismiss the motion, but it had allowed Denhardt's attorneys to protest his innocence in front of the grand jury. Under the circumstances, it was the best they could do. Shortly after noon, the grand jury retired to a separate chamber followed by Kinsolving and his longtime secretary, Madelyn "Miss Tillie" Baldwin, serving as stenographer. The defense attorneys watched Miss Tillie follow the group into the room. If she was there to take notes, then by law, they could request a copy of the transcript.

For four hours on January 18, the grand jury listened to five witnesses: Barney Browning, George and Nettie Baker, the prosecution's blood expert, Dr. James A. Kennedy, and John Messmer, who carried a briefcase and two suitcases when he was called into the room. His baggage caused a furor of speculation among the reporters. "Messmer arrived in New Castle carrying a bulky briefcase and two suitcases, one of which was reported to contain General Denhardt's bloodstained overcoat and the other the stained clothing Mrs. Taylor wore the night of her death, November 6," the *Courier-Journal* reported.[161] One after another, the witnesses disappeared into the room and closed the door behind them while the defense team waited and wondered.

Later, Rodes Myers made one last attempt to convince Kinsolving to let his client testify alone before the grand jury. Kinsolving quickly refused. "We will be delighted to have General Denhardt come in and testify like anybody else—with the Commonwealth and a stenographer present," he said.[162]

"We just can't agree to that," said Myers as he turned and walked away.

Kinsolving shook his head as he watched him go. The last thing he wanted was for Denhardt, a skilled lawyer and silver-tongued politician, to be alone with the grand jury. The hours passed, and by late afternoon Kinsolving had a feeling that things were going to go his way. As the grand jury completed its session for the day, he was feeling so confident that he announced to reporters that the grand jury would likely hear eight or ten more witnesses, and he predicted an indictment would be returned against the general on Tuesday.[163]

The next day, a mixture of freezing rain and sleet battered the courthouse windows as the witnesses for the day gathered in the courtroom. The flooding situation was worsening in Louisville, and the Ohio River was eight feet above flood stage. The dirty water blocked nearly all Jefferson County roads and had shut down most traffic. The city was bracing for a major crisis, and the first of two relief stations was ready to provide food, shelter, and medical treatment. While the Ohio River continued its dramatic rise, the rivers that fed into the Ohio also rose steadily. The Kentucky River in Henry County was now out of its banks and moving inland. People were worried about the impending disaster and the mood in the courtroom was tense and solemn. The night before, John Messmer hurried home to Louisville to deal with his own personal crisis. His home in the West End of Louisville was directly in the path of the raging river. Over twelve square miles of the area, including his street, were about to be submerged beneath the muddy waters. But in Henry County, Judge Marshall called the court to order and the grand jury continued to hear testimony.

Witnesses for Tuesday included Verna's daughters, Frances and Mary Pryor, Dr. H. B. Blaydes, Oldham County Deputy Sheriff Clayton Renaker, Smith Keightley, and Coroner Ricketts. The reporters were already familiar with this group of witnesses, but there was a surprise witness they did not know. "Clarence Roberts" had been handwritten at the end of the typed list of witnesses. He was the final witness of the day, and when he walked out of the grand jury room, reporters besieged him with questions.

"Clarence, why did they call you?"

"Clarence, what did you testify to?"

Looking bewildered at all the attention directed at him, the boy replied, "Why, I saw the fountain pen . . ."

"Clarence! You're not supposed to talk," snapped Doc Garr before he could continue.[164] But it was too late. The reporters immediately jumped to the conclusion that Clarence had seen a fountain pen pistol owned by General Denhardt, and that it was involved in the case.

"Roberts's reference Tuesday renewed speculation on reports that General Denhardt once owned a fountain pen pistol which has since been lost. County attorney Thomas pooh-poohed the reports, and intimated they must have come out of detective story magazines," the *Courier-Journal* reported.

Jimmy Thomas did his best to dispel the notion of a fountain pen pistol as fantastic, but the cat was out of the bag. Both the press and Denhardt's attorneys now knew what Kinsolving would use to account for the second gunshot.

Everyone waited expectantly when the grand jury ended their session at three p.m., filed into the courtroom, and gathered in a circle before Judge Marshall. They handed up three indictments that day, two for minor cases and one against the general for willful murder. Judge Marshall formally asked them, "So say you all?" The twelve jurors nodded their heads at the judge, indicating a unanimous indictment. Henry Denhardt was not in the room when the jury returned and the reporters went running to find him. He was sitting in a small restaurant across the street, casually sipping a beer.

"General Denhardt, did you know the grand jury has returned an indictment against you?"

"General Denhardt, do you have a statement?"

Denhardt smiled at the reporters. "Oh, they did?" he said nonchalantly. "Well, see my attorneys."[165]

It was late in the day, and Judge Marshall announced that he would wait until Wednesday morning to arraign the general. Berry and Myers wanted a copy of the transcript as soon as possible, and asked Jimmy Thomas when it would be available. He replied with a smile, "You know, it's the strangest thing, I had the stenographer in there all the time, and I forgot to tell her to take a single note!"[166]

Berry and Myers looked at him incredulously and shook their heads in disgust. It was a dirty trick, but it was tit for tat. The prosecution had gotten them back for the unexpected subpoena issued for Messmer. Without the transcript, the testimony of two expert witnesses, Dr. Kennedy and John Messmer, would remain unknown until the trial. Denhardt's attorneys would also have to wait and wonder what Clarence Roberts knew about a fountain pen gun.

On Wednesday morning, General Denhardt arrived in New Castle for his arraignment. He was well dressed in a dark suit and overcoat and looked composed as he took his seat at the table in front of the judge's bench. State highway policemen stood at each of the courtroom exits, and two took their places near Judge Marshall. The judge turned to his circuit clerk and said, "Let's have the indictment." Denhardt smiled as he rose to his feet to receive the charge from the judge.

"You have been charged by the grand jury of Henry County with the crime of willful murder. You have attorneys?"

Denhardt nodded that he did.

"You are free on bail?"

Denhardt nodded again.

"I will set this case for trial next Monday morning, and meanwhile let the present bond stand."

Judge Marshall turned to Kinsolving and asked if that was satisfactory. "Yes," replied Kinsolving, "until that time at least."[167] The arraignment took five minutes, and when Denhardt and his attorneys left the courtroom, the state police escort followed him out the door.

But the trial would not be held as planned on Monday, January 25. For the first time in months, the latest news in the murder case slipped from the front pages of the newspapers as the flooding worsened. The counties around Louisville became a haven for homeless refugees. Instead of working on the defense of the general, John Berry, as chairman of the Henry County Red Cross, worked desperately to accommodate hundreds of refugees arriving by train in Henry County. Judge A. S. Morgan implored the people of Henry County to follow the rules established by

Berry in order to protect the health and property of the locals. A number of committees to deal with the crisis were established, and Wirt Turner served as chairman of the finance committee.

By January 24, Louisville was completely isolated from the outside world with nearly 40 percent of the city under water. In the Brown Hotel, where Dr. McCormack had his apartment, the water rose to a depth of three and one half feet in the lobby. In John Messmer's neighborhood, people were rescued at the rate of one hundred families an hour. But the waters continued to rise, and would not stop until the raging Ohio River finally crested at 57.15 feet, twenty-nine feet above flood stage. On January 25, martial law was declared, and President Roosevelt responded to Governor Chandler's plea for federal assistance.

The Great Flood of 1937 was a catastrophe, but it was a boon for Denhardt's defense team. It gave them the delay they wanted, and it allowed them more time to prepare a difficult client for the fight of his life. It would be late April before Denhardt's case for willful murder was finally called to trial in New Castle, and the delay would prove to be more beneficial for Henry Denhardt than for the prosecution.

Chapter 13

THE TIMELINE

In February, Kentuckians began the massive task of cleaning up the debris and mud left behind by the murky river waters. Victims of the disaster grimly searched through what was left behind, and worked to salvage what they could of their former lives.

Early in the same month, Beckham Overstreet decided there was nothing he could salvage from his working relationship with General Denhardt. On February 15, he wrote to Denhardt demanding his legal fees and complaining of the general's conduct. "Your conduct towards me has not only been inexcusable but reprehensible, and as to that, I am not going into detail. You and I both well know the facts." But Denhardt brushed aside Overstreet's demands and refused to pay, claiming he had volunteered his legal services.[168]

On February 24, Overstreet wrote to Berry and enclosed a copy of the lawsuit he had prepared to file against Denhardt in Oldham Circuit Court. Overstreet noted, "You will observe that I have prepared this petition so as to conceal the threats against my life which General Denhardt has made, thereby avoiding publicity and to save any injury or hurt to his case by reason of his personal violence toward me, because I am fearful if that fact came out, it would substantially injure his case, and I want you to know I am doing all I can to withhold that from the public."[169] He added that if his case went to trial, he would be under oath and it would be necessary to disclose all the facts.

Berry sincerely regretted the loss of Overstreet, and probably worried that the story of Denhardt's threatening behavior would reach the press. He tried to mediate the dispute, and with Clarke Otte, offered to meet with Denhardt and Overstreet. But Denhardt refused to negotiate and casually brushed aside the threat of another lawsuit. The general was going to Florida for a vacation, and Overstreet's threats were not going to stop him. He left John Berry a forwarding address and quietly left the state for a stay with friends in Jacksonville. When Overstreet followed through with the threat and filed suit for his legal fees, his case was promptly dismissed. Overstreet remained mum about Denhardt's threats against him, and John Berry breathed a sigh of relief.

The news of the general's vacation drew a stark contrast between those who were privileged and the majority of people who were not, between the treatment of this particular defendant and the treatment of other defendants in murder cases. While the general spent time vacationing in Florida, they served time in jail. Denhardt was also treated differently by his attorneys. If he had been another client accused of murder, the fee would already have been set and a lump sum amount paid to the attorneys. But in February as his defense team worked diligently to prepare for the April trial, they were still waiting to be paid for their services.

For his three remaining attorneys, the general's case was a five-alarm fire with blazes coming from all directions—managing a difficult client, investigating, working with experts, developing strategy, dealing with the press, and contending with local animosity against their client. The defense of General Denhardt had become a full-time job for Berry, Otte, and Myers. And while they worked long hours taking care of the innumerable details and problems, their investigators combed LaGrange looking for useful tidbits of gossip, which they summarized in a memorandum to the defense team.

Mrs. Coleman lives directly in the rear of Mrs. Carfield. Mrs. Carfield buys her buttermilk from Mr. Coleman. There is a Mr. Robertson who conducts the creamery across from the Carfield Hotel. A Mr. Baxter Taylor told him that, he, Baxter Taylor, was in the Sada San Restaurant in St. Matthews the night of the tragedy and that when they were in the restaurant and that when Mr. Taylor either spoke to Mrs. Taylor or either Mrs. Taylor spoke to him, the general was very rude and had some sort of argument. Mrs. Taylor then, in Mr. Taylor's presence, explained to the general who the man was and so forth, and the general made the statement in Baxter Taylor's presence, that Mrs. Taylor didn't have the right to speak to anyone.

For about a week prior to November 6th, the employees of the laundry, according to Mrs. Powell, noticed that Mrs. Taylor was very much worried. She did not appear anxious to see the general and furthermore, she had not kept herself as tidy as was her custom in the past. She seemed to be worrying about something. Then the day the general came, she told the employees in the laundry that she would not see him, but a little later changed her mind and said, "Well, I will see him because I don't want any scene here in the laundry or anywhere."

The woman Mrs. Taylor discharged from the laundry is Mrs. Roberts. Her daughter works at the post office. Mrs. Powell said that Mrs. Taylor told her that she, Mrs. Taylor had heard several people in the neighborhood say that she was having an affair with somebody over at the laundry.[170]

Most of the information they gathered was useless small-town gossip in the wake of a tragedy. When their investigators returned with pages of notes, the attorneys were faced with separating truth from exaggeration and fiction. In addition to encouraging his weary attorneys to plow through the local gossip, Denhardt sent them to-do lists, urging them to find court records and evidence of mental instability in Verna's family. In one of his lengthy lists, he asked his attorneys to focus on the "insanity" of Doc Garr, and to search for evidence of suicides in the Garr family history: "#10. The first name of the father of Mrs. T. should be ascertained at once, together with the place of death and the time thereof. Also such other facts should be ascertained as regards the manner of his death, trouble in collecting insurance, etc., as may be possible."[171]

Both teams of lawyers worked hard to track down every source and every witness. But for H. B. Kinsolving, it was most important to interview witnesses who could help retrace the footsteps of Verna and Denhardt on November 6. These were the last people to see Verna alive. They might offer insights into what happened that day, as well as reveal important information about her state of mind. Kinsolving's timeline for November 6 began in the morning at the Taylor home, before Verna left for Louisville with the general.

On that Friday morning, the day began normally at the Taylor house. Mary Pryor remembered that her mother was upbeat and happy that morning. "She was in fine spirits, and just as happy as she could be . . . feeling better than I had seen her feel for a long time."[172] Her younger sister, Frances, noticed nothing unusual about her mother that morning, saying, "She was very well, I thought."[173]

Verna's trips to Louisville on Fridays followed a pattern. She stopped by the Kentucky Military Institute to check on the Community Laundry's account and collect the payment. She continued to downtown Louisville and did her banking.

For Mary Pryor and Frances, this day began like any other Friday when their mother was leaving for Louisville on business. Verna ate a hearty breakfast and said goodbye to Frances when she left for school. At nine thirty, she left the house with General Denhardt.

Sometime between nine thirty and ten o'clock, Verna and the general stopped by Mildred Connell's house in LaGrange to pick up a package. Verna had promised her friend that she would return the package to a Louisville department store. The two women chatted briefly on the porch. "I noticed no difference. She seemed just the same," Connell said.[174] Several weeks after Verna's death, Connell discovered that her friend had returned the package. "I never received the credit slip, but my bill was credited when it came the first of the month from Stewart's."[175]

At ten a.m., Verna stopped by the laundry to attend to last-minute business before she left town. Mary Pryor recalled, "I was still at home and I heard the phone ring, and we are on a party line with the laundry, and of course I answered it, because I didn't think anyone was there, and it was my mother putting in a long distance call."[176]

Sometime between ten and ten thirty, the couple finally left LaGrange. Their first stop was at the Kentucky Military Institute in Lyndon. Arthur Rueve, the business agent for the school recalled that Verna arrived around eleven forty-five, and spent approximately fifteen minutes in his office. He had worked with Verna for six years and described her that morning as being cheerful as usual. While he checked the business account, Verna stood at his office window and looked toward the parade ground.

"We had a parade on that day, and she just looked out and mentioned how nice the boys looked," he recalled.[177] Rueve knew she had a driver waiting for her to return, but never saw the man in the automobile.

Mrs. D. F. "Bess" Lee last saw Verna two weeks before her death when they had lunch in LaGrange. She remembered her cousin was cheerful that day and seemed to be in good health. On November 6, Lee was looking forward to seeing her again at a bridge luncheon. She expected Verna to arrive at her house in Louisville at twelve thirty.

"At twenty-five minutes after twelve I answered the phone and it was General Denhardt, telling me that Mrs. Taylor would be unable to keep her engagement with me because of a headache," she recalled.[178] Lee asked if she could speak with Verna. Denhardt told her she was in the car and couldn't come to the phone. He mentioned twice during the brief conversation that he did not feel well.

Harry Gorman was supervisor of the savings department at the Citizens Union National Bank in downtown Louisville, and Verna had been his regular customer for three or four years. She arrived at the bank with Denhardt around one o'clock. Gorman described her as "very pleasant, agreeable, always in a good humor, and it was really a pleasure to wait on her."[179] He recalled that Verna's demeanor was no different than usual on November 6. She deposited seven hundred dollars into her savings account and discussed plans for investment.

The next person to see Verna that afternoon was attorney J. Ballard Clarke, a longtime friend. Around four fifteen or four thirty, Clarke was walking toward the Pendennis Club with a friend when "Mrs. Taylor came up and caught hold of my arm and greeted me—said, 'Hello, How are you?'"[180] The three chatted as they crossed the street together and walked to the Pendennis Club. When the group parted, Verna continued walking in another direction. General Denhardt was nowhere in sight. Although Verna complained of a headache, Clarke did not notice anything unusual in her manner. "She was just as natural and sweet and lovely and gracious as she always was."[181]

R. H. Kirchdorfer, the owner of the Sada San Restaurant in the St. Matthews area of Louisville, did not know Verna Taylor personally, but he recognized her when she entered his restaurant with the general around six o'clock.

"After I served them their meal, I walked away to wait on a man at the cigar case. I glanced over and noticed they hadn't started their meal, and I kind of wondered why."[182]

The two sat for three to five minutes without eating.

"I noticed that Mr. Denhardt was looking over at Mrs. Taylor, but I didn't see anyone talking," Kirchdorfer recalled.[183]

Denhardt had purchased a bottle of liquor at a store across the street from the restaurant, and he later admitted that he borrowed a glass from the barkeeper and poured a drink.[184] But Kirchdorfer did not notice Denhardt drinking in his restaurant and he did not appear to be intoxicated. He heard Verna make a long-distance call from a telephone at the front of the room.

"I heard her say that she would be unable to chaperone . . . that she had a headache and was unable to chaperone the dance, but whoever she was talking to should stay there until she came," he said.[185] The couple left the restaurant around six thirty.

Frances, Verna's youngest daughter, was on the other end of the call. She had plans to go to a dance that night, and her mother and Denhardt had promised to be chaperones. Frances recalled that when Verna telephoned around six fifteen, "She said she had a headache, and that she and General Denhardt could not chaperone the dance, and for us to get somebody else."[186] Verna told her that they were leaving Louisville, and she expected to be home in an hour. Frances waited for her mother, but finally left for the dance when Verna did not arrive. At midnight, she was at the dance when she heard the news of her mother's death.

The next person to see Verna that evening was Barney Browning. Sometime between eight forty-five and nine o'clock, Verna appeared at the door of his service station asking for help with a stalled car.

None of the witnesses that day noticed anything unusual in Verna's behavior, and most knew her well. But there were gaps in the timeline that Kinsolving and Messmer could not fill. They knew that Verna had ordered flues for a boiler sometime during the afternoon. The flues were delivered to the laundry that night and installed on Saturday morning after her death. While he retraced the path of the couple, Messmer also discovered that Denhardt rented a hotel room in downtown Louisville for forty-five minutes or an hour. Sometime around four p.m., he was in a room at the Kentucky Hotel. Why Denhardt would rent the room was one of the mysteries troubling Kinsolving. The possibility that Verna might have been there with him was embarrassing and upsetting to Verna's family, and she was no longer alive to defend her reputation. But the family knew with certainty that Verna would never spend time alone in a rented room with Henry Denhardt.

"It worried me, but I knew nobody would believe anything against her," Roy Garr later said.[187]

There were other mysteries that not even John Messmer and his investigators could uncover. After Verna and Denhardt left the Sada San Restaurant, Messmer's witness trail ended. Where were they from six thirty until Verna appeared at Browning's Service Station two and a half hours later? The drive from Louisville should have taken around an hour. Why did they drive through LaGrange to Henry County when Verna's daughters were expecting her home?

Unfortunately, there was only one person alive who could answer these troubling questions and fill the gaps in Kinsolving's timeline of November 6. Whether Henry Denhardt would tell the truth about what happened that day remained to be seen.

Chapter 14

A MOTIVE FOR MURDER?

Henry Denhardt's attorneys had an important advantage over Kinsolving—they knew Denhardt's story from beginning to end. But they also knew that his version of events was a potential landmine that could damage their case. A month before his April trial, while he was scribbling to-do lists and instructions to his overworked attorneys, Denhardt committed his story to paper in a rambling thirty-three-page memorandum. It was more a disjointed and muddled stream-of-consciousness piece than an organized statement from an attorney and former judge. The chronology of events was difficult to follow, and in some places, made little sense. But true to form, the general depicted himself as the victim, the wronged party, and everyone else was to blame.

The document contained several self-serving and self-aggrandizing comments, including "She then reached over and put her arms around my neck and kissed me and said, 'Next to God, you are the best man that ever existed'" and "I asked why she had deceived me in this manner, she said, "That was very wrong, but I was simply trying to lead you on, therefore I deceived you as I did.""[188] The memorandum was the general's dramatic story of love, deceit, and betrayal, and he was the maligned hero. It contained accusations and scandalous anecdotes that no one would ever have the opportunity to deny.

Denhardt included unflattering stories about Verna, Mary Pryor and her fiancée, Allen Brown, Frances, Reuben "Bookie" Taylor, Chester Woolfolk, and Doc Garr. Doc was a special focus of the general's enmity, and he repeatedly made certain that his attorneys knew Garr was "crazy" or had "mental troubles." It was probably Denhardt's revenge against Doc for signing the murder warrant that started the legal process.

Berry, Otte, and Myers were surprised by Denhardt's eagerness to dictate or write an exposé that was personally embarrassing and damaging to his substantial ego. The accusations were astounding, but if the general was telling the truth, he had been the innocent and unwitting party in a love triangle that included his forty-year-old fiancée and a twenty-six-year old "boy."

Denhardt's political career had careened to an end in early 1936, but the summer that followed was filled with new beginnings. His meeting with Verna Garr Taylor in mid-June was totally unexpected, a lightning bolt into the humdrum of his retired farm life in Oldham County.

"On the tenth of June, Garr came to my farm and told me that his mother had a house for rent; that he understood my sister and I were about to rent a place in LaGrange," Denhardt wrote.[189]

Doc was too busy to go with him to see the house that afternoon. He suggested that the general stop by Verna's house to pick up the key.

Denhardt was immediately attracted to the lovely widow, and their initial meeting was followed by dinners, movies, and drives in the countryside. While he does not admit it, Denhardt was probably flattered by the attention of a beautiful woman twenty years his junior. Walking into a public place where his cronies could see Verna on his arm was undoubtedly a gratifying experience.

During the summer courtship, both were absent for weeks at a time—Verna on vacation in New York, and Denhardt on military maneuvers at Fort Knox. In August, when he returned from Fort Knox, Verna's vivacious and talkative sister visited for three weeks, and, according to Denhardt, jealousy problems began. "I tried to be nice to Mrs. Taylor's sister, Juanita, because of the fact that she was her sister. I did not have the slightest thought of any flirtation or anything improper with her. Yet, Mrs. Taylor appeared to become exceedingly jealous of our friendship." He described arguments over Juanita where Verna stormed at him "in a most furious and loud manner."[190]

There were also arguments over his friendly relations with his ex-wife. "I had to go to Bowling Green and Logan County on some business. She insisted that I make the trip in one day. I told her that it would be almost impossible for me to attend to my business there and go and come in one day. I told her that I would have to drive two nights and that it would be too hard a trip. She finally agreed that I might go with the understanding that I would not call on my former wife or even telephone her as was my custom and that I, of course should not kiss her, that also was my custom when I saw her."[191]

One of the most bizarre and unflattering anecdotes was also about Verna and his ex-wife. "After I had given her [Verna] the engagement ring, she informed me that when an engagement was broken, or in the event of a divorce or death an engagement ring should revert to the man giving it and she insisted that I write my former wife in regard to the diamonds, wedding presents given by my friends and certain other silver and articles of value that my wife had asked to keep during her life." Denhardt claimed that Verna insisted he write the letter and allow her to read it before he mailed it. "She was still urging me to push this matter right up to the fatal day." The general did not bother to explain how anyone could remember in 1936 wedding presents they received in 1905.[192]

He devoted nearly two full pages to stories of Verna's jealousy and demands. There is a subtle anger in the text that questions his motives for telling the stories. The general needed to support his version of Verna's depression and suicide, but the tales of jealousy did nothing but portray her in the worst possible light. They looked like payback from an angry man.

Denhardt alleged that he kept a "little notebook" of the events during the summer and fall. He recalled that on October 23, he returned from Bowling Green and met Verna at the Pendennis Club for dinner. She was cold and distant. "I did not ever understand what the real trouble was until after she told me of her love affair, with Ches. She told me that Ches had brought her to town that day and now I can account for her change of attitude by reason of the fact that Ches had brought her to town, and of the conditions which must have occurred during my absence." Denhardt claimed he realized that "Ches was even then, about two weeks ahead of the suicide putting on the pressure. . . . The real climax came less then [*sic*] two weeks later when the ring was displayed and he then realized fully that he had to put real pressure, or else lose her or his job."[193]

There were also ongoing discussions over investments and property rights, and where the couple would live. Denhardt claimed that Verna wanted to build a house on his farm. The general gallantly refused to use her money to build a house, but promised to deed part of his farm to her so that the money she invested in a house would be protected. After more discussion, the two decided to remodel the original house on the farm. "In fact, we both drew plans of what we would like in the way of changing the house."[194]

Verna also supposedly urged him to deed half his farm to her. "She said that she thought it would be right in as much as she was giving up a good business to marry me, for me to convey half of my property to her."[195]

Denhardt wanted to know whether this proposition meant she

would not marry him unless he deeded his property to her. "I told her I never believed in pre-nuptial contracts, that I had always said I would never make one and that I had no intention whatsoever of making one with her. I asked for a decision, she thought for a while and then said that she wanted me regardless of my property." Denhardt claimed that he forgave Verna "because she had had a hard time and that I felt that because of this she was simply trying to make certain the securing of her financial future."[196]

In looking back at events during the summer and early fall, Denhardt wondered if Verna had ever really loved him, or if she viewed him as a retirement plan. But he claimed that by early November, the marriage plans were still ongoing and the two would be married within weeks.

On the night of November 5, the general was returning from Louisville when he noticed Verna and Woolfolk rounding the courthouse in LaGrange in the laundry truck. Both vehicles stopped, and Verna rolled down the window. After a brief exchange, Denhardt invited himself to her house and said he would be by shortly. Denhardt wrote that he later learned a key piece of news that confirmed his suspicions. The other employees had already left, and Verna and Woolfolk were alone at the laundry that evening.[197]

When he arrived at Verna's house, Denhardt described her as "very much disturbed" and he believed something was wrong. She told him that Woolfolk was in love with her and was very jealous of Denhardt. She had shown her ring to some of the employees at the laundry that morning and word of it had reached Woolfolk. He was very jealous and did not want her to marry. "She said that every time I came near or even telephoned, she watched him and that he would shake like a leaf and get white as a sheet, and that she was afraid he might do something drastic, that he had been in love with her for years. I asked her what her feelings were toward him and she said she liked him, that he had come over to the house and played cards in the kitchen when she was lonesome and that she had used his car, and that he had been very faithful to her in her business."[198]

Denhardt related an odd anecdote that he claimed was part of this discussion. Verna's brother-in-law, Reuben "Bookie" Taylor was a "great admirer" of Woolfolk and had invited him to attend his "boy parties." Woolfolk went to one of them, but over time, there had been a "change of feeling" between Bookie and Woolfolk. Bookie asked Verna to deliver a letter to Woolfolk from him. Denhardt wrote, "I asked why Bookie didn't deliver his own letter. She said that Bookie stated that Ches loved the ground she walked on and he wanted Ches to be his friend, and that she could do more with him than anybody else." She gave Woolfolk the letter, but he handed it back and advised her not to read it. "I asked if she had and she said she had. I asked her what kind of letter it was. She said, 'What kind do you think it would be?' She said it was simply a love letter."[199]

It is a bizarre anecdote in a document filled with odd stories. Denhardt may have included it to point out that even Verna's brother-in-law was aware of the influence she had over Woolfolk. He may also have used it to show that Woolfolk was the kind of man who would receive a "love letter" from another man. It is also possible that Denhardt included the story about Bookie because he was angry at Verna's family and in the mood to air everyone's secrets.

After this startling revelation, Denhardt claimed they dismissed the Woolfolk situation. "The matter worried me greatly; however, we parted on good terms with our usual goodnight greetings."[200] He included a description of the couple's "goodnight greetings" in his memorandum. "There was hardly a night after our engagement, in fact, I do not recall any night, that we did not part without each saying to the other that we loved each other better than we ever did anyone in all our lives. We also used the expression, 'God keep you and bless you.' We each promised the other to pray for each other each night. This I did every night from the time of our engagement and she did the same for me. And each told the other that we were happier than ever before in life. This was our attitude and relationship to each other until the very last."[201]

The next morning the two left LaGrange for Louisville. Verna had plans to review the laundry's business account with the Kentucky Military Institute, make a deposit at a bank in downtown Louisville, and attend an afternoon bridge party at her cousin's home. Denhardt recalled that Verna complained of one of her frequent headaches, and said she had not slept well the night before. But according to the general, it wasn't until their stop at the Kentucky Military Institute that the day went completely haywire.

Denhardt recalled that, while Verna was inside the school's business office, he walked around the building to exercise. When Verna returned, she asked him if he had seen her standing at the window. He told her he had not. "She then stated that she was making up her mind in regard to a very serious matter which concerned me. I asked her what it was. She then told me of her love affair with Ches which she stated had been going on ever since about two years after her husband's death. She said that she thought she was in love with Ches up to the time I came along." The night before, she had argued with Woolfolk about her engagement with Denhardt and he had "roughly handled her and mistreated her" after the other employees left the laundry.[202]

Denhardt claimed he was flabbergasted at the confession and had no idea that the two were involved. "I could hardly believe it was anything but a terrible dream, yet, it was true that the woman to whom I had confessed everything early in our affair, so that there might be no 'rude awakenings' for her later when we might become really serious, and on whose account I had been better than ever in my life, and had absolutely avoided every appearance of evil, had been intimate constantly with a twenty-six-year-old boy."[203]

Verna told him that no one living knew about her affair with Woolfolk. "She said only one person had ever accused her of this and that she told this woman she was crazy. Her name was Mrs. Shelby Allen, now dead."[204] Mrs. Shelby "Bessie" Allen of LaGrange died in March 1933. If the story Denhardt alleged was true, Allen saw or heard something suspicious around the time that Verna and Woolfolk became involved.

After Verna's confession, he understood that there had been warning signs he ignored during the summer romance. Denhardt recalled the time in late June when Verna and Frances were leaving on vacation for New York. Denhardt thought they were leaving on Thursday night and wrote Verna a farewell letter. But on Friday morning, he saw Frances in downtown LaGrange on her way to the bank. Puzzled, he drove by the laundry to see if Verna was there, but Chester Woolfolk was alone. Woolfolk told him Verna had just left.

Denhardt looked out the window and saw Verna running as fast as she could in the direction of her house. She stopped running when he called her name. Verna told him that her visit had been delayed, and that her chauffer (Woolfolk) was going to drive her to Cincinnati to meet the train. Her excuse for running was that she did not want him to see her looking disheveled from working at the laundry. "I frequently after that told her that she looked better that morning than I ever saw her. I know now why she stayed over and ran. This boy was the only person at the laundry as they worked only part time."[205]

He also remembered that several days before Verna's death, he had stopped by the laundry with Bertha, and Verna sat in the car with them and visited. Woolfolk pulled up beside them in the laundry truck. "When he came, Verna scarcely looked at either Bertha or me, but kept her eyes almost constantly on Ches.

Whether she did this through fear of his doing something to me or because she loved him so, she could not take her eyes off of him." After Verna's death, Bertha remembered the peculiar scene and remarked, "Did you notice her watching him last Tuesday when we were at the laundry?" Denhardt noted, "I think I understand now why she did."[206]

After leaving the Kentucky Military Institute, when Verna "saw how she had absolutely crushed me, she became more thoroughly depressed than before, and said she couldn't possibly go to Mrs. Lee's party."[207] He urged her to go to the bridge party, hoping it would help her depression. But she could not face the other women, and asked Denhardt to call and say she wouldn't be able to attend. Denhardt telephoned Lee from the Pendennis Club. During the conversation, Lee asked about his health and he told her he was sick that day. "The facts about the matter are that I really had been sick all day, ever since I had heard about Ches."[208]

November 6 was evidently a day of confessions by Verna and revelations for the general. Verna supposedly confessed that Doc had arranged their initial meeting. According to Denhardt, she said "her brother had planned having me meet her ostensibly to rent the house and that it was on his insistence that she had started going with me."[209] Doc's reason for matchmaking was the financial security that a relationship with Denhardt could offer.

Verna also supposedly told him that the business and property suggestions had been "forced on her by her brother Dr. Garr" to ensure her future.[210] But according to Denhardt, Doc was unaware of Verna's scheme to find a place for Woolfolk on their farm in the hope that he "would not cause trouble."[211] Early in his memorandum, Denhardt noted that Verna "spoiled and humored Dr. Garr because he had had trouble with his wife and seemed to need her help more than did the others."[212]

That has a ring of truth. But it does not make sense that

Doc would be able to force his self-sufficient sister to say or do anything against her will. The scheme to placate Woolfolk sounds improbable, but not impossible if the allegation of an affair was true.

On the drive to downtown Louisville and "just after she had told me about her affair," Denhardt's car had a punctured tire.[213] He walked to a nearby service station and had a worker come to put on a spare. In his memorandum, he does not mention that there was any discussion while they waited.

According to Denhardt, Verna's depression continued throughout the day, and she spoke several times of suicide, claiming she had ruined her life—"Oh, I have made such a mess of my life, I simply can't stand it."[214] But she also urged him to marry her while they were in Louisville. Denhardt wrote, "I said that I didn't even have a new suit of clothes to wear" and thought it would look foolish to elope. "She then stated that I didn't intend to marry her at all, if I didn't marry her that day." Denhardt insisted that they were still engaged and she had his ring. They had plans to marry in a few days when Verna's younger sister arrived for a visit. He urged Verna to wait until she arrived.[215]

In the late afternoon, before they left the Pendennis Club, Denhardt purchased an inner tube at a nearby tire store. The parking lot attendant at the club changed the tires and installed the inner tube. He wrote, "While we were waiting in the car and while the tires were being changed I had to take out my keys, the one belonging to the glove box being the same as the one that locked the back part of the car . . . When I did this she motioned at the glove box and said that I need not take the keys with me she wasn't going to do anything." The general implied that Verna motioned toward the gun he carried in his glove box.[216]

They stopped for dinner at the Sada San Restaurant, and Denhardt borrowed a silver dollar from Verna to buy a half-pint of whiskey. "I told her that I was sick and felt so depressed that I thought I was entitled to have a drink. She said, 'Yes, I think you are, and there is not a reason why you shouldn't take one to help you over the shock.'"[217]

It is true that Denhardt purchased whiskey across the street from the restaurant with one of Verna's silver dollars. But why would Verna, who did not approve of drinking, allow or encourage him to purchase whiskey? Later in his memorandum, Denhardt wrote, "She lectured me about taking a drink, had me agree to go to church with her after we married."[218] It would be out of character for Verna to encourage anyone to drink in her presence. Denhardt implied that Verna encouraged him to drink out of a sense of guilt over her confessions. But it is also possible that she felt badly because she was ending their relationship and the general was not taking it well.

Denhardt purchased his whiskey and the two left the restaurant for LaGrange with Verna driving. "We stopped along the road several times and talked as was our custom she did not seem to be in a hurry to get home." Verna supposedly became even more despondent and told the general "she would be dead within fifteen minutes after she got home."[219]

During this conversation, Denhardt claimed she suggested a suicide pact where they would die together. "I replied by saying that I knew nothing that she had done which would cause her to commit suicide and certainly I had been good and kind to her in every way, and I couldn't understand why I should die. She said that I was right that she didn't want me to die that I had been better to her than anybody ever was." Denhardt also told her that if she killed herself while she was with him, people would blame him for her death.[220]

Verna supposedly asked his help in writing a suicide note. Denhardt was a lawyer, and he "could tell her what to say in a note that she would leave behind. I, of course, discouraged this proposition . . ."[221] This statement is one of many in the memorandum that defy belief. It is hard to imagine that Verna asked Denhardt to help her write a legally correct suicide note.

When they reached LaGrange, Verna wanted to continue driving on Highway 22, which, according to Denhardt, was one of her favorite drives. By this time, it was very dark, and the two-lane road leading out of LaGrange into Henry County was winding and narrow. It may have been Verna's favorite drive during the day, but at night, it required slow and cautious driving. It is hard to believe that a woman with a headache would enjoy the drive. It's more likely that Verna continued driving at the general's suggestion, and to allow him time to recover from his half-pint of whiskey.

Denhardt stated that Verna continued to be so despondent that he insisted she turn the car around at the Pendleton Schoolhouse to go home. The car stalled with a dead battery, and Verna walked to Browning's Service Station next door to get help. Denhardt said he did not get out of the car because he was sick, and because Verna did not want anyone to know he had been drinking. The latter part of this statement was probably true. It also supports the theory that Verna continued driving through LaGrange to give the general time to sober up.

The car was pushed to George Baker's driveway, and the couple talked while they waited for a battery. "After we had sat in the car in the Baker driveway for some minutes she seemed to be more calm and collected and apparently alright." Verna asked him to go to Baker's door and telephone the garage "and tell them to hurry up with the battery." Denhardt left the car and walked toward Baker's house. "I had gotten nearly to the door when she called for me to come back. When I went back she was gone."[222]

Denhardt claimed he stood by his car and called for Verna several times, but it was very dark and he could not see her. Bernard Shepherd drove slowly past the Baker's driveway and saw the general standing near his car.

A short time after the Shepherd car passed, Denhardt heard

a shot fired from the east in the direction of Browning's Service Station. He claimed that he "immediately" walked to Baker's door for help, and Baker came out of the house "almost immediately" after the gunshot. The general rushed back to the car to look for his gun. He asked Baker for a light to go and find Verna. While they were discussing the situation, "a second shot, a muffled one, was fired."[223]

When Hundley returned with the battery, "we drove down the road toward the garage and back and tried to look on each side to see if we could find her or her body. We failed to discover it and later Mr. Baker with a light, together with Hundley, Shaver and myself went down the road and we found her body."[224] Denhardt made no mention that he waited at the car while the battery was installed before he made the second search and found Verna's body.

According to Denhardt, he left Verna's body alone and unattended in the ditch because "I supposed some of them would remain near in fact I felt they would, anyhow, I just couldn't stay I had to get back to my car where I could sit down. I was, of course all-to-pieces."[225] The statement that "some of them" would remain near Verna's body makes no sense. Hundley had already left for LaGrange to bring help, and Baker walked ahead to check on his wife. There was no one left at the scene but the general and Cuba Shaver, the automobile mechanic.

Ricketts, Keightley, and Denhardt sat in Ricketts's car and discussed what had happened. Denhardt recalled, "I described hurriedly the occurrences of the night, told of her threats to kill herself and where I was when the shots were fired. We talked a few minutes, then I said to Mr. Ricketts, what do you want me to do now, do you have any further need for me tonight?' He said, 'No, you are at liberty to go.'" Denhardt asked for someone to drive him home, and Cuba Shaver agreed to do so. "I was sick, depressed and worried. It was but natural I get someone to drive me."[226]

Denhardt claimed he had reserved a room at the hotel in LaGrange because of the plans to chaperone Frances's dance. But he wanted to get home and talk with Bertha. The road to the general's house was impassable because of the snow and mud, so he told Shaver to stop in the front field, and he walked to the house. He took Verna's purse with him and gave it to Bertha.

"Upon arriving home that night, of course, I told Bertha of the terrible affair." Bertha was shocked and concerned, but tried to calm her brother and encouraged him to rest. He finally went to sleep after a sedative and whiskey.[227]

The next morning, Denhardt was still under the influence when Coroner Ricketts, Sheriff Harrod, Deputy Stivers, and D. F. Lee arrived at his house. He described the chaotic scene. "I found myself standing in the middle of the floor with some several men rough handling me. Mr. Cole finally came in and I told them I would do what he said, he got them to let me get in bed, but before this these birds had, so Bertha said, searched my bed, she asked what it was all about." Denhardt claimed that the men shoved Bertha aside as they pushed into his bedroom.[228]

D. F. Lee was present on behalf of Verna's family and wanted to know the truth. "I frankly told him that Ches did not want her to marry me, and had been giving her trouble. I told him I supposed they knew she and Ches had been in love. He said he was afraid that this was the trouble." Denhardt claimed his friend Dr. McCormack believed the family was so "aggressive" because he had told Lee the truth. "He feels they are trying to save her reputation by making me the 'goat.'"[229]

On Monday, November 9, Denhardt allowed Messmer to perform his paraffin test. Afterward, Coroner Ricketts asked to see the general's overcoat. "In the hurried examination, I did not see the small drops of blood which may have been there. I held up my finger and said there is where the blood came from."[230]

Denhardt claimed that on the night Verna died, he was holding her hand when she noticed that his finger was bleeding. He used his handkerchief to staunch the flow. He still had the stained handkerchief in the pocket of the trousers he wore that night. "I may have cut my finger on the sharp edge of the windshield electric heater where the wire from the battery is attached. I really don't know how it was done."[231]

Denhardt claimed that Verna had been living a double life for three years. He gave his attorneys several reasons to support his version of suicide: her alleged affair with Woolfolk, fear of what Woolfolk might say or do, and concerns about her rebellious teenage daughters. Verna fretted over Mary Pryor's relationship with Allen Brown. She worried about Frances, and considered sending her to a private school in Shelbyville. Denhardt believed he had brought happiness into her unhappy and complicated small town life. "She said that after I came into her life I had brought a great deal of happiness and cheer and had been nicer to her and done things for her which had been lacking in the years before."[232]

Woolfolk could offer companionship, but he could not give Verna money and security. Denhardt offered her both, and while he wanted to believe she truly loved him, he would never be certain. "Whether she meant any part of it at all or was faking it all does not matter now but I do believe that she ran up the road that night to kill herself rather than doing so at or in the automobile because she did not want to cause me any trouble. She did think and know that I had been good to her always."[233]

In the days ahead, Denhardt and his attorneys would have to make a strategic decision—whether he would testify at his trial or remain silent at the defense table. As the defendant, the general was not legally required to take the witness chair. But all agreed that it was only human nature for a jury to be suspicious of a murder defendant who had nothing to say in his own defense.

If the general testified to everything he claimed, it would ruin Verna's reputation, and he would have to admit in a crowded courtroom that he had acted like a foolish older man in love with a younger woman. The publicity would be excruciating.

But there was a dangerous angle to the memorandum that concerned Berry, Otte, and Myers more than Verna's reputation or Denhardt's fragile ego. It really didn't matter whether Verna and Woolfolk had been involved in a love affair, or whether the whole story was a figment of Denhardt's paranoid and suspicious imagination. It was most important that this was their client's version of the truth, and he believed in the affair. But if the general testified that Verna Garr Taylor had used and betrayed him, he would be handing Kinsolving a solid motive for murder. This was the dilemma the defense team faced as the trial approached.

Chapter 15

IN THE EYE OF THE HURRICANE

In late March, H. B. Kinsolving and John Messmer caught the train to Pittsburgh, Pennsylvania, for a meeting with one of their expert witnesses, F. C. Buckmaster. Buckmaster was a chemist and an expert in performing the paraffin test. For the previous twelve years, he had worked with the district attorney's office in Allegheny County.

There was no doubt that John Messmer was also competent and experienced at performing a paraffin test, but Denhardt's attorneys would attack his lack of formal education. Buckmaster, on the other hand, was a graduate of Columbia University. His educational background was impressive and his professional credentials were beyond reproach. Kinsolving needed Buckmaster to approve Messmer's paraffin testing techniques and methods before Messmer testified.

In the Pittsburgh laboratory, Kinsolving fired Denhardt's revolver and Messmer performed a paraffin test on his hand. Buckmaster watched closely for any errors as Messmer made several casts of Kinsolving's right hand. At the end, he pronounced Messmer's techniques sound; he obviously knew what he was doing.

Buckmaster was confident as he shook hands with Kinsolving and promised to see him in Kentucky in late April. He was an experienced witness, used to dealing with fractious defense attorneys. He had testified in fifteen murder cases, and an estimated three thousand criminal cases in the courts of Pennsylvania, Ohio, and West Virginia.[234] He did not expect to experience anything in New Castle, Kentucky, that he had not faced in the past.

When they returned from Pittsburgh, Messmer tackled the problem of how to determine the distance from which Verna was shot. Late one afternoon, he met Doctors Blaydes and Walsh, and Dr. A. J. Miller, the University of Louisville pathologist, at the police rifle range in Louisville. They killed a sow on the rifle range and drained her blood by slicing a large vein in the neck. She was shaved, washed clean, and fastened to a large board. Messmer took squares of Verna's pink slip and black crepe dress and draped them over the hog's carcass. He loaded Denhardt's pistol with the same type of cartridges found in the gun on the night of November 6 and measured off distances. Messmer fired into the hog through the fabric from three, six, nine, and eighteen inches. He also fired a contact shot by pressing the barrel of the pistol against the body of the hog.

After each explosion of gunfire, the men studied the effects on the carcass and made notes. They measured any discoloration around the entry wounds and observed embedded particles of gunpowder or tattooing around the wounds. They compared the effects of each distance on the slip, the black dress, and the skin of the hog. Dr. Walsh placed pieces of the dress and slip in sealed cellophane envelopes and marked the distance of each shot on the outside.

Denhardt's experts performed their own experiment on the carcass of a hog using the general's gun and pieces of Verna's dress. It was an example of primitive ballistics tests and dueling expert witnesses, and their conflicting testimony would eventually leave an already befuddled jury even more confused.

Both teams of attorneys spent the weeks before the trial

preparing their expert witnesses, and making certain that they completed the tests on the .45-caliber pistol and ammunition, the bloodstains on Denhardt's overcoat, and the clothes worn by Verna on the night she died. The defense experts also performed paraffin tests after firing Denhardt's revolver.

But the issue that consumed both the defense and prosecution throughout the late winter and the early days of spring 1937, was venue—where the trial would be held. The alleged crime was committed in Henry County, and the place designated for the trial was New Castle, the county seat. Denhardt and his attorneys were determined to move the trial to another location, while Kinsolving and Verna's family were equally determined to keep it in Henry County.

In late March, Henry Denhardt wrote to John Berry urging him to do everything in his power to change the venue. He worried that even if they prevailed, no other Kentucky county would be a more favorable venue. "It seems that the whole district has been completely canvassed and vicious propaganda spread," he complained.[235] Denhardt claimed that the situation was so bad that he would as soon be tried in Henry County as three of the surrounding counties. But while there had also been talk in Spencer County, thirty-four miles from New Castle, he believed it was his best option. He urged Berry to convince Judge Marshall to move the trial to the small town of Taylorsville in Spencer County. Denhardt proclaimed dramatically that "it would be the greatest miscarriage of justice in the history of Kentucky" if he failed to get a change of venue.[236]

In order to move the trial, the defense had to convince Judge Marshall that the general could not receive a fair trial in Henry County. They were certain that the frenzied public demonstration at the examining trial would weigh heavily in their favor. Berry and Kinsolving spent months collecting affidavits of people in the area—Kinsolving attempting to prove that the general could receive a fair trial in Henry County and Berry trying to show that it would be impossible to find a jury free of bias. Berry's mission was the more difficult one. While some of the local people grudgingly agreed that it would be hard for Denhardt to receive a fair trial in Henry County, they refused to sign their names to an affidavit. He eventually found fifty people, and he attached their affidavits to a motion for change of venue that he filed at the Henry County Circuit Clerk's office in April.[237]

In his motion, Berry pointed out that during the inquest and examining trial, state troopers were positioned in and around the courthouse, and stood near Denhardt in case of violence. Large crowds of people thronging the courtroom and hallways made it difficult to maintain order. McClure James, a special correspondent for *Newsweek* magazine, had signed one of affidavits. James wrote that when he arrived in New Castle for the examining trial, the town was filled with people and the courtroom overflowed with spectators. Everywhere he went in New Castle, he heard groups of angry people discussing the case and vigorously arguing that Denhardt should receive the electric chair. Walking in town during the noon recess, he noticed that one of the windows of a local business had prominently displayed a .45-caliber revolver. Underneath was a placard that read: "This is the type of gun that was used to kill Mrs. Taylor."[238] James was also present for the courtroom demonstration after Jimmy Thomas's rousing speech, and from all he had seen and heard in New Castle, he believed there was a strong local animosity against Denhardt.

In his response to Berry's motion, Kinsolving pointed out that no matter where the trial was held, it would attract large crowds of people. The presence of a large crowd would not intimidate or influence the trial jury. Kinsolving argued that there was no public hostility against the general in Henry County, and he could receive impartial justice there as easily as he could anywhere else. He also addressed Judge Morgan's decision to move Denhardt to the Jefferson County Jail. Kinsolving argued that Denhardt was moved so that he could be closer to medical treatment from Dr. McCormack, not because he might be taken by force from the local jail.[239] Judge Morgan's affidavit was one of the seventy-five attached to Kinsolving's response. According to Morgan, the threats of violence against Denhardt were from counties other than Henry.[240] Mary Pryor Taylor Brown also signed an affidavit stating that her mother did not have business contacts or intimate friends in Henry County who would influence a jury. The Garrs and Taylors had only two distant relatives living in the county.

The motions and affidavits were filed with the court, and Judge Marshall would hear the issue of venue on the first day of trial.

As the trial date approached, New Castle, one of the smallest rural towns in Kentucky, began to prepare for the biggest event in its 139-year history. The town had one hotel that had been booked for weeks. Reporters stayed in small trailers set up for them in the New Castle area or stayed with locals. Denhardt's defense team planned to headquarter in the town of Eminence, four miles away. The local *Oldham Era* reported:

> New Castle will witness the largest crowd it has ever had if reports are true. Representatives of the Associated Press and other news gathering organizations will be present as well as special writers and photographers for many of the largest newspapers in the country. Representatives of magazines will also be on hand. Special wires are being leased and every possible method of transmitting the proceedings of the trial is being arranged for. The case has attracted nationwide interest and will hold the front page on daily newspapers until the conclusion of the trial.[241]

An emergency telegraph room was set up in an office behind the second-floor courtroom for reporters and their telegraph operators to relay breaking developments during the trial.

Henry Denhardt continued to appear confident and nonchalant with the reporters who dogged his every step. But he was not as confident as he appeared. While the citizens of New Castle braced for the invasion of outsiders and the attorneys made last-minute preparations, General Denhardt put his personal affairs in order. On April 16, he quietly revised his original will by handwriting a codicil. He was a sixty-one-year-old man facing execution or life in prison. Even if he managed to pull off an upset at his trial, he feared that the Garr brothers would always be out there waiting, somewhere in his future.

In the handwritten revision of his will, Denhardt left his entire estate to Bertha, his devoted sister. Bertha and Dr. McCormack were designated executors, with his brother Jesse as their surety. If sufficient funds were available, they were to be used to aid in the eradication of tuberculosis in Kentucky. But if the estate exceeded $25,000, he wanted to remember someone else. The general handwrote a bequest of $2,500 to Rosalie W. Chestnut of Jacksonville, Florida, "my faithful secretary for several years."[242]

The general had recently returned, tanned and relaxed from his vacation in Jacksonville, where he had stayed with Omer and Rosalie Chestnut. The two were originally from Florida, but had lived in Bowling Green, Kentucky, where they met and became friends with Denhardt. They had no children, and Rosalie was forty years old in 1937, the same age as Verna Taylor. In his codicil, Henry Denhardt chose to remember Rosalie, but not her husband. And in his bequest, he did not write her name as "Mrs. Omer Chestnut," the usual way to address a married woman in 1937, but rather "Rosalie W. Chestnut." When he was satisfied with the revisions, he placed the will among his personal papers.

But even while he was putting his affairs in order, by the trial date General Denhardt was still arguing with his attorneys over the amount he was willing to pay. He had checked on fees for similar services in important cases, and the largest fee he found was for $3,000 or $3,500 for a group of four attorneys. This amounted to less than $1,000 per attorney. The general offered to pay his three attorneys $2,000, less than $700 each. He added insult to injury by saying that he really did not believe any of them had been forced to neglect their other cases on his account.[243]

Berry and Myers were disappointed and frustrated, but Clarke Otte was furious. He was so irate that Denhardt later claimed that just hours before the trial, Otte encouraged Berry and Myers to walk away from the table and leave him if he did not pay them $5,000.[244] Eventually, they persuaded Otte that it would be a terrible blow to Denhardt, and look bad for all of them if they walked out and left him without counsel. Denhardt was in the worst situation of his life, and desperately needed Otte to handle the scientific testimony of the experts. Berry and Myers were confident that the payment might be late, but Denhardt was good for it and would pay as promised.

While Denhardt's attorneys worried about payment in the days before the trial, Kinsolving worried about his witnesses and the complex and confusing details of the case. George Baker was his lead witness, and for the first time, Baker would be expected to hold up under a withering cross-examination. Baker could be relied on to speak honestly, and a local jury would identify with him as a simple man in a tough situation. But he was also a poor historian when it came to time and distance. The defense, of course, would move for a dismissal based on Baker's remark about being with Denhardt when the second shot was fired. But no judge who wanted to be reelected would dismiss Denhardt's case.

As the trial approached, nagging questions remained that Kinsolving couldn't answer, and holes in the timeline for the evening of November 6 that not even John Messmer could fill. The lengthy time Denhardt and Verna spent driving from Louisville to Henry County was one of them. It also concerned him that the defense was up to something with Chester Woolfolk, Verna's handsome laundry truck driver. Too many questions had been asked around LaGrange to ignore the possibility that Denhardt's attorneys might use information they had been gathering about Verna and Chester Woolfolk to try and establish a romantic connection.

Kinsolving was unaware that, in January, Berry had urged Denhardt to give Otte money to hire a private investigator. Berry wrote to Denhardt, "The secret angle of the case should now be investigated exhaustedly and the investigation cannot be made by any person known to be identified with your defense."[245] In Berry's opinion, the investigation of the "secret angle" was so delicate that he believed Denhardt needed a professional investigator.

Whether Denhardt took Berry's advice and spent the money to hire an investigator is unknown. But in the months between January and April, someone working for the defense was digging for information about Verna and Woolfolk. An investigator noted that a friend was asked to sit with a distraught Woolfolk on the day after Verna died. Questions were asked about how often Woolfolk's car was parked in Verna's driveway.

For Kinsolving, the pressing issue was how the defense intended to use this information. But it was hard for Kinsolving to imagine the egotistical general admitting in court that Verna preferred someone other than him.

While he was worried about where the questions about Verna and Woolfolk were leading, Kinsolving was also concerned with how the family would hold up in court during the trial. Verna's daughters would be called as witnesses on the first day of trial, but they were also determined to sit through the rest of the testimony. Kinsolving, Clarke, and Turner knew there were going to be things said and exhibits introduced that no daughters of a beloved mother should have to hear and see. It was one thing to hear that their mother had been shot, but quite another to see her bloody clothes and pieces of her skin paraded into court for all to see.

It promised to be as rough a trial as any in the history of Henry County. The reporters would no doubt be sympathetic to the family, but they would also eagerly watch their reactions to make the stories more sensational. There would undoubtedly be times when the Garr brothers would want to jump from their chairs for Denhardt's throat and call him a dirty liar, especially if he intimated a romantic relationship between Verna and Woolfolk. Judge Marshall would not put up with any outbursts in his court. He ran a tight ship and no matter how sympathetic he was to the family, a commotion in his courtroom could mean jail time. If the crowd was rowdy, he would simply empty the room. There would be no demonstration like the one at the examining trial. The Garr brothers would have to keep control of their emotions and let the attorneys do their work.

Six months had passed since Verna died, and it had been a time of long hours spent investigating, interviewing witnesses, and drafting motions and responses. There had been countless arguments between the attorneys, courtroom appearances, and even a catastrophic flood. But those months had been calm in comparison with what they were all going to face. Kinsolving, Clarke, and Turner were about to leave the quiet eye of the hurricane and face the full fury of the winds in New Castle.

Part II

NEW CASTLE

If any person be guilty of willful murder,
he shall be punished with death or confinement in the
penitentiary for life, in the discretion of the jury.

—

Kentucky Revised Statutes
Section 1149
1936[246]

Chapter 16

JUDGE MARSHALL TAKES A SWING, APRIL 19, 1937

The Henry County Courthouse in New Castle is tall and stately, an Italianate-style building of red brick that over the years has aged to a rich dark burgundy. Its handblown glass windows, trimmed in white, have offered a view over the center of town since 1875, when the courthouse was built to replace another that had burned to the ground. The dark brick building is topped by an imposing, white Beaux Arts cupola that soars into the sky. The tiny town square below was once filled with busy dry good stores, diners, and law offices. The cupola can be seen for miles from the narrow roads that wind through the rolling fields around New Castle.

Circuit Judge Charles Cotesworth Marshall had made the drive to Henry County for many years from his home in Shelbyville. On cloudless days, somewhere just outside of Eminence and several miles away from New Castle, the towering cupola would appear in the distance like a beacon, summoning him to court in Henry County.

In April 1937, Judge Marshall was aging and white-haired at sixty-nine years old. For thirty years as the circuit judge of Kentucky's twelfth district, Marshall had spent his days driving the back roads to courthouses in five rural counties. The courtroom was his kingdom, and the Henry County Courthouse was one of the fiefdoms where he ruled as a benevolent dictator, ensuring that justice was dispensed according to his high standards. It did not matter to Marshall whether Henry Denhardt was guilty or innocent. His job was to make certain that Denhardt received a fair trial in his courtroom.

For Judge Marshall, son of a family of attorneys, and a collateral descendant of famed United States Supreme Court Justice John Marshall, the law was serious business. He had tried many difficult cases during his career, and the Denhardt trial would be one of his most challenging. It was a point of pride for Marshall that the Court of Appeals turned back few, if any of his cases, a testament to his ability as one of the finest jurists in Kentucky.[247] Judge Marshall tolerated no foolishness in his courtroom, and he was easily irritated by anyone who dared to cross his brightly drawn line. He often expressed his impatience in court by snapping at querulous attorneys, "Get along gentlemen. Let's move along." In the coming weeks, the attorneys during the Denhardt trial would hear the phrase many times.[248]

After so many years as a circuit judge, Marshall had experienced all that his profession had to offer, both good and bad. But that was before he arrived in New Castle for the first day of his Henry County docket. From the moment he drove into town and finally found a place to park, he could tell that his usual requirements of order and decorum were about to be severely challenged. Everywhere he looked, there was chaos. The streets were clogged with horses, mules, wagons, buggies, automobiles, and a mob of people moving slowly but steadily toward the courthouse. The normally quiet courthouse lawn was completely changed. There were musicians singing, booths and vendors selling food, and even a snake charmer performing for the crowd.

In thirty years on the bench, he had never witnessed a spectacle to equal this one and Marshall was appalled. A man's life and reputation were at stake in his courtroom and his future depended on the outcome. But the gravity of the occasion was lost on this crowd that had turned a murder trial into a carnival. New Castle, a town of scarcely several hundred residents had exploded almost overnight into thousands of laughing and chattering men, women, and children intermingled with jostling reporters, photographers, and hucksters. By the time he had finally elbowed his way through the crowd to the courthouse door, Judge Marshall was in a terrible mood.

The scene inside the courthouse hallway was as chaotic as the one outside. As Marshall pushed his way through the crowd, the flash of the photographers' cameras was blinding. When a photographer from the *Chicago Daily Times* ventured too close with his camera, the judge finally snapped. Clenching his fist, he swung wildly at the man, and the reporters pressing around him in the crowded hallway scattered. In the confusion and uproar, the photographer pivoted sideways and the blow glanced off his shoulder.

"Now get out of here or I'll throw you in jail!" shouted Marshall.[249]

He had made his point, and the subdued reporters parted respectfully in front of him as he walked up the iron stairs to the second-floor courtroom. When he had composed himself, and taken his usual seat at the judge's bench, he apologized for his actions and set the rules for the trial. He understood that the journalists were there to get a story and cover Denhardt's trial, but they were to take no photographs of him in the courtroom or inside the courthouse while the trial was in progress. "Yes, sir," the reporters said respectfully.

Judge Marshall could do nothing about the uproar outside the courthouse, but he took pride in his orderly control of a courtroom. In his years as a judge, he had never requested armed police during a trial, and he was not going to start.

Henry Denhardt had founded Kentucky's Highway Patrol and there was a loyalty to him among the officers. They had appeared with their guns in court that morning unsolicited and stood around the room. The judge called the state troopers to his desk and explained that he had no need for them; they could surrender their weapons or leave the courthouse premises. The troopers refused to surrender their guns, voted to leave, and marched out of the courtroom. Judge Marshall was unconcerned.

The local newspaper reported, "Sheriff Evan Harrod stated that he was confident that he and his deputies could handle the situation and if necessary he could summon the sheriffs from adjoining counties for assistance. He stated, however, that he anticipated nothing but an orderly trial throughout."[250]

Once Judge Marshall had settled the issue of photographers and armed police in his courtroom, he turned his attention to the huge crowd. He warned them that they were to be on their best behavior. This was serious business and there were to be no outbursts or laughter in his courtroom. "I don't want any demonstrations or evidence of approval or disapproval," he lectured them sternly.[251]

"Now, the first item to discuss today is venue, and I have a motion from the defense, and a response from the state," he continued. "Gentlemen, let's proceed." But if Marshall thought that the venue hearing would move at a normal pace, he was mistaken. For five grueling hours, he struggled through testimony in favor of and opposed to moving the trial to another location. At times, both Marshall and Denhardt dozed as the hours slowly passed.[252]

Rodes Myers asked John Berry to take the witness chair and speak about his difficulties in obtaining affidavits. Berry said, "I think 98 percent of the people in this county are against General Denhardt. Many of them have concluded he is guilty and should be punished severely. Rumors go so far as to charge General Denhardt with nine murders of women." He also mentioned that he had experienced hostility in Henry County for representing Denhardt.[253]

Sheriff Harrod was called as a witness and testified that while there was "an unfriendly feeling toward General Denhardt" among the spectators at the examining trial, he had no trouble controlling the crowd.[254]

When the testimony and arguments finally ended, everyone waited anxiously for the judge's decision. If he granted a change of venue, the trial would be delayed, but if he ruled against Denhardt, the selection of a jury would begin. As Kinsolving hoped and John Berry feared, Marshall refused to move the trial from Henry County.

The judge solemnly addressed the attorneys: "I have no doubt that in this county the defendant will receive a fair and impartial trial. Outside of the anxiety of the citizens to find out what was going on, and the outcome of the investigations, there was no hostility. It may be true that many persons expressed opinions. Maybe a greater number expressed that he was guilty because the defendant has made no statement. Today nobody knows what his statement will be."[255]

The general had made public expressions of innocence solely to the newspapers. But during his inquest and examining trial when he had the opportunity to speak, he remained silent. No one other than his attorneys really knew what Denhardt would say in his defense.

Earlier in the day, Denhardt had appeared confident. Laughing with reporters about his weight gain and "robust appearance" since the examining trial, he said, "I have a clear conscience and I sleep well." In the same comment to the press, he blamed his indictment on politics. "There would never have been an indictment except for the activities of some of my political enemies."[256]

However, when Judge Marshall ruled against his motion for a change of venue, the general's face went pale and flushed red. He had counted heavily on moving the trial, and after the demonstration in the courtroom during the examining trial, he had a good argument. But Judge Marshall had made his decision, and with the trial remaining in Henry County, the outcome looked dismal for General Denhardt on the first day. The next item on the agenda was to select a jury.

Selecting the jury for General Denhardt's murder trial took two laborious days, and eighty-one men were summoned into court before twelve were finally selected for the jury panel. The attorneys quizzed the men closely, knowing that each potential juror could be the difference between a guilty or innocent verdict, and life or death. Judge Marshall did not leave the interrogation of the potential jurors to the attorneys, but took an active role in the tedious process. If a man hesitated, or seemed unsure, the judge demanded that he give clear answers without "beating around the bush."[257] Each man was invariably asked if he had formed an opinion on Denhardt's guilt or innocence. Many would slowly drawl, "Well, I can't say that I have." The reply never failed to irritate Judge Marshall. "Well," the judge barked back in each case, "you're the only man that can say. Now answer the question and answer it properly! Did you form an opinion or did you not?"[258]

As the long hours passed, a response would occasionally amuse the crowd, and titters of laughter would ripple through the courtroom. The onlookers soon found themselves on the short end of the judge's temper. "I warned you at the start that this was not an exhibition. This is a serious occasion. This is the trial of a man for his life, liberty, and reputation, and let's have no more instances of risibility or amusement!"[259] The crowd quieted quickly. No one wanted to lose his or her seat before the trial began.

Each prospective juror was also questioned whether he had conscientious scruples against the death penalty. Those who did were immediately excused from jury duty. When it was finally finished, and the pool of potential jurors had been thoroughly vetted by the attorneys and the judge, eleven local farmers and one service station operator stood ready for jury duty. All were male, white, and most were middle-aged. They were all men of practical, commonsense knowledge with little formal education. One man had completed the twelfth grade, and the others ranged in educational accomplishment from the fourth grade to the eighth. Understanding the testimony of scientists and medical experts would be a challenge for these men. But for the prosecution and the defense, they were the best choices available from the jury pool.

Late in the day after the jury had finally been selected, Judge Marshall turned to the defense table and asked the attorneys to enter a formal plea on behalf of their client. Denhardt, neatly dressed, and cheerful throughout the final long day of jury selection, sat watching at the table with a hand propped against his cheek. He listened as Rodes Myers said firmly, "Not guilty!"

The judge turned to the jury, "Gentlemen, raise your right hands. Will you hear testimony, consider it carefully, and a true verdict render according to the law and the evidence?"[260] It was a solemn moment, and the impatient judge had been waiting for days to finally reach this point. But even after the jury was selected and sworn, and Denhardt's official plea entered in the record, there was one last defense motion to hear.

"Mr. Myers, I believe you have another motion for the defense before we dismiss for the day."

The ruse Jimmy Thomas had pulled with the stenographer and the grand jury in January still irritated the defense attorneys. Myers presented a motion to quash the indictment. If the stenographer took no notes, then she was in the grand jury room illegally as an observer, he argued. Any indictment drawn during the time she was in the room should be invalid. Thomas sat listening to Myers's argument with a face that betrayed no emotion. Judge Marshall wearily shook his head and overruled the motion. "Exception," Myers murmured, and retired to the defense table.

Throughout the long and tedious days of motions and jury selection, the courtroom remained filled, but not jammed with onlookers. By six p.m., when Kinsolving finally read the lengthy indictment charging Brigadier General Henry Denhardt with the willful murder of Verna Garr Taylor, only two elderly men still sat listening in the courtroom. The rest of the spectators had tired and left for home.

Before adjourning, Judge Marshall turned a stern eye to his jury. He warned them not to talk about the case among themselves or with anyone who might approach them for information. There were too many reporters looking for tidbits of information, and he did not want any of it coming from this jury. The last thing Marshall wanted was to have to try the case again because of juror misconduct.

When they had solemnly nodded in agreement and court finally adjourned at six thirty on April 22, Judge Marshall had conducted the longest court session of his career. After what he had already witnessed outside the courthouse, in the hallways, and in the courtroom with the lengthy arguments, motions, and continuous exceptions, he knew that the Denhardt trial was going to be contentious, and one that would surely try the limits of his patience.

Chapter 17

STATE OF MIND

The next morning, a large throng of people pressed through the doors of the second-story courtroom in New Castle, jockeying for seats and standing room. In front, near the judge's bench, were two rectangular, wooden tables. General Denhardt waited impassively at one with his attorneys; his brother and sister sat nearby. Kinsolving, Turner, Clarke, and Jimmy Thomas sat at the other table. A large contingent of Garr relatives were present in the courtroom. They had left their jobs, their homes, and their farms at spring planting time, some driving many miles to be present. A number of them were only distantly related to and vaguely knew the Garr family of LaGrange, but they were there to support their relatives and see that justice was done.[261]

The *Courier-Journal* reported: "Commonwealth's Attorney Kinsolving said today that the prosecution's case will be conducted, so far as possible, in chronological order. First witnesses, according to that plan, will be those who saw General Denhardt and Mrs. Taylor in Louisville the day of her death, and at home before the couple left for Louisville."[262]

With his initial group of witnesses, Kinsolving's strategy was to reveal Verna's state of mind on November 6 for the jury and establish a chronology of the events. On the first day of testimony, the defense team was evasive on whether Denhardt would take the witness chair. For a verdict in favor of the Commonwealth, Kinsolving would have to prove that Denhardt was guilty of murder beyond a reasonable doubt. Denhardt's team would be working hard to introduce every possible element of reasonable doubt.

"All rise!" called the bailiff, and everyone rose respectfully as Judge Marshall briskly entered the courtroom in his black robes. He adjusted his usual seat on the bench, beneath the formal portraits of past Henry County judges, and placed a brass spittoon within striking distance. With a stern look over his glasses at the spectators and the attorneys waiting expectantly before him, and with a voice that resounded throughout the large courtroom, Marshall banged his gavel and barked, "Gentlemen, let's call the case of *Commonwealth versus General Henry Denhardt*."

Kinsolving would deliver the first salvo for the state with his opening argument. Clutching his glasses in one hand, he walked to the area in front of the jury box and looked at the quiet, serious men sitting in front of him. He began his speech with the usual formal salutation in open court: "May it please the court, and you gentlemen of the jury." For the next two hours, Kinsolving slowly paced the wooden floor in front of the courtroom as he spoke. He introduced the victim, told the story of how she met the defendant, detailed the tragic events of November 6, and reviewed the witnesses and evidence.

"His silver-rimmed spectacles dangling from his hand, his voice cool, rapid, and dispassionate, the stocky, square-shouldered, sandy-haired prosecutor detailed his attack in pithy, simple language to the sober-faced farmer jury before him," the *Courier-Journal* reported. "He made no gestures for their benefit, or for the benefit of the crowd that from early morning filled every seat in the big square courtroom and overflowed into the aisles."[263]

Kinsolving promised that the prosecution would show General Denhardt was seen returning to his car from the direction of the death scene; that he lagged behind in the search for Verna's body; that he denied killing her before he was accused; and that his overcoat was stained with blood. With the evidence, he would convince the jury that Denhardt murdered Verna Taylor with the first shot heard that night, and that he moved her body and appeared at the stalled auto, firing the second shot from a small-caliber fountain pen weapon.[264] But Kinsolving's narrative came to an abrupt halt when he mentioned that Coroner Ricketts would relate the story of his visit to Denhardt's farm on the morning after Verna's death.

Defense attorneys quickly shouted objections, anticipating that Kinsolving was about to tell the jury that Denhardt was intoxicated. They asked for a conference with the judge in his chambers. After hearing the arguments from both sides, Judge Marshall ruled against Kinsolving.

"Mr. Kinsolving," Marshall said sternly in chambers, "I will not permit a statement about the defendant's intoxication to be made during this trial."[265] Kinsolving would have liked the jury to know that Denhardt was roaring drunk just hours after Verna died, but he was not surprised when Judge Marshall ruled against him. It added spice to the story and reflected on the defendant's character, but it was not pertinent to Denhardt's guilt or innocence.

When they returned to the courtroom, Kinsolving continued his opening argument. He turned to the topic of John Messmer and his paraffin tests, and once again, there was a continuous stream of objections from the defense table. Marshall overruled most of them, but the interruptions were distracting, and made Kinsolving's lengthy opening argument even longer as he struggled to review his witnesses and evidence for the jury. He finally concluded: "I am convinced when this proof is submitted to you gentlemen in this case that you will be convinced from this proof that Mrs. Taylor did not come to her death by her own hand, that she could not have possibly killed herself and did not kill herself; but that the defendant, who was present with her and whose gun was used, as the proof in this case will show, was the man that fired the fatal shot into her body that took her life."[266]

The opening argument had been long and contentious. It was an indication that the trial would be hard fought, both sides locked in a fierce battle to either clear the general, or send him to the electric chair. Judge Marshall asked the defense attorneys if they were ready to make their opening argument. Rodes Myers declined, but reserved the right to make an opening argument later in the trial.

Kinsolving asked for his first witness, Roy Stewart, to be called into court. Roy Stewart was a handyman who did odd jobs and repairs at the Community Laundry. He initially worked for Verna's husband, but after Rowan Barclay Taylor's death, Verna became his employer. He had known Verna for fifteen years, and he arrived at the laundry on the night of November 5 after receiving a message from her. She asked him to check the boiler and see if he could install a new stack and three flues. He was at the laundry for thirty minutes, but concluded that he did not have the tools to do the work. He described Verna as a "very jovial" person, and never moody or melancholy. When he met her on the street in downtown LaGrange, she always smiled and greeted him.[267] Her demeanor was no different on November 5, the last night he saw her alive.

Kinsolving took his seat, and Clarke Otte walked briskly from the defense table to cross-examine the witness.

"You say you were there about thirty minutes?" he asked.

"Yes."

"You were there alone, I understand; back in the boiler room alone?"

"No, sir. She was with me."

"Did you see Chester Woolfolk there?"

"Yes, sir. He was there the entire time I was there."

"He was there when you left?" probed Otte.

"Yes, sir."[268]

The defense had wasted no time in introducing Chester Woolfolk into the trial. Whether it was an indication of future problems on that front remained to be seen.

Kinsolving asked for his next witness, Mary Pryor Taylor Brown to be sent into court. Verna's oldest daughter was twenty-one on the day she testified. She was tall, slender, and attractive, neatly dressed and wearing a stylish hat. Mary Pryor was nervous, but steady and determined as she approached the front of the courtroom and took her oath to tell the truth.

Kinsolving crossed the floor to the witness chair and gently began his questions. Mary Pryor recalled her first meeting with the defendant in May or June 1936, when he came to her home to inquire about renting a house. After his initial visit, he began stopping by several times a week. Her mother would go with him to the country club, or for automobile drives to Louisville and visits to the Pendennis Club in that town.

Kinsolving asked Mary Pryor if her mother had ever made threats to kill herself and she quickly replied, "Why, no, of course not."

"Had she any trouble or any illness, or was there anything that caused her grief or sadness around that time?"

"No, none whatsoever."[269]

The laundry business was doing well, and her mother did not have any debts. Verna employed four men and nine women, purchased the supplies, and looked forward to making improvements at the business. On the day of her death, she purchased flues to be installed in the boiler. They were delivered to the laundry on the night she died and were installed the next day.

Kinsolving asked, "Miss Mary Pryor, had there been any disagreements or fusses of any kind, or quarrels, between your mother and the defendant previous to her death, and immediately prior to her death, to your knowledge?"

"Yes—"[270]

Before she could continue, there was a storm of objections from the defense and arguments between the attorneys. Kinsolving was determined that the jury would know about the argument Mary Pryor overheard between her mother and Denhardt. The defense was equally determined that they would not and Myers continued to object. "We are objecting, unless she can state from her observation of the two."

"Objection overruled," said Judge Marshall.

"Exception," retorted Myers.[271]

When the arguments continued, Marshall finally stepped in, weary of the bickering attorneys. He looked over his glasses at the witness and asked, "Now Miss Mary Pryor, what occurred in your presence, and in the presence of both of you, if it did occur that way?"[272]

With Judge Marshall's question, Mary Pryor was finally able to tell the story of the argument she overheard between her mother and Denhardt from the next room. She told the jury that she heard her mother order him out of the house that night.

When questioned about the engagement ring, she recalled that it was on her mother's hand when she left the house with Denhardt on the morning of November 6. But when Kinsolving asked how her mother was dressed that morning, Mary Pryor's steely resolve suddenly collapsed. She began to weep, causing a sympathetic murmur in the courtroom. When she had composed herself, she was able to describe her mother's black crepe dress and black wool coat for the jury.[273]

By the time Clarke Otte began his cross-examination, Mary Pryor's resolve had returned and she was ready for his questions. She denied that her mother was ever depressed and remembered her as a happy person. There were no changes in her personality in the days leading up to November 6. Otte insinuated that perhaps Verna was depressed and hid it from her daughter. Mary Pryor replied, "If my mother had been melancholy, I would have known it because I knew my mother so well."[274]

Otte returned to the questioning and asked, "Do you know Chester Woolfolk?"

"Yes, I do."

"Did he ever come there frequently and play cards?"

"He has been there at our house."

"Frequently," he said with a hint of sarcasm.

"Well, he checks in every night."

"Checks in. What do you mean by 'checks in'?"

"He collects the money during the day, and he of course—"

"He was a good friend of the family, wasn't he?" Otte continued.

"Yes, he was."

"You all treated him like a member of the family, didn't you?"

"Yes."

"Did he ever teach your sister any music?"

"He gave her a few lessons on the saxophone."[275]

The morning passed quickly, most of it taken by Kinsolving's opening argument. When Mary Pryor's testimony ended, Judge Marshall announced a lunch recess, and dismissed the ladies in the courtroom several minutes early to prepare the noonday meal.[276] The rest of the crowd pressed their way out of the courtroom shortly after the ladies left.

Otte's snide questions about Chester Woolfolk had been the most interesting part of the testimony that morning. While Kinsolving worked hard to establish Verna's state of mind, Otte worked equally hard to distract the jury with the Woolfolk questions. There was little doubt that he was trying to lead the minds of the jury down an avenue of speculation, a place where Kinsolving and Verna's family did not want them to go.

Chapter 18

THE LONELY HIGHWAY

After the lunch recess, Kinsolving called his first afternoon witness, Maude Bell. Bell had worked at the Community Laundry for eleven years, and for five years, she had seen Verna Taylor nearly every day. Bell was matter-of-fact, outspoken, and not easily intimidated. She was also opinionated, and by the time she took the witness chair, she had already decided that General Denhardt had murdered her employer.

Kinsolving asked, "What kind of woman was she, as to disposition?"

"As sweet as could be."

"How did she meet people?"

"Very pleasantly, nicely, ladylike."[277]

In the weeks and days leading up to her employer's death, Bell had not noticed any change or difference in Verna's personality or demeanor. Bell lived nearly a mile outside of LaGrange, and it was customary for Verna, Chester Woolfolk, or occasionally both of them to drive her home in the laundry truck. Bell had heard Verna speak of the repairs and improvements she was planning at the laundry. She knew that Verna was in the process of ordering materials and contracting the work.

"When did you last see her, see Mrs. Taylor?" queried Kinsolving.

"The night before she was killed."

"What was she doing at the laundry on that night?"

"Well, we had all been working there, and she was sitting at her desk when I left."[278]

When Kinsolving was finished with his direct examination, Clarke Otte left his chair beside Denhardt and strolled to the front of the courtroom. He knew Bell was one of the employees present when Verna showed them the engagement ring on November 5. He quickly asked, "Was Chester Woolfolk there at the time?"

"No, sir. I don't think so. I don't remember him being there."[279]

Otte quizzed her about Verna's habit of concealing the ring in a handkerchief in the front of her dress. He also asked Bell a number of questions about November 5 and what she observed when Verna showed her employees the ring. But Bell was becoming tired of Clarke Otte and his prying questions. When he asked her if any of the "girls" wept or cried when they saw the ring, she replied in a huff, "If they did, I didn't see 'em. I didn't see no weepin' or cryin'."[280]

The spectators in the courtroom burst into laughter and Judge Marshall banged his gavel furiously. The laughter quickly subsided, and he lectured the crowd. "Just a moment. I want to say to you ladies, and gentlemen too, that you must control your risibles. If there is anything that affects your sense of humor, control it, just like you would in a church . . . You are not disorderly, but this is not a place for amusement on the part of any lady or gentleman in the courtroom."[281] With a delivery to his spittoon, Marshall nodded at Otte to continue. Otte finished by asking Bell whether she had heard any comments about Verna moving to the general's farm. She agreed that she had heard something said about it.

Sixteen-year-old Frances Taylor was Kinsolving's next witness. Frances and her sister appeared slender and delicate, but they were actually tough and courageous survivors. For the past six months, their lives had been a living hell. They had buried their mother, struggled through her exhumation and autopsy, and suffered through the inquest, examining trial, and indictment against Denhardt. The reminder of how their mother died assaulted them daily in the newspapers. But Frances continued in high school, and Mary Pryor took over the daily operation of the Community Laundry.[282] Frances walked into the courtroom with her head high and took her seat in the witness chair.

Kinsolving began with the day her mother died, the day of the dance at the Mary D. Shop. "Was your mother or the defendant involved in your plans for the evening in any way?" he asked.

"They were supposed to chaperone the dance."[283]

Kinsolving asked if her mother suffered from headaches. The *Courier-Journal* reported her response: "She said headaches bothered her mother, but that Mrs. Taylor had no financial worries so far as she knew. Several times, she said, she accompanied her mother and the general on motor trips."[284]

In particular, Frances recalled attending a football game at Kentucky Military Institute with her mother, Denhardt, and two of her close friends a few weeks before Verna died.[285]

On cross-examination, Otte doggedly returned to the topic of Chester Woolfolk and his relationship with the family.

"Now, Miss Taylor, did you take lessons on the saxophone?"

"I did."

"Who taught you?"

"Chester Woolfolk."

"Did he ever play cards there at home?"

"No, sir."

"Never has?" Otte asked with exaggerated disbelief.

"No, sir."

"Did he visit the home very much?"

"Well, he would come there and check in at night, then he taught me . . . gave me some lessons on the saxophone."[286]

Otte was obviously fishing for information with his questions about Woolfolk. It was irritating, but Kinsolving could do nothing but listen impatiently. When Otte finally finished, Kinsolving's concern shifted to two of his most important afternoon witnesses: Barney Browning and George Baker.

Browning and Baker had testified at the examining trial, but neither had ever been cross-examined. Kinsolving knew that Denhardt's attorneys would be ready with questions. Browning's appearance went well, but on cross-examination, it was obvious that John Berry wanted the jury to remember that Denhardt was sick on the night of November 6. He returned Browning to the point where he asked Verna Taylor why Denhardt did not help push the car.

"You asked why he didn't help?" asked Berry.

"Yes, sir. I did ask what was wrong with the man that he couldn't help."

"And she said that he was sick."

"Yes."[287]

"Thank you, Mr. Browning," said Berry as he returned to the defense table.

"Your Honor, the state calls George Baker as its next witness," said Kinsolving. As his name echoed out into the hallway, Baker walked into the crowded courtroom and made his first appearance in the trial as the state's cornerstone witness.

In the months since the examining trial, Baker's tenuous grasp of time and distance had not improved. In response to a question of how far something was from him, Baker was likely to say "just a piece." Answering a question about how much time had passed, he might reply "just a short bit." But he was honest and straightforward, and a jury composed almost entirely of farmers would identify with him.

George Baker was more confident since his initial appearance at the examining trial. He knew what to expect, was less awed by his role as the prosecution's lead witness, and was willing to offer additional details. For the first time, he included the important information that Verna asked him if there was a telephone at his house while they were still on the highway. Baker testified that she asked the question within earshot of Denhardt before they pushed the car to his driveway.

"Mrs. Taylor said something about the phone when they said they couldn't—he couldn't pull the car to LaGrange, she said something about a telephone, if there was a telephone, and I told her there wasn't any telephone closer than Pendleton . . ."[288]

His description of Denhardt waiting while the battery was installed was more dramatic than at the examining trial.

"He was just standing there around the automobile, looking up and down, and he said to me several times, he would say, 'My, my! Ain't that awful!' He said, 'The finest woman I ever knew.' He mentioned that to me several times while they were fixing the automobile."[289]

Kinsolving easily guided him through his account of the night Verna died and his involvement in the tragedy. Baker had his usual struggle with time, but the shock of seeing Verna's body lying in the ditch had made an indelible impression. The description of what he witnessed was detailed and compelling.

"She was lying on her back with her hips laying in a swag of the ditch, like, in a puddle of water and snow, her head laying slightly over a bump, with the chin laying upwards. Her head was laying from the road and her feet towards the road."

"Can you describe the position of her limbs and arms?" asked Kinsolving.

"Yes, sir, I can. Her right limb was laying out straight. Her left limb was laying in a cramp, something like that; just laying back with her foot almost to her knee. This arm were laying in this shape and one shoe setting right in here by the body. This hand was laying straight."

"Did you see her gloves?"

"Yes, sir. One glove was grasped in this left hand . . . the other was laying on the ground by her feet."

"What about her shoes?" Kinsolving asked.

"One shoe was on her foot and one shoe was laying by her body."

"What about her hat? Did you observe it?"

"Yes, sir. Her hat was laying back under her left shoulder, like; under her head and shoulder like . . ."

Baker's voice trailed away.

"Did she have on a coat of any kind?"

"The coat was thrown back, apparently. It seemed like she was on the coat. I thought at first she didn't have on a coat. The coat was back under her . . ."[290]

As expected, John Berry's cross-examination was detailed and thorough. He asked Baker to look at a map of his farm, driveway, outbuildings, and Highway 22 as it passed in front of his property. Berry questioned him about his farm and the rooms in his house. Baker pointed at the places on the map with a straightened wire coat hanger. Berry queried him closely about the place in his yard where he met the general after the loud gunshot. Baker pointed at the map.

"The tree is right here, you see, here. Right in here is the tree, and I walked right out here and we met out here. The gatepost, you see, is right here. I wouldn't be positive, you know. It was very dark; but we met right in there somewheres."[291] He got down from the witness chair to place a book on the map that represented Denhardt's car in his driveway.

"What direction did that second shot come from?" asked Berry.

"Well, I couldn't tell that it come from any direction. It just sounded like it was a dead shot; sounded like a .22 rifle in a barrel, to me."[292]

Baker wasn't able to estimate how close he was to Denhardt when he heard the second shot. He was walking from his house and did not notice Denhardt at the car until he heard the second shot and looked up. However, he recalled that Denhardt was moving toward his car from the direction of Verna's body when he looked up and saw his head and shoulders.

Before he left the witness chair, Baker estimated that it was possibly ten minutes from the time he saw Denhardt at his side porch until the car driving from LaGrange passed his house; ten minutes between the passing of the car and the loud gunshot; and three to five minutes after the gunshot before he stepped outside. But Baker also made it clear that he was simply guessing at the time. Berry did not ask the question about his comment at the death scene, and Kinsolving was content to let it pass.

Arthur S. Rueve, business agent for the Kentucky Military Institute, was the eleventh witness called by the prosecution on the first day of trial. On cross-examination, Clarke Otte was fixated on what Verna saw as she looked out of Rueve's office window. He was determined to make Rueve agree that Verna looked toward the parked automobile rather than the parade ground.

"Where was the car parked that she came in?"

"It was always parked right outside my office window, in the driveway."

"She could look out the window from where she was standing and see the car?"

Rueve replied, "No, she looked in a different direction."

"The driver of course was on the front seat of the car?"

"The only way I know she had a driver was when she got in she was on the other side, and she didn't drive," said Rueve.

Otte persisted. "But you do remember that she looked out the window."

"Yes, I do, on account of when she made the remark about how nice the boys looked on parade."

"No further questions," said Otte as he walked back to the defense table.[293]

Nettie Baker, Kinsolving's next witness briefly reviewed the events at Browning's Service Station, and told the story of how her husband pushed the Denhardt vehicle to their driveway. She remembered hearing their dog bark and thinking that something was wrong. When her husband went to check on Trixie, she overheard Denhardt ask if they had a telephone in the house.

John Berry pushed back his chair and walked from the defense table for cross-examination. Nettie Baker had done well as a witness, but she had never been cross-examined and waited nervously for his questions.

Berry asked, "Mrs. Baker, you at no time went out into the yard?"

"No, sir."

"And the door of the room in which you were sitting, or the doors and windows of the room in which you were sitting, were closed."

"Yes, sir."[294]

"Mrs. Baker, how long was it after your husband went out to see about the pup barking and returned in the house and told you of seeing General Denhardt that the car passed?"

"Well, I didn't look at the time, but it wasn't but a short bit."[295]

Berry pressed her for an estimate of the time. She finally guessed that it was two or three minutes until the car passed her house. During his testimony, George Baker had estimated the time at ten minutes. The jury was left with an estimate of two to ten minutes from the time George Baker saw Denhardt at the side porch until the car drove past the Baker home.

Kinsolving's next two witnesses were Bernard and Lottie Shepherd, and by the time they were called that afternoon, their testimony had become crucial to both sides. The husband and wife were the driver and passenger of the mysterious automobile that slowly passed the Bakers' house just before the loud gunshot. On the night of November 6, the couple had been visiting Bernard's mother on a farm near LaGrange. Their drive home took them by the Baker farm and the site of Verna's death. As he approached the Baker house, Bernard Shepherd saw Denhardt's automobile parked at the end of the driveway and slowed to thirty-five miles per hour, fearful that the car might back into the road. In his headlights, Shepherd saw a large man in an overcoat with one hand in his pocket. The man was standing motionless beside the car on the passenger side.

"Did you see any other person at or around that car at that time?" asked Kinsolving.

"I did not."

"Were the lights burning on your automobile?"

"Yes, sir."

"Did you observe any other person on the highway between the Baker residence and the Browning filling station as you went up the road?"

"I did not."

"Any other cars on the road?"

"No, sir."[296]

During John Berry's cross-examination, Bernard Shepherd remembered that the passenger door to Denhardt's car was open. As Shepherd drove toward the intersection, his headlights did not illuminate anyone walking on the highway. When he reached the intersection, he turned left toward home in front of the Browning Service Station.

Lottie Shepherd also recalled the large man in an overcoat standing alone on the passenger side of the automobile. She did not see anyone walking on the highway or standing next to it as they continued east toward the intersection.

The Shepherds' testimony was puzzling, and rather than clarifying the events of the night Verna died, it only added to the mystery. If Verna was no longer in the car and not walking on the highway, then where was she just before she died? It seems highly unlikely that a woman dressed in her best clothes and wearing heeled shoes would voluntarily climb into a dark ditch filled with snow, water, and mud. If someone had forced her into the ditch, it couldn't have been the general. He was standing in Baker's driveway and Verna was nowhere in sight. If Verna was frightened and fled Denhardt's car, she could have flagged down the Shepherds for help. She had stopped Hundley in the road earlier; there's no reason to believe she would hesitate to do it again.

The Shepherds should have seen both Denhardt and Verna if Kinsolving's theory was correct and Denhardt chased her down the highway. George Baker gave a rough estimate that ten minutes after the Shepherds' car passed his house, he heard the first loud gunshot. Nettie Baker estimated that it was two or three minutes. If Denhardt was motionless by his car, the minutes did not begin to tick until the Shepherds' car had passed. Once they were gone, Denhardt would have had to sprint into absolute darkness, find his victim, kill her, pull her body into the old roadbed, and return quickly to his car. The jury was left to wonder whether all of this was physically possible for the sixty-year-old overweight man sitting calmly at the defense table.

After her tragic death, Verna Garr Taylor was called "the most beautiful woman in two counties." This photograph of Verna at thirty-six was taken during the summer of 1932. *(Courtesy of the Garr-Taylor families)*

Henry Denhardt in 1894 at eighteen. This formal photograph was taken at a Bowling Green studio and marked what was probably a happy family occasion— the graduation of the youngest Denhardt child from high school. *(Courtesy of the Denhardt family)*

Lieutenant Henry Denhardt in 1898 dressed in the uniform of the Kentucky State Guard. *(Courtesy of the Denhardt family)*

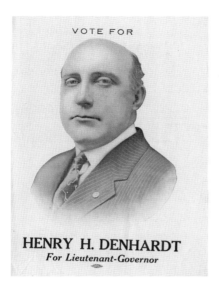

VOTE FOR

HENRY H. DENHARDT
For Lieutenant-Governor

Broadside from Denhardt's 1923 campaign for lieutenant governor *(The Filson Historical Society, Louisville, Kentucky)*

A Smith & Wesson .45-caliber US Army Model 1917 in the hands of a woman who is the same size as Verna Garr Taylor—five feet eight inches, 145 pounds, with an arm length of twenty-six inches. The exact dimensions of Verna's hands are unknown, but the hands of the model are probably close in size. According to the defense's suicide theory, Verna turned this large pistol on herself—using one hand—at a nearly impossible angle of left to right. *(Photo: Vivian Knox-Thompson)*

Chester "Ches" Woolfolk, the mystery man of the Denhardt
trial was never called as a witness. His role in Verna's life
remains a mystery decades later. *(Photo:* Courier-Journal,
April 25, 1937, Gannett–Community Publishing.)

The Garr brothers from left to right: Jack, Dr. E. S. "Doc," and Roy pose for photographers in the Shelby County Jail. *(Photo:* Courier-Journal, *September 22, 1937, Gannett–Community Publishing.)*

Old Shelby County Courthouse, Main Street,
Shelbyville *(Photo: Donna Shifflette)*

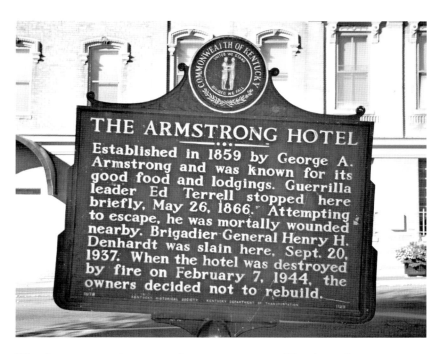

THE ARMSTRONG HOTEL
· · ·
Established in 1859 by George A.
Armstrong and was known for its
good food and lodgings. Guerrilla
leader Ed Terrell stopped here
briefly, May 26, 1866. Attempting
to escape, he was mortally wounded
nearby. Brigadier-General Henry H.
Denhardt was slain here, Sept. 20,
1937. When the hotel was destroyed
by fire on February 7, 1944, the
owners decided not to rebuild.

The historic marker near the intersection of Sixth and
Main Streets in Shelbyville *(Photo: Donna Shifflette)*

Verna Garr Taylor is buried in the Valley of Rest Cemetery, LaGrange, Kentucky. *(Photo: Vivian Knox-Thompson)*

General Denhardt is buried near his parents and siblings in Fairview Cemetery, Bowling Green, Kentucky. *(Photo: Donna Shifflette)*

Chapter 19

FIREWORKS IN THE COURTROOM

J. B. Hundley was an opportunist, a man hoping to make some extra cash out of his role in the tragedy. He believed his testimony was of such importance that Denhardt and his lawyers would pay for it. Hundley had been in contact with Denhardt's defense team since early 1937. In a letter written from Akron, Ohio, on March 14, Hundley asked John Berry for $190 to settle a debt: "Unless I can get $190.00 to pay him off, I don't see how I can be of any help. I know my evidence & what I can do will help Mr. _____ more than that. I will have to know by Thursday or Friday. I have tried to help because you know I came down there & it cost me more than I received. But thats o.k. Am willing to do all I can."[297]

On June 16, 1937, over a month after the end of the trial, Hundley followed up with another letter to Berry mailed from Frankfort, Kentucky:

"Dear friend, I went back to Akron but didn't get to go to work. Mr. Berry I am planning on opening a barbershop in Frankfort & would appreciate if we could settle right away. I will need it to get started."[298]

Whether Kinsolving was aware that his witness was working with the defense team behind his back is unknown. It's likewise unknown whether the defense actually paid Hundley, or whether he just assumed they would. His role in the events of November

6 was well documented by other witnesses, and his opinion of the importance of his testimony was exaggerated. Hundley heard George Baker make the comment that Denhardt could not have killed Verna Taylor because he was with him when the second shot was fired. His testimony would become important for the defense only if George Baker denied making the statement. Baker may have had problems estimating time and distance, but he was an honest man. If Hundley or Denhardt and his team believed he would lie under oath, they were very wrong.

Hundley was so eager to tell his story that he had barely settled in the witness chair before he blurted, "You want me to tell the whole story? Well, I was coming up over the hill there . . ."

"Now just wait a minute! Let him interrogate you," said Judge Marshall, irritated by Hundley's breach of courtroom etiquette. Kinsolving was also surprised and started slowly, asking him to spell his last name. Hundley spelled his name for the record and waited.

"Your initials are J. B.?" asked Kinsolving.

"J. B., and they had it 'J. D.' this morning," replied Hundley.[299]

A witness who could not wait to testify and wanted to be certain his name was correct for the record was unusual, but once Kinsolving had control of the situation, Hundley began to answer his questions.

J. B. Hundley was unmarried and a barber by trade. In November 1936, he was employed in LaGrange where he had lived for three years. In early 1937, he moved to Akron, Ohio.

A Louisville reporter commenting on the odd beginning of Hundley's testimony noted: "Hundley, who embarrassed the Commonwealth by starting to relate how he 'came over the hill' before any questions had been asked him, reviewed the stalled car scene on the highway, and confirmed Baker's testimony about Mrs. Taylor's gloves."[300]

When Verna's body was found, Hundley suggested that the

coroner and funeral director should be called and volunteered to drive to LaGrange. When he returned with Keightley, Denhardt, Shaver, and Baker were standing in the driveway. He recalled hearing Denhardt protest his innocence. "Well, when we was getting out of the car, Mr. Denhardt said, "I couldn't have killed her, because I loved her too much."[301] Hundley's description of the position and condition of Verna's body in the old roadbed closely matched George Baker's testimony.

"Was there any blood visible there on the clothing or on the ground at the point where you found her body?" asked Kinsolving.

"I didn't see any. It looked a little damp around where the bullet went in."[302]

On cross-examination by John Berry, Hundley recalled that when he arrived at Baker's driveway with the battery, Denhardt said that he had heard gunshots up the road and wanted to see about them. "He didn't say, 'Let's go see about the woman.' He says, 'Let's go see about the shots.'"

"Did he at any time, then, mention Mrs. Taylor or refer to the lady that was with him?"

"No, sir."[303]

Berry returned him to questions about the position of Verna's body in the ditch. Hundley remembered that she was clasping a glove in her left hand. He did not notice that she was wearing a hat until they moved her body onto the gurney. It was crushed on the ground beneath her body.

"What did Mr. Denhardt say when Mr. Keightley asked him what had happened?"

"He just said Mrs. Taylor killed herself."[304]

At the end of his cross-examination, John Berry finally asked the question Kinsolving had been anticipating.

"I will ask you, Mr. Hundley, if you had any conversation with Mr. Baker, or heard any remarks or statements he made that night—"

"Objection!" shouted Kinsolving quickly.

". . . that were made in the presence of General Denhardt?" Berry continued.

Judge Marshall nodded. "Objection sustained. I will have to sustain it. Come up here a moment."[305]

This was going to be a hotly contested issue, and the judge called both sides into his chambers out of the hearing of the jury. After hearing Berry's arguments in favor of letting Hundley answer the question and Kinsolving's opposition, Judge Marshall made his decision. George Baker was waiting with witnesses outside the courtroom. If Berry wanted to ask him if he made the statement, George could speak for himself. When George was recalled for cross-examination, Kinsolving asked for an exception to the judge's ruling. John Berry had his opportunity to ask the question during cross-examination. For some reason he failed to ask it, and Kinsolving did not believe Berry should be given another bite at the apple. But Judge Marshall ruled against him, and George Baker was recalled.

The atmosphere in the courtroom was tense when Baker entered for the second time late in the afternoon. His first appearance had gone well and no one had asked him about his remark, but he knew it was only a matter of time until someone did. From the expressions on the faces of the attorneys, it looked like that time had arrived. John Berry waited by the witness chair.

"Mr. Baker, I will ask you if on the night that Mrs. Taylor's body was found, while they were loading the body into the ambulance or down at your driveway when Mr. Hundley and Mr. Shaver had come, while Mr. Denhardt was present, if you made the statement: 'I don't know this man and I don't know this woman, but Mr. Denhardt couldn't have killed this woman, because I was with him when the second shot was fired.'"

"Yes, sir, I did," Baker replied without hesitation.[306]

"Well, he has a right to explain it," said Kinsolving. That

prompted Baker to turn to the judge and ask timorously, "Can I explain it?"

"Why no," said Marshall, looking surprised.[307]At that point, the storm began in earnest. Berry argued that it was a statement and there was nothing to explain. Kinsolving retorted that Baker had a right to make any explanation he cared to.

"There's nothing there to explain," said Berry emphatically. "He just said he said it, and that's all there is to it."[308]

Kinsolving asked the judge to admonish the jury that it should ignore the statement.

Rodes Myers entered the fray. "There's nothing to admonish them about!"[309]

The arguments grew more heated and Judge Marshall interrupted, trying to reason with the attorneys.

"Mr. Berry called the witness back for cross-examination. He had a right to ask him the question the first time, and he did not. He overlooked it. Then he undertook to prove what was said by another witness, and I wouldn't permit him; then he calls the witness back and asks him the question, and he answered it," said Marshall in his most judicious voice.

But Kinsolving wasn't finished. "That's right, and I think it is a matter that affects, if anything, his credibility."[310]

"We haven't got up the question of credibility at all," said the judge in a strained voice. "It is a statement that he says he made. I don't know why he made it. Stand by." The judge motioned the attorneys to his chambers.[311]

But when they returned to the courtroom, the melee started again. George Baker looked bewildered in the witness chair, while the arguments raged back and forth over his head. Kinsolving was not going to yield without a fight. If possible, he wanted Baker to elaborate on his statement, or have it removed entirely from the record. The prosecutor was drifting into dangerous territory with a tired, short-tempered judge who was already at the end of his limited patience. Turning to Baker, who looked thoroughly miserable, Kinsolving asked, "Mr. Baker, are you of the opinion now that the defendant, Denhardt, could not have . . ."

"Objection!"[312]

The *Courier-Journal* reported what happened next: "Judge Marshall, his left eyebrow lifted and his right drawn down in a frown that laid it on his cheek, brought his fist down upon the bench, his eye fixed upon Kinsolving in a glittering blue glare. 'Mr. Kinsolving!' rasped the judge. 'You know that's improper! Don't you dare do anything like that in my court.'"[313]

But Kinsolving did not retreat, even before the wrath of Judge Marshall. "It was purely a matter of opinion that he expressed."

"It was not!" said the judge. "He didn't ask for his opinion. He just asked what he said; that was all. Stand by. You can't ask a question like that."[314]

Clarke Otte entered the battle and made a motion to discharge the jury and continue the case.

"Motion overruled!" shouted Marshall. "He never answered the question." The judge glared at Otte when he requested another exception.[315]

At the end of the first major battle of the day, George Baker's remark remained in the court record untouched and the jury could make of it what they would. Baker was finally excused and retreated quickly from the courtroom.

Court was adjourned at five forty-five, and Sheriff Harrod escorted the weary jury past the clamoring reporters in the hallway. It had been a long first day of testimony, but the entertaining clash between the attorneys at the end had made the wait worthwhile for the spectators.

Overall, it had been a successful day for the prosecution. As planned, Kinsolving's early witnesses established that people who had known Verna for years noticed nothing unusual in her demeanor on November 5 and 6. She was a dedicated mother who was the sole provider for her household and paid for her children's clothes and education. The jury learned that she was an accomplished businesswoman who made competent decisions for her business and employees. Several witnesses testified that she was planning improvements at the laundry and purchased the supplies on the day she died. It seemed unlikely that she would kill herself several hours later.

But Otte's continuous questions about Chester Woolfolk were a fly in Kinsolving's ointment. Kinsolving knew that Otte was playing a game of cat and mouse with the witnesses, but he did not know that the information Otte used for his questions came directly from Denhardt's memorandum. For Kinsolving, it was as though Otte knew a nasty secret, and his cross-examinations unsettled the witnesses, and made the reporters in the courtroom wonder why he was so interested in Verna's young laundry truck driver. The reporters would draw their own conclusions and focus on Woolfolk in their stories about the first day of the trial. Whether Otte's ploy would have an effect on the jury remained to be seen.

Chapter 20

CHESTER WOOLFOLK

On the second morning of the trial, it was obvious that Clarke Otte's questions about Woolfolk had managed to provide a distraction from his client's guilt or innocence. Chester "Ches" Woolfolk had become the mystery man of the trial and the focus of rumor and speculation.

A *Courier-Journal* article reported, "Interest here in Woolfolk's part in the courtroom drama . . . dwarfed all other aspects of the case today, and prospects were that the courtroom would be jammed by Henry County people eager to see what turn the case will take next."[316]

In LaGrange, reporters searched frantically for any information they could find on Woolfolk. It quickly became obvious what the townspeople thought about Otte's questions; the reporters met a solid wall of silence and hostility. When they asked for directions to Woolfolk's home, they received indefinite answers or none at all. They finally located the Woolfolk home and spotted Chester's car in the garage, but his mother told them that he was not there. When they asked her if he would be at the laundry on Monday to report for work, they were told that he wasn't going to work. The journalists reported, "The commonwealth, Special Prosecutor J. Ballard Clarke says, has instructed the young man 'not to talk with newspapermen' and efforts to locate him have been futile."[317]

Twenty-six-year-old Chester Woolfolk was a resident of LaGrange, and a member of one of its older and established families. He had worked at the Community Laundry for several years, and was known to be a friend of the Garr and Taylor families. A large photograph of him in the weekend edition of the *Courier-Journal* covered nearly the entire front page. It portrayed a handsome young man with an enigmatic half smile and dark hair combed fashionably back from his forehead. The reporter was quick to speculate on defense team strategy. "The attorney's questions were clearly directed at establishing the existence of a personal friendship between the young truck driver and the lovely widow, with the apparent intention of presenting him as another sweetheart of Mrs. Taylor's and a rival of the general's."[318]

The strategy would allow Otte to allege that complications in the relationship between Verna and Woolfolk led to her suicide. If necessary, he could also point to Woolfolk as a romantic rival who had a motive to kill Verna. It was extremely clever and provided the all-important element of reasonable doubt.

For the press, the possibility of a scandalous love triangle added spice to an already sensational story.

The *Zanesville Signal* reported, "Adding further to the mystery, another special prosecutor, Wirt Turner, Saturday denied the state was interested in Woolfolk, but the next day [J. Ballard] Clarke said, 'Woolfolk, on my instructions, stayed in Wirt Turner's office all day.'"[319]

Kinsolving and his team were obviously on the defensive and unsure what to do about Woolfolk. For the present, they instructed him to stay away from reporters and kept him secluded in Turner's law office.

Across the narrow street from where Woolfolk waited, a guitarist played, the snake charmer performed, and the ladies of the Missionary Aid Society worked hard to keep up with the demand for their sausages and apple pies. The members of the

Associated Press and local news agencies rechecked their wires and connections, and the large crowd pushed their way through the courthouse doors and up the iron stairway.

At nine a.m., the jury entered and took their seats in the wooden jury box. The mob in the courtroom rose to their feet as Judge Marshall entered and banged his gavel to bring the room to order. Since his threats to eject anyone unable to control his or her "risibilities," the crowd had been subdued and respectful. Judge Marshall intended to make certain they remained that way.

"All right, call your first witness," he said, looking toward the prosecution table.

Kinsolving's witnesses for the second day included Sheriff Walter Briggs and Roy Garr. Both were present to testify about the heel prints found by the road on the day after Verna died. As expected, Rodes Myers immediately objected. The site had not been secured, and hours had passed since Verna's death. But Marshall overruled him and allowed both men to describe the heel prints and their location beside the road. Sheriff Briggs's testimony went well, but Roy Garr struggled with his first appearance as a witness in a trial.

Roy was a plainspoken, rural Kentuckian who viewed his world in black and white, right and wrong. From the beginning, Roy had trusted in the legal system to prosecute Denhardt, and discouraged the hotheads who wanted to take justice into their own hands. While he supported the legal process, he was quickly learning that during a trial, lies could be presented as the truth, and the truth could be colored to the advantage of the one making the argument. The jury was left to sort out the difference. The legal shenanigans of the attorneys went far beyond the simple understanding of Roy Garr who viewed Denhardt's guilt in as straightforward a manner as he lived his life. He firmly believed that Denhardt had murdered his sister, and in return, Denhardt owed a debt to society and the Garr family.

Jack Garr was with Sheriff Briggs when the heel prints were discovered, but it was Roy who was called as a witness. When he took his seat in the witness chair, Roy was prepared to talk about the heel prints and offer his version of what they meant. He was soon to discover that a court of law can be a frustrating place for a man who has an opinion to express.

"Well, we could see her heel prints, where it was evident that she had . . ."

"Objection" said Rodes Myers.[320]

Roy tried again. "Well, we saw heel prints there, where they had backed up four or five times."

"Objection!"[321]

"Well, each pair were apparently even, you know, and they looked like they had stepped back a foot each time."

"Objection!"[322]

"She was backing towards the . . ."

"Objection!"[323]

Judge Marshall exhaled, trying to keep his temper. "No, not 'she was.' Just tell us about the tracks."

"Can you just tell which way they pointed?" asked Ballard Clarke, trying to help his witness.[324]

Roy asked for permission to step down from the chair and show the jury. Judge Marshall nodded, and Roy stood in front of the jury box and stepped backwards five or six times to show the jury how the heel prints appeared.

"Thank you, Roy," said Clarke.

Rodes Myers made a formal motion for all of the testimony to be excluded. It wasn't clear who made the tracks or that the ground was even in the same condition as it was on the night of November 6.

Judge Marshall rubbed his chin for several moments as he pondered the defense motion. "Well, for the present, your motion is overruled."

"Exception," said Myers in frustration and turned to walk back to the table.

On the second day, Ballard Clarke called two witnesses to testify about the fountain pen gun, but both were disappointing. By the end of their testimony, the jury had only learned that Denhardt owned a fountain pen gun. It was an embarrassing moment for the prosecution when Judge Marshall ruled that most of the fountain pen gun testimony was irrelevant.

Funeral director and embalmer W. S. Keightley was a key witness for the prosecution. He spoke with Denhardt at the death scene, embalmed Verna's body, and was at the general's farm on the day of his paraffin test. He also provided one of the more dramatic moments of the trial when Verna's bloodstained clothes were displayed in court.

Kinsolving turned to where Sheriff Harrod stood watching. "Mr. Sheriff, I will ask you to call Mr. Messmer, and have him produce that clothing here."[325]

Rodes Myers quickly jumped to his feet. "Your Honor, may I approach?" The judge nodded, and all the attorneys followed him to the bench. Myers leaned toward Judge Marshall, and in a low, urgent voice said, "Judge, he is getting ready to bring in here and introduce in evidence clothing worn by the deceased on that occasion . . . The clothing is of no substantial value whatsoever. It is purely inflammatory, and we object to its introduction."[326]

Marshall quickly overruled him.

The defense attorneys and Henry Denhardt watched helplessly as John Messmer solemnly walked in the room carrying a suitcase. Kinsolving opened it, and slowly and dramatically held up each article of bloody clothing for the mesmerized jury to see. Spectators seated in the back of the room craned their necks or stood to get a better view.

"Mr. Keightley, I will ask you to examine this black crepe dress and tell the jury whether or not that is the dress worn by Mrs.

Verna Garr Taylor when you found her body on the road and took it to your undertaking establishment."

"Yes, sir, this is the dress."[327]

He held up the black coat with its lamb's wool collar, the black toque hat found underneath Verna's body, her heeled shoes, underwear, and pink slip. As he presented each article for the jury to examine, he asked Keightley to confirm that Verna had worn it on the night of November 6.

The reporters watched the family closely for their reaction to the macabre scene. One paper reported, "When they were pulled out of a suitcase, the pink slip still stiff with blood, the bullet holes in dress and coat plainly visible, Mrs. Taylor's daughters were sitting just behind the Commonwealth table. The younger daughter bit her lip and clasped her sister's hand. Both restrained tears."[328] By the time Kinsolving was finished, he had successfully demonstrated to the jury that there were no powder burns on Verna's clothes. Judge Marshall admitted the bloody clothing as evidence.

During Keightley's cross-examination, Clarke Otte asked very specific questions about what he had witnessed when Messmer performed the general's paraffin test. Keightley described the paraffin sticks, the alcohol stove and how it was lighted with a match either from Messmer's pocket or the kitchen. But after Messmer lit the match, and before he performed the general's paraffin test, Keightley did not see him wash his hands. One of the reporters later explained in his news article, "Otte's questioning was directed at the possibility of outside nitrates (as from the match) entering into the test and giving a false positive reaction."[329] Once again, Otte was planting the seed of reasonable doubt, and this time it was directed at the validity of Denhardt's paraffin test.

Judge Marshall called for the lunch recess, but no one sitting in the courtroom wanted to leave and lose his or her seat. A number of people brought rope that they could lower from the second-story windows and haul up picnic baskets of food. The delighted photographers snapped pictures of smiling men and women, dressed in their best clothes, leaning out the open windows with rope that they lowered to the courthouse lawn below. It was the perfect solution to avoid losing a seat, and Sheriff Harrod and his deputies ignored the foolishness.

There were times, however, when Verna's family wanted to escape and leave the trial and New Castle behind, if only temporarily. Months later, Roy would recall the day his family decided to drive to the town of Eminence for lunch during the trial.

"One day in Eminence we were eating lunch, my two brothers and my two nieces, Mrs. Taylor's daughters, were eating lunch at a table in the center of the restaurant," he recalled. "And in walked Denhardt, and he walked in pretty near to us, saw us and he backed out of there, and no more than he saw us he threw his hand on his hip that way, didn't turn and walk out as a man would, he backed out, never did turn around till he got out of the door. We didn't have a gun or knife on us, we sat there with our heads down and let him go out."[330]

By the time the brothers finally raised their heads and looked out the plate-glass window, Henry Denhardt was retreating quickly across the street. After the unnerving scene at the diner in Eminence, Roy and Doc vowed never to be caught unarmed and defenseless again. If they believed Denhardt was anywhere in the vicinity, the brothers kept their pistols close. It was a fateful decision that would ultimately change the course of their lives and many other lives forever.

Chapter 21

BLOOD SPOTS

Coroner Ricketts, another key witness for the prosecution, was called into court. While Smith Keightley's testimony provided one of the more dramatic moments of the trial when Verna's clothing was displayed, Coroner Ricketts unintentionally provided comic relief. Kinsolving asked Ricketts to tell the jury about the day he had visited the general's farm, watched the paraffin test, and took custody of the overcoat. Ricketts was another practical and plainspoken Kentuckian like Roy Garr. When he examined Denhardt's overcoat, there was no doubt in his mind that he was looking at splotches of dried blood. But Rodes Myers objected. Ricketts was not an expert in bloodstains.

"Now, Your Honor, we want to object to his saying what that was, unless he is competent and made the tests," Myers said.

Judge Marshall agreed with Myers. "Mr. Kinsolving, I'm going to sustain the objection to his calling it 'blood.'"

"Judge, I will amend the question to use the word 'spots' instead of 'blood.'"

"Yes, that's the proper thing," Marshall agreed.[331]

But Ricketts struggled with his answers when it was obvious to him that there was blood on Denhardt's overcoat.

"What was the size of the spots on the overcoat?"

"They varied in size. Now there was clotted blood in one of these buttonholes. I don't know which one," replied Ricketts.

"Objection!"

Judge Marshall admonished the coroner. "Well now, Mr. Ricketts, you are not an expert as to blood."

"Well . . . blood spots" said Ricketts, and the spectators in the courtroom burst into laughter at his dilemma.[332]

Furious, Judge Marshall banged his gavel, and pointing it at the crowd, he delivered one of his sternest lectures.

"Now ladies and gentlemen, I don't want to have to warn you again. I again tell you that this is not an exhibition, nor is it being conducted for your entertainment or amusement. If you want to stay in the courtroom and hear this, you had better keep quiet. If anybody in your neighborhood creates a disturbance by laughing or talking enough to disturb the court, if you want to stay in here you had better point out the fellow who has been guilty of it, and I will send him out, just him." He turned his attention back to Coroner Ricketts.

"Now, Mr. Ricketts, don't refer to those spots as blood, as you have no actual knowledge yourself as to whether it was blood or not. Refer to them as 'spots.'"[333]

By the time Clarke Otte began his cross-examination, Coroner Ricketts was growing tired of the interminable questions. Otte asked him to look at Verna's pink slip and tell the jury whether it was torn or cut with scissors. Ricketts examined the slip and said that it had been both torn and cut.

"Was it cut that night?"

"No, sir, it wasn't cut that night, but there was a torn place in it."

"What kind of a torn place was it?" Otte continued.

"How is any other torn place?" replied Ricketts in exasperation.[334]

Before Judge Marshall's lecture, the crowd would have laughed at Ricketts's reply, but they remained quiet and listened as the judge warned the witness not to argue, but to simply answer the questions. Ricketts nodded, and continued by saying that the torn place in the hem of the slip was five or six inches; he had noticed it in the morgue when Verna's clothing was removed.

Otte returned to his former testimony about the bruise on Verna's thigh. Ricketts believed the bruise was made before her death. He described it as approximately six inches in diameter, but not a uniform circle. Ricketts suddenly stood up from the witness chair.

"What do you want to do now?" said Otte, bewildered by his sudden move.

"What do I want to do?"

"Yes."

Ricketts calmly replied, "Well, I just got up to rest."[335]

A number of the spectators put their heads down or covered their mouths, but the courtroom remained quiet. Otte was furious at Ricketts. He began to fire questions relentlessly, attempting to unsettle him and discredit his testimony. He moved quickly from one topic to another, asking him about the death scene and Denhardt's statements, the pistol and how he could look into the cylinder without the bullets falling out, the position of the body, and whether the gun was pointing toward the road. To his credit, Ricketts gamely and patiently answered the questions. Otte finished by asking whether Messmer was being paid for his services as an investigator. It was a valid question, because the experts scheduled to testify in the coming days would be paid for their services.

Ricketts replied, "I asked him what the charges would be and he said, 'There will be no charges; that the state or the city of Louisville were paying his salary."[336]

"No further questions," said Otte and returned to the defense table.

Both Ricketts and Keightley were solid witnesses for the prosecution, corroborated one another, and held up well under

Otte's cross-examination. But their testimony left another question for the jury to ponder. Both men agreed that there were a few spots of blood on the front of Verna's pink slip, but neither saw blood on the outside around the front bullet hole. John Messmer would later agree that when he examined Verna's clothing under a microscope, there was only a round bullet hole in the front of her black dress.[337] If blood spurted from her wound and made the spots on Denhardt's overcoat, as the prosecution believed, why weren't there at least traces of blood on the front of her dress?

Dr. Blaydes was Kinsolving's final witness on Saturday, April 24, and everyone present knew that he was there to testify about the autopsy. Kinsolving began with some preliminary questions, and they proved to be more interesting than Blaydes's role in the autopsy. Before Verna's funeral on Sunday, Dr. Blaydes was called by the family to look for bruising on her throat.

"Where did you examine her?" asked Kinsolving.

"At Miss Verna's home."

"Did you inspect any wounds on her body at that time?"

"I examined her neck for bruises," said Blaydes.

"Did you see any wounds on her body at that time?"

"Yes, sir. Not at that time, no."

"Did you subsequently assist in her autopsy?"

"Yes, sir."[338]

Investigators also mentioned the mysterious bruising on Verna's neck in a terse defense memorandum of March 31, 1937, when they were interviewing witnesses in LaGrange for information: "Mrs. Carfield, who operates the Carfield Hotel, saw the finger marks on Mrs. Taylor's throat. He [*sic*] was there when Dr. Blaydes and Dr. Hartman of Campbellsburg made the examination."[339] If there were "finger marks" on Verna's throat, they would have been a significant find. During the autopsy, Blaydes and Walsh documented the bruise on Verna's thigh, but their report made no mention of bruising on her throat. Unfortunately, during his questioning, Kinsolving focused on Blaydes's role in the autopsy, and the question of whether there were bruises on Verna's neck was never resolved.

Kinsolving patiently guided Blaydes through his findings during the autopsy. In the doctor's professional opinion, the gun was not held against Verna's body when she was shot.

On cross-examination, John Berry was waiting with his transcript from the examining trial. He asked Blaydes if he had testified that day that although he did not examine the wound with a microscope, he was certain there were carbon deposits under the skin. Blaydes agreed, but wanted to explain why he thought so at the time. "I am better informed on it now than I was then."

"Have you since examined the body?"

"No, sir, but I have looked up the chemical action of formaldehyde on a ragged or fresh wound. Strong formaldehyde produces a dark brown deposit on all fresh surfaces."[340]

Blaydes admitted that at the time of the autopsy he was uncertain what the discoloration signified. For clarification, he removed skin from around the wounds and sent the sample to Louisville for analysis. Dr. Blaydes was a respected physician and surgeon, but medicine and the scientific analysis of wounds had evolved over the thirty-three years since he had graduated from medical school. During his testimony, it became apparent that Blaydes was a simple country doctor caught up in a complicated murder trial without the expertise of a trained pathologist.

Chapter 22

THE SPARKOGRAPH MACHINE

A steady spring rain fell outside the courthouse on Monday morning, April 26. Men and women in their best suits, dresses, and hats ran through the downpour, hurrying to reach the front doors before they were completely soaked. By nine a.m. when Judge Marshall banged his gavel to start the third day of trial, all of the seats were filled, and once again, there was standing room only for those who did not arrive early.

Both teams of attorneys had lined up expert witnesses, including chemists, toxicologists, pathologists, serologists, and ballistics experts. These experts travelled to tiny New Castle from Chicago, Pennsylvania, Washington DC, and New York. The amount of scientific knowledge on display at the trial astounded local reporters and they began referring in their articles to the "laboratory trial" of General Denhardt.[341]

On that rainy Monday, Kinsolving introduced the first of his expert witnesses, and the laboratory phase of the trial started.

Witness Clyde T. Erwin presented a modern marvel called the Sparkograph Machine, capable of photographing a bullet and the accompanying gases leaking out of the barrel at the moment of discharge. In March, Sergeant Messmer brought Denhardt's revolver to Erwin's laboratory at the Peters Cartridge Division of Remington Arms. While Messmer fired the gun,

Erwin made photographs with his Sparkograph Machine. The gun was connected electrically with the machine through a timing switch.

The Sparkograph indicated that while Denhardt's pistol did not release a large amount of gas ahead of the bullet, it released enough to be seen in the photographs. A reporter who viewed the photographs noted, "Each of the pictures put in evidence today showed a silhouette of the Denhardt gun. In one case, the bullet had not left the barrel, but a cloud of gas already had begun to spread about the cylinder. In another, the bullet was several inches away, just ahead of a dense cloud of muzzle gas."[342]

Erwin's photographs proved to the jury that Denhardt's pistol was capable of leaving the powder stains necessary for a valid paraffin test. Erwin also told the jury that there were two types of gunpowder in the cartridges of the general's pistol on the night Verna died. A lengthy and complex discussion on both types—one a single-based nitrocellulose gunpowder and the other a multi-base nitrocellulose-nitroglycerine gunpowder—left the jury bewildered.

Erwin's testimony on gunpowder types set the stage for Dr. Walsh to enter as a witness and discuss the autopsy results. He testified, "The bullet entered on the left side and came out on the right, in back, and in going through it hit the heart, the ventricle, the big chambers of the heart, and tore those apart; then hit what is called the aorta. It missed the rib in front, rib number seven; then went out in between the fifth and sixth ribs, and we found a little piece of bone under the skin in back."[343]

Walsh also testified about the experiment with the hog's carcass at the rifle range. The *Louisville Courier-Journal* reported, "The pork was in a preservative solution in pint jars. The scraps of fabric were neatly done up in cellophane envelopes, which the LaGrange physician testified he had sealed after tests."[344] When Judge Marshall's heavy volume of the *Kentucky Revised Statutes* failed to hold these envelopes suspended over the judge's table, they were thumbtacked to a cardboard map.

Kinsolving's questions led Walsh through each stage of the experiment and a description of the wound in the hog at each distance the pistol was fired. His conclusion from the autopsy and the experiment was that Verna did not die from a contact shot.

Dr. A. J. Miller, another expert witness for the prosecution, discussed the experiment on the hog and compared the shots to the pieces of skin cut from Verna's wounds. Kinsolving led him through his findings. "Doctor, I will ask you if there was brought to you this exhibit, which is in evidence here, which contains a section of the skin taken from the body of Mrs. Verna Taylor."[345] The doctor agreed. He pointed out that one of the pieces of skin had a hole in the center and was pushed inward where the bullet had entered. The skin was distorted by the suture during embalming. It was a grisly moment in the trial as Kinsolving held up the brown bottle containing sections of Verna's skin. When some of the spectators gasped, Judge Marshall did not even look at them. He simply nodded and admitted the brown bottle as an exhibit.

"In wounds that I have seen following from a revolver held very close to the skin, or in contact, the tissue beneath the skin is ballooned," Dr. Miller said. "That is, there is a big cavity just beneath the skin."[346] He testified that he did not find any evidence of ballooning in the sections of Verna's flesh. Over loud objections from Denhardt's attorneys, he gave his expert opinion based on the experiment with the hog and his examination of Verna's skin. He concluded that "the gun was more than nine inches from the body, and probably more than eighteen."[347]

Dr. Walsh also testified that there was no evidence of ballooning. He testified that he had microscopically examined the discoloration found during the autopsy. "The discoloration seems to be both a combination of the reaction of the tissues with the formaldehyde, and burned carbon and powder. It extended perhaps a quarter of an inch around the outside of the wound."[348]

Not surprisingly, the defense witness's opinion differed from that of the prosecution's witnesses. Dr. O. M. Wheeler's conclusion for the defense was that a contact shot killed Verna and that the muzzle of the gun was held against her dress.[349] Denhardt's attorneys argued that the discoloration found during the autopsy was gunpowder or carbon deposits caused by a gun held to Verna's breast during a suicide.

The first day, Otte did his best to imply that there was more than an employer and employee relationship between Chester Woolfolk and Verna. During cross-examinations of Walsh, Erwin, and Miller, Otte and Myers worked hard to point a different finger of blame at John Messmer. Messmer was present at the experiment with the hog, fired the pistol while Erwin took photographs, and delivered the pieces of Verna's skin and her clothes to Louisville for expert analysis. Messmer was present at nearly all of the experiments conducted on behalf of the prosecution. It was easy to make him a scapegoat.

Otte began his cross-examination of Erwin by implying that there was something unusual about a missing photograph made with the Sparkograph Machine.

"Where is the other one?" he inquired.

"I believe that's at the laboratory."

"Have you the film for it?"

"No, not here."

"Why didn't you bring it with you, Mr. Erwin?"

"It didn't show anything."

"When was the decision made not to bring that one? Who decided that, Mr. Erwin?"

"Mr. Messmer and myself decided."

"Mr. Messmer decided he didn't want that one brought and told you to leave it at the laboratory," Otte said emphatically.

"He didn't put it that way, no. He just said it wouldn't be necessary to bring the photograph because it didn't contain any information."[350]

Rodes Myers cross-examined Dr. Miller and continued the defense strategy against Messmer.

"Messmer brought you the specimen, I believe, of the skin," said Myers.

"Yes, sir."

"He also brought you the dress."

"He didn't bring it to me. I saw it."

"He had it in his possession," Myers insisted.

"Yes, sir."

"He also had the slip in his possession when you saw it."

"Yes, sir."

"He also did the firing of these shots on the pig."

"Yes, sir."

"He is the man who selected the cartridges that went into that pistol."

"I don't know. I don't know whether he was or not," said Miller, tired of the probing questions.

"Did you see him load it?"

"Yes, sir."[351]

It was an effort to introduce reasonable doubt with John Messmer as the scapegoat for the defense. It did not matter whose reputation was compromised or whose future was destroyed. The attorneys were ruthless in their defense of Denhardt and it did not matter how many bodies littered the legal playing field. When Dr. Miller left the witness chair, he had evidently had enough for one day. Like Judge Marshall, he couldn't resist taking a swing at a photographer as he left the courthouse.

The *Courier-Journal* reported, "Brawny, camera-shy Dr. Miller, who left New Castle this afternoon with hands over his face after striking Freddie Parker, five-foot-six photographer for the *Courier*

Journal, and then daring Parker to have him arrested, was ordered to return for possible further testimony tomorrow."[352]

During the long days of trial, the defense presented a formidable front, but spectators in the courtroom were unaware that trouble was brewing between Denhardt and Clarke Otte. Denhardt later complained that during the trial, Otte "kept constantly talking about fees and money, and told me this would be necessary if I wanted real service."[353]

However, as witness after witness faced his deadly cross-examination, there was no indication that the dispute affected Otte's performance. The lawyer from Louisville had quickly become the "heavy" of the trial. He was a master at conjuring smokescreens to confuse a witness and jury. Otte's cross-examinations left witnesses irritated and confused with his ability to take an innocent reply and twist it into something more sinister. He had an amazing grasp of facts and details, and kept the witnesses unsettled with his snide remarks and condescending manner.

During the early phase of the prosecution's case, the jury made notes, listened intently, and understood the witnesses and testimony. But by Monday afternoon, they were struggling to connect the question of Denhardt's guilt or innocence with heated arguments and questions about gunpowder, ballistics, leakage gas, ballooning of tissue, and photographs made by the Sparkograph Machine. Otte and Myers were doing their best to make the jury wonder whether John Messmer was incompetent or involved in a conspiracy to "frame" their client.

Messmer and F. C. Buckmaster were scheduled to testify about the paraffin tests. Otte could not wait to cross-examine John Messmer. He intended to "blow him out of the water," just as he had promised General Denhardt.[354]

Chapter 23

CLEAN HANDS

The paraffin tests were key pieces of physical evidence in a case that was largely circumstantial, and Kinsolving needed to prove their validity to the jury. When Keightley testified that John Messmer did not wash his hands after lighting a match before making Denhardt's casts, it opened the door for Otte to question the results of both paraffin tests. Verna's test was suspect because her hands had been washed. Now Denhardt's test could be challenged because Messmer's hands hadn't been washed.

Kinsolving and Messmer attempted to bolster the validity of Verna's paraffin test with an experiment on the hands of Marguerite Keightley. On April 20, she fired Denhardt's revolver two times behind the funeral home in LaGrange. Afterward, her hands were washed with the same soap used to clean Verna's hands, then lightly dried with a towel. Within the hour, Messmer made a paraffin mold of her shooting hand, and Marguerite Keightley's paraffin casts showed two of the nitrate deposits.[355] While Kinsolving could point to the experiment as proof that the results of Verna's tests were valid, he was in dangerous territory with Denhardt's paraffin test. But there was no turning back, and he called chemist F. C. Buckmaster as his next witness.

Buckmaster gave the puzzled jury a lesson in advanced chemistry. He described his preparation of the molds or casts, and the chemicals used to produce the blue spot reaction. Kinsolving asked him to describe how he prepared the diphenylamine-sulphuric acid reagent.

He responded, "Our method of procedure is to drop a small amount of diphenylamine—to be exact, a half a gram—in a mixture of 20 cc. of sulphuric acid, concentrated chemically pure sulphuric acid, and one hundred cc. of distilled water, which makes a clear solution almost in appearance identical to distilled water."[356]

The reporters noticed the bewildered expressions on the faces of the jury and courtroom crowd. "The quiet, rural crowd sat thoughtfully, a hint doubtful, as it tried to thread its way through the maze of formulae and technical phrases that proceeded in half-caught snatches from the witness stand."[357]

But while the chemistry lesson was confusing, the jury clearly understood Buckmaster when he said, "The first necessary step is for a person to wash his hands thoroughly so there could be no conflicting nitrates on his hands . . ."[358] But Buckmaster reinforced the validity of Verna's test results. In his opinion, the light washing of hands with a liquid soap would not remove the nitrate content.

Buckmaster's livelihood depended on the reliability of the paraffin test. He admitted that outside substances such as soot, matches, or even some toothpaste brands could react with the chemicals. But in his opinion, gunpowder residue left behind a different reaction to the chemicals. It left a characteristic blue comet tail that developed almost immediately for a positive test. When Buckmaster was dismissed, Kinsolving asked for Sergeant John Messmer to be sent into court.

The testimony of the lead investigator was eagerly anticipated. Everyone turned to watch as square-jawed, brown-haired, and bespectacled forty-year-old John Messmer walked resolutely toward the witness chair.

Outside, the rain had continued since early morning and had

developed into a howling, full-blown spring storm. The ominous dark clouds brought wind and rain that battered the old glass windows. Spectators standing near them moved to a safer vantage point where they could see and hear the witness. Before Messmer finished his testimony, they expected there would be a storm inside the courtroom to match the intensity of the one outside.

Kinsolving did not hesitate when he asked, "Do you usually wash or cleanse your hands before making those tests?"[359] Messmer admitted that it was absolutely necessary to wash the hands before performing a paraffin test, but he hedged when he answered.

"Yes. Well, I just try to keep my hands clean at all times. I make no special effort to see that they are absolutely clean just immediately before the test."[360]

Clarke Otte was eager to cross-examine Messmer, perhaps too eager. His cross-examination began with an argument.

"Well, in addition to the lamp, looking for forgeries and the preliminary test for blood, do you engage in the field of ballistics?" asked Otte.

"In the field of the identification of firearms and bullets. Ballistics is the science of a projectile in motion, and I don't go into that."

"I didn't ask you what ballistics was. I asked you if you do any work along that line."

Messmer retorted, "Ballistics is the science of a projectile in motion, and I don't go into that."

"I never asked you the definition of ballistics, Sergeant. I just wanted to know if you engaged in ballistics."

Kinsolving quickly objected that Otte was arguing with his witness.

"I am not arguing with him! He is arguing with me!" Otte exclaimed furiously, turning to Kinsolving.

Judge Marshall stepped in to settle the fray. "Now, Mr. Otte, the witness just said he did not. He has answered the question."

"Now I understand it," Otte nodded, trying to save face. "I was just objecting to his manner of answering my question, telling me the definition of ballistics when I hadn't asked him for it. I am satisfied he knows it."[361]

His previous cross-examinations had been excellent, sometimes brilliant, and it was not a good moment for Otte with a witness he badly wanted to discredit. But he knew Messmer's weakness and gradually began to probe his way toward it. Otte asked him about the equipment he normally carried when he was called to perform a paraffin test and where it was stored. He asked whether he used an alcohol stove with sterno, and whether he used a match to light the stove.

Otte finally said, "You didn't wash your hands out there that day, did you?"

"No, sir, I did not."[362]

When Clarke Otte asked Messmer whether a negative nitrate reaction on a cast conclusively proved the person had not fired a gun, Messmer admitted it did not. Otte nodded knowingly and looked at the jury. "No further questions."

F. C. Buckmaster was recalled, and Kinsolving asked him about the blue specks Messmer found on Denhardt's casts. Buckmaster quickly replied, "In my opinion, the specks, in the position as described, with the characteristic comet-tale formations with the diphenylamine or Lunge reagent, would be characteristic of gunpowder residues on the paraffin molds."[363]

Buckmaster also testified about Messmer's paraffin testing techniques. "In my actual experience in watching his operations, I was of the opinion that he was not only a careful, conscientious worker, but a man thoroughly experienced and trained in the line of work he was doing."[364]

Although Messmer and Buckmaster stood steadfastly by the validity of the paraffin tests made on the hands of Verna Taylor and Henry Denhardt, neither could say that a paraffin test was foolproof. Both were excellent witnesses, but the problem was with the reliability of the paraffin test. They both admitted that nitrates could also be found in other common items around a home, and Messmer admitted he did not wash his hands after lighting the match for his alcohol stove. While both were sure that the chemical reaction was different with items other than gunpowder, it still planted a seed of doubt in the jurors' minds. If a negative paraffin test couldn't conclusively prove a suspect had not fired a gun, the jury could ask themselves whether Denhardt's positive test proved that he had.

The morning of the fourth day of trial began like all the others. A tired jury filed into the room, Judge Marshall took his place at the bench, and there was the usual shuffling of papers and whispered conversations at the prosecution and defense tables. But that morning, there was an air of expectation in the packed courtroom. Kinsolving was in the final turn toward home, and the defense attorneys would soon take center stage. Everyone knew that when they did, the witness they had waited so long to hear would make his appearance. But Kinsolving had one more expert witness waiting to testify. There was also a significant question missed during Roy Garr's testimony.

Ballard Clarke briefly recalled him to tell the jury that Verna was right-handed. The jury had already heard that the trajectory of the bullet was from left to right and Verna clutched a glove in her left hand. It would have placed her in a nearly impossible position to shoot herself one-handed with the large weapon.[365]

After the noon lunch hour, Kinsolving called his final expert witness into the courtroom. A local reporter described the testimony. "The last major evidence against Denhardt was given Wednesday by E. R. Donaldson, special agent of the Federal Bureau of Investigation, who testified that chemical analysis of bloodstains found on Mrs. Taylor's clothing and an overcoat worn by Denhardt on the night of her death were of the same classification."[366]

Both Henry Denhardt and Verna Garr Taylor had Group A type blood. In 1937, no test could distinguish whether the blood on Denhardt's overcoat belonged to Verna Taylor or to him.

At the end of four long, grueling days, the prosecution rested their case against General Denhardt. Most of the evidence against him was circumstantial, and the strongest evidence of guilt came from his own actions and statements at the death scene. The prosecution had done an excellent job of establishing that Verna was perfectly normal, and not depressed or suicidal before her death. Doctors Walsh and Miller were convincing that Verna did not die from a contact shot. In their opinions, her death could not have been a suicide.

Late in the afternoon, the attorneys from both sides retired to the judge's chambers for arguments and motions. Judge Marshall quickly overruled a motion by John Berry to dismiss the charges based on George Baker's statement. Berry argued that if the prosecution's lead witness claimed their client couldn't have shot Verna Taylor because he was with him when the second shot was fired, the case should be dismissed. But Marshall stood firm. It was time for the defense to present its case.

Henry Denhardt's attorneys were fighting a desperate, unpopular, and uphill battle to save him. Public sentiment was against him, and the only question for the majority of people following the trial was whether he would go to prison or die in the electric chair. Denhardt was never the "alleged" killer, but rather the "assumed" killer of lovely Verna Garr Taylor. But Denhardt's attorneys were well prepared, and they began their case with a wise request. They wanted the jury to visit the place where Verna had died.

Chapter 24

THE TESTIMONY OF
GENERAL DENHARDT

On Wednesday morning, April 28, Judge Marshall announced
that he would grant the defense motion for the jury to visit the
death scene. But the thought of his jury outside the safety of the
courtroom prompted another stern lecture. He ordered Sheriff
Harrod and his deputies to arrest any reporters seen taking
photographs of the jury, and no sightseers were to be allowed
in the area.[367] The twelve men were loaded into cars under the
sheriff's supervision and driven to George Baker's farm.

The place where Verna Taylor died had been the focus of
everyone's attention for days. But by the end of Kinsolving's case,
the jury had only heard estimates of the distance from Baker's
driveway to where her body was found. Keightley said, "I judge
about, possibly a hundred yards from the entrance, maybe further.
I don't know just the distance."[368] Coroner Ricketts gave a
different estimate. "I guess about four hundred feet" said Ricketts
on the witness stand.[369] George Baker testified, "Well, I judge it
was—I never measured it, but I judge it was something like 550
feet, probably 600 feet. I never did measure it or step it, but I'm
going by the fence posts along the road."[370]

The actual measurements were not as important to Kinsolving's
case as they were to the defense. Denhardt's attorneys wanted

the jury to see and walk the distance. They wanted them to look at their overweight, sixty-one-year-old client and imagine him running that distance, murdering a woman, and arriving back in Baker's driveway within several minutes. John Berry asked Rev. James E. Wright, a local minister to make exact measurements of the distance Denhardt would have to cover before and after the murder. It was 689 feet from the center of Baker's driveway to where Verna's body was found.[371] The actual distance was thirty-one feet shorter than the length of two football fields from one goal line to the other. If the jury believed Kinsolving's theory, portly, red-faced Henry Denhardt covered 1,378 feet on the night of November 6, and was not out of breath when Baker came out of his house.[372] And while numerous witnesses noted that the ground was wet and muddy from rain and melted snow that night, no one saw mud on Denhardt's clothes or shoes.

Judge Marshall and Henry Denhardt strolled together on the highway and watched as the jury walked the Baker's yard and the highway in front. A solitary wooden stake in the old roadbed marked the spot where Verna's body was found. Sheriff Harrod walked with the jury, answered their questions, and pointed out landmarks of interest in the case. It was a quiet, pleasant escape from the tedium of the courtroom and the chaotic scene in New Castle. When they finally nodded that they were finished, the jurors were loaded again into the automobiles. It was time to travel the short distance back to the courthouse and the hard chairs of the jury box. Denhardt's attorneys had waived their opening argument, and their client would be the first witness for the defense.

At one p.m., Henry Denhardt left the familiar safety of the defense table and walked with his head high and shoulders squared toward the cane-bottomed witness chair. It was the climactic moment in the murder trial, the high tide in the drama that had surrounded the case for six months.

"Between him and the jury stretched a few feet of matting—the only open space in Henry County's square courtroom," the *Courier-Journal* reported. "Elsewhere there were faces, a sea of faces, ranked to the rear wall, jammed in the exits, flanking the judge, pressing about the Commonwealth and defense tables. Two women fainted in the stifling crush. Sheriff Evan Harrod struggled to curb the mass that pushed like toothpaste from a tube, through the courtroom's rear entrance, just at the judge's right."[373]

Denhardt was calm as he took his oath, but reporters watching closely noticed that his raised hand trembled slightly.[374] He sat quietly in the witness chair with his knees crossed, toying with a pair of horn-rimmed glasses and looking out over a sea of curious, but hostile faces. Bertha and Jesse Denhardt were there for support, and his attorneys looked back at him with encouragement.

Henry Denhardt was both an attorney and a politician with a strong background in public speaking, and there was no doubt that he would be able to handle himself as a witness. Six months had given him ample opportunity to prepare for the day. He knew the strong points in Kinsolving's case; he knew what he would have to say to cut the net closing around him. He remained calm and focused as his longtime friend Rodes Myers approached the witness chair. For the next three hours and twenty minutes, the spellbound jury and spectators would hear Denhardt's rambling, self-serving, and sometimes bizarre account of his romance with Verna Garr Taylor, and his version of the day and night she died.

Myers began by asking Denhardt questions about his distinguished service in the military and as an elected state official. He questioned him about his failed marriage to Elizabeth Glaze Denhardt and about his sister who lived with him. When Myers finally asked him how he met Verna Garr Taylor, Denhardt launched into his account of the tragic romance. While Denhardt admitted that there were occasional "tilts" between the couple, he denied that there were ever any real problems. He admitted that there was occasional jealousy over his friendliness with Verna's sister, Juanita, but didn't regard it as anything serious. When Myers asked if there had been discussions about Juanita, the general replied, "Well, Mrs. Taylor had asked me not to be so friendly with Juanita, and didn't like Juanita's—well, Juanita was very vivacious, very talkative, a fine woman, and we talked a good deal and she didn't like for me to do that any great deal; but I regarded that as trivial and it was not of a serious nature."[375]

The argument Mary Pryor overheard in the next room was "simply a rehash of this little difference about Juanita."[376]

"Mrs. Taylor and I had a little tilt. It wasn't any serious one, and it ended in a few minutes, and we separated as usual that night. There was no breaking off or no one ordered me to leave the house. No one ever did order me to leave the house. I was a welcome guest," he said.[377]

"Is that the only argument that you and Mrs. Taylor had, if you would call that an argument?" asked Myers.

"Well, that is all of any consequence that I recall. She didn't want me to see my [ex-]wife or telephone her when I went to Bowling Green, and I promised not to. I had always gone to see her. We were on friendly terms, and I would telephone her and go up and call on her when I went there. She was always glad to see me and is now, and Mrs. Taylor understood that and she didn't want me to do that, and I promised not to."[378]

The letters Verna wrote to Denhardt during her summer vacation were entered as evidence, and Denhardt read them aloud to the jurors. For the first time in the trial, the jury heard from the victim, her thoughts read aloud by the man accused of killing her. A reporter from Louisville offered his impression of Verna after hearing the letters. "From the letters, she appeared as a person who loved flowers and open fireplaces and homely things, was young enough to enjoy fireworks and worry about diet and weight

('I have been eating so much I am afraid to step on the scales') and who thought with pride of her general at the head of a parade of soldiers."[379]

Denhardt testified that the couple had discussed where they would live after their marriage and initially planned to build a new home on his farm. They decided instead to remodel the existing historic house. "We had drawn plans for the remodeling of the house. That is, we had both on paper planned what we would like. She had visited the home several times for the purpose of getting acquainted with what it needed, what she wanted. We had a great deal of pleasure in planning our future at the home."[380]

Denhardt said there were no serious problems in his relationship with Verna until November 5. That morning, he stopped by the laundry and talked with her until noon. Denhardt drove her home for lunch before he left LaGrange for Louisville. Myers did not ask about and Denhardt did not volunteer the reason that his business in Louisville could not wait until the next day. Denhardt arrived back in LaGrange around eight p.m. and as he was driving into town, he saw Verna and Chester Woolfolk in the laundry truck. He drove past and waited on the court square to speak with Verna. Later when he went to her house, she was "very nervous and in an unhappy state of mind."[381] When he asked her what was wrong, she told him that Chester was in love with her and jealous of their relationship. He was upset that she had shown her ring to the employees earlier that day.

"I said, 'Well of course I know you don't care anything about him.' She said, 'No, except as a friend.' She liked the boy. He had been a faithful worker for her, had been very kind in his treatment of her, and she felt sorry for him. He had come over to the house occasionally and she used his car, but her feeling for him was only that of kindness as an elderly woman would feel toward a younger man. She told me he was just 26 years old."[382]

He continued, "We talked of that a few minutes that night,

not long. I didn't pay any serious attention to it. I thought nothing especially of it."[383] The couple discussed the Woolfolk situation, but parted on good terms with their "usual good-night greeting."

"You say the usual good-night greeting. What was that? What did that consist of?" prompted Myers.

"Well, Mrs. Taylor was a very religious, good woman. She went to church and she taught a Sunday school class up until I think she quit some months before, but up until the time she went to New York, I think she had taught pretty regularly. She had a wonderful influence over me and tried to help me in every way. I thought, and still think, and will always think she was one of the best women I ever knew, and I loved her, because she was so good. We never left at night without saying 'God bless you,' and we always agreed to pray for each other, and we would, of course, express our love for each other, and we kissed goodnight."[384]

Kinsolving's team was keeping a close watch on the Garr brothers, knowing they would be furious at the things Denhardt was saying in open court about their sister. The brothers stared directly at Denhardt as he spoke, but they remained silent even through the most infuriating parts of his testimony.

The next morning when Denhardt arrived at Verna's house for the trip to Louisville, she complained of a bad headache, was very nervous, and told him she had not slept the night before. After leaving LaGrange, their first stop was the Kentucky Military Institute. Denhardt sat in the car while Verna went inside to conduct business. While he was waiting, he claimed that he also walked around near the car to exercise.

During Rueve's testimony, Clarke Otte had focused on what Verna might have seen as she looked out the window. Rather than watching the boys on parade, Denhardt claimed she stood by the window where she could see him walking.

"She came out after some time and told me she had had some few little matters to straighten up—shortages, claimed shortages—

and it had taken a little longer; but she said, 'While I was in there, I stood by the window and looked out, and I saw you walking around.' In the conversation which extended on down the road, she said she was deeply troubled, worried very greatly, because of the mistreatment accorded her the night before by Ches; that it was the first time he had ever mistreated her or been rude to her in any way, and it seemed to hurt her a great deal."[385]

Denhardt claimed that Woolfolk's "mistreatment" of Verna was due to their upcoming marriage, and that she told him that Woolfolk had told her he would not permit it to take place. Verna said that she did not realize Woolfolk was so deeply in love with her until just a few weeks before. But when she showed her ring at the laundry on Thursday, he knew she was really going to marry Denhardt. She did not know what Woolfolk was going to do and tried to give Denhardt back the engagement ring.

"She said, 'Now Henry, I haven't told you this, because it meant nothing to me.' But she said, 'He is acting so badly I don't know what he is going to do, and if this affects you any, I will give you your ring back.'"[386]

But he convinced her to keep it.

"I asked her, I said, 'Do you love me as you always said you do?' She said, 'I certainly do.' I said, 'If you do, keep the ring. We'll work out the Ches matter. He isn't going to do anything, and I don't care what he does, so long as you love me;' and she insisted that she did. I said, 'Keep the ring.' And she did keep it."[387]

Denhardt was a blustering, short-tempered man of action. If he was in love with Verna, and she was "mistreated," it is hard to believe he wouldn't have threatened to confront Woolfolk and settle the matter himself. It would not be in character for him to simply pat Verna's hand and reassure her that everything would be fine.

Denhardt's testimony continued. He said that after the conversation about Woolfolk (which at the trial did not include any mention of a clandestine affair), Verna became more despondent, nervous, and distraught. Shortly after they left Kentucky Military Institute, Denhardt had a puncture in his back tire and walked to a nearby filling station for help.

"When you returned to the car, what was Mrs. Taylor doing?" asked Myers.

"Well, she had opened the glove compartment of my car and had in her lap a pistol that I had kept in there for a few days, and was toying with it, and I said, 'What are you doing with that pistol, Verna?' She said, 'Well I was just looking at it.' I said, 'You oughtn't to do that, because I don't think you know anything about a gun,' and I put it away and locked the compartment. She said that sometimes she felt that she would kill herself. I said, 'Why that's foolish. You won't do it.' She said, 'I would if I had the courage of a distant relative who did shoot herself through the head.'" [388]

Denhardt testified that most of their discussions that day were about Woolfolk, and "how he had misconstrued her kindness to him. He had taken for granted things which she didn't mean, and he had misconstrued her kindness into a feeling that she might be in love with him. She said she wasn't, and had only been kind. She said nobody had ever thought she was or suggested that she was except one lady. She called her name, and she said something to her once, but she said she told her she wasn't, and that was all there was to it." [389]

They arrived in Louisville at the Pendennis Club, and Verna asked him to telephone Bess Lee and tell her she couldn't attend the bridge luncheon because of her headache. Denhardt urged her to go, hoping that the bridge party would divert her mind from the Woolfolk problem, but she refused. Denhardt called Lee and told her that Verna didn't feel well and wasn't able to come to the bridge party. Lee asked to speak with Verna, but Denhardt told her she was waiting for him in the car.

After the telephone call, the two walked a block to Stewart's Department Store where Verna returned Mrs. Connell's package. They stopped at the Walgreens inside the Seelbach Hotel for lunch, and Verna was able to drink only a cup of tea.

"Were you feeling badly that day? Was anything the matter with you, or not?" Myers asked Denhardt.

"Well, I had been over to Taylorsville on Wednesday, that snowy Wednesday just after the election, and I had driven through a snowstorm over there and contracted a cold, and was really not well at all."[390]

After Verna's visit to the Citizens Union National Bank, the couple separated on the street with a promise to meet in the parking lot beside the Pendennis Club at four thirty. Denhardt did not know where Verna went after she left. Neither Myers nor Denhardt mentioned the rented hotel room. When Denhardt reached the parking lot later that afternoon, she was waiting for him in the car, "plunked down in the car, just leaning against the side of it, just in a thoroughly depressed state of mind."[391]

According to Denhardt, Verna was also desperate to marry him that day. He told her it would look foolish for a mature couple to elope, and that they should wait until her sister arrived in a few days. "She said to me, 'Henry, if you don't marry me now, you don't intend to marry me.' I said, 'I intend to marry you. I will marry you.' And I said that to her then, and repeated that to her several times during the night when she would go over the fact that she didn't believe I would."[392]

"Was any mention made of eating dinner anywhere?" asked Myers.

"I tried to induce her to go with me to the country club. She refused. She said she wouldn't go, couldn't go. I insisted that she go. I said, 'It's bright and cheerful out there and it will help your feelings.'"[393]

But according to Denhardt, Verna continued to refuse. "She

said she hadn't had anything all day except two cups of tea, one at breakfast and one at Walgreens, so I finally persuaded her to stop there at the Sada San Restaurant, in St. Matthews, to get something to eat."[394]

With Verna's permission and her silver dollar, he purchased a half pint of whiskey across the street. But he insisted it was purely for medicinal purposes to help with his cold symptoms. While they were sitting at the table in the restaurant, Verna complained of her headache, and said "she was not in the humor or mood to do anything that night." Before they left, Verna called home to tell Frances she was not feeling well, and they would not be able to chaperone her dance.[395] It was the last conversation Frances had with her mother.

Verna was driving Denhardt's car when they left Louisville for LaGrange. On the way, they stopped on a small, deserted side road to talk, and were there for fifteen minutes or half an hour.

"She told me at that time that she would be dead in fifteen minutes after she got home, and I told her that that was foolish, and that if she loved her children and mother and me, as I knew she did, that she would dismiss that foolish thought from her mind. We talked there for some time, and she finally dismissed it, except she said, 'If I do, I'm going to leave a note.' So that was about all that happened. We sat there a good deal of the time saying nothing."[396]

Verna was driving the car when they resumed their trip toward LaGrange.

"Did you stop in LaGrange?"

"No. We usually turned in when we came from Louisville, turned in there at the schoolhouse to go to her house. She sort of started in, but said, 'Let's go on up 22, take a little ride,' and she went on up 22, which was an accustomed drive for us."[397]

When they reached the crossroads six miles outside of LaGrange, Verna was still very depressed and Denhardt thought they should go home. He told her to turn into the school yard next to Browning's Service Station. But when she tried to turn around, the lights went out and the car stalled. Denhardt said that Verna had volunteered to go for help at the service station. He was sick, and it was more likely that the people in the service station would know her. Denhardt made no mention that Verna did not want anyone to know he had been drinking. When Browning and Baker came to help, he did not push the car because he was sick, "and in the next place I am getting pretty old and I always get somebody to fix my car or push it for me . . ."[398]

"Do you know anything about the mechanism of an automobile?" asked Myers.

"No, sir."

"The battery or lights?"

"No, sir. Oh, I know something about it, but I am not a mechanic."

"You don't know how to repair them?"

"No, sir. When my car stops, I stop, for I haven't any knowledge of a car."[399]

Denhardt asked Verna whether she wanted to ride to LaGrange with Hundley, but she refused. As they sat in the darkness in Baker's driveway, Verna suggested that they make a suicide pact and die together.

Denhardt recalled his words to her and their subsequent conversation. "'You've got nothing to die for, and I don't understand this talk, and as far as I'm concerned, certainly I don't want to die and you shouldn't want me to die.' And she then said, 'No, you don't deserve to die.' She said, 'This ring you gave me is the nicest thing I ever received in my life,' and she said, 'You yourself have been better to me than any person in the world.' She kissed her ring then, and reached over and put her arms around my neck and kissed me, and said I was the best man that ever lived. That was her greeting, almost her last greeting to me . . ."[400]

Denhardt claimed that Verna asked him to walk to Baker's door and see if there was a telephone to call LaGrange and check on the battery. However, Verna already knew the Bakers had no telephone. George Baker testified that she asked about a telephone when they were stalled on the highway. He told her the nearest telephone was miles away.

Denhardt said that he left Verna in the driver's seat alone while he walked toward the Baker house, but before he reached the side door he heard her call him back to the car. "She said, 'Henry, Henry, come here.'"[401] As he started back, George Baker came to the door, and Denhardt stopped to ask him about the telephone. When Myers asked him what was causing the Bakers' dog to bark, Denhardt replied, "My presence there, I imagine."[402]

He returned to the car, but Verna was gone. "I called 'Verna! Verna!' but there was no reply."[403] He said he thought she had gone up the road for personal reasons and would return in a few minutes. The Shepherds drove past and he looked up the road in their headlights trying to see Verna. He watched the car continue east and turn the corner at the intersection in the distance. A minute or two later he heard a loud gunshot.

"Well, I felt that the worst had happened, I was dazed at it, and amazed and surprised . . ."[404] He turned immediately and walked toward the house for help and met George Baker coming out of his door. As they approached one another in the yard, he heard a second shot, different from the first.

"Well, he said, 'Did you hear that shot?' I said, 'Yes, I did. Did you?' Speaking of the first shot. Then I said, 'Isn't that awful!' I realized what had happened, and it was the worst thing that ever happened in my whole life. I said, 'I'm afraid she has taken my gun and gone,' and in the meantime, I had looked in and found it had gone, and she had taken that gun."[405]

Denhardt insisted that George Baker had come out of the house within a minute of the first loud gunshot.

"General Denhardt, did you fire the shot that killed Mrs. Taylor that night?" asked Rodes Myers.

"I did not."

"Did you kill Mrs. Taylor that night at any place on that road, and put her body over there?"

"I did not."

"Did you have any struggle with her whatsoever?"

"Certainly not."[406]

He said that he hadn't climbed down into the ditch to check on Verna because he knew she was dead and he could do nothing. He thought it best to leave the body as it was until the coroner came. Denhardt claimed he denied killing Verna in response to George Baker's comment. He took a golden opportunity to say it again for the jury.

"Mr. Baker had repeated on several occasions, 'I don't know this woman and I don't know this man, but I was with this man when the second shot was fired. He couldn't have done it.' I said, 'Certainly I couldn't have done it.' I wouldn't have done it, anyhow, because I loved her too well . . . ."[407] Denhardt agreed that he told Ricketts and Keightley that the opposition of Verna's daughters to the engagement led to her suicide. He did not discuss the "Ches affair" because he did not know them and considered it a personal matter.[408]

Myers asked him about November 7, when Coroner Ricketts brought D. F. Lee to his house and Denhardt spoke with him privately.

"Don't tell what you said, but did you relate to him in substance, what you have told the jury?" asked Myers.

"Briefly, yes, sir. I couldn't finish it, because I turned over and *wept bitterly*."[409]

"Objection, Your Honor," said Kinsolving. "Any unnecessary statement he made about what happened afterwards is self-serving."[410]

Marshall agreed and partially sustained the objection. When Myers continued with another question about Denhardt's conversation with D. F. Lee, Kinsolving objected again. This time, Marshall overruled Kinsolving. It appeared the jury would hear the details Kinsolving was working so hard to exclude. But without explanation, Myers agreed to withdraw any further questions about D. F. Lee and continued instead with questions about the general's overcoat.

Myers asked him if he knew how the bloodstains got on his coat and the general had a ready answer. He cut his finger trying to repair a wire on his car's defroster. According to Denhardt, he did not realize his finger was bleeding until Verna drew his attention to it. He assured the jury that the blood found on his overcoat belonged only to him. But Denhardt did not testify that he showed his cut finger to Ricketts on the day of his paraffin test as he claimed in his memorandum. Finally, Myers asked him whether he owned a fountain pen pistol. Denhardt admitted owning the gun, but said it was a gas gun and he would never use a loaded shell. When he left Frankfort in early 1936, the fountain pen gun was packed with other items from his desk drawer and stored in the attic of his house where it remained.

Denhardt's testimony was carefully orchestrated. He did not accuse Verna of an affair with Woolfolk, omitted any arguments over business and property, and downplayed any references to Verna's jealousy or demands. The portions of his memorandum that could embarrass him or damage his case were intentionally excluded. His testimony differed from his memorandum on several critical points, particularly in his account of the night Verna died. It was well planned by Denhardt and his attorneys, and as expected, he was an excellent witness.

According to him, Mary Pryor never heard him ordered out of the house by her mother because it did not happen. George Baker's testimony was wrong because he came out of the house immediately after the gunshot. Denhardt never heard Verna ask about a telephone, even though he was present when Baker told her that the nearest one was miles away. His current version of why Verna committed suicide was no longer due to family interference, but because of the professed love of Chester Woolfolk.

Denhardt's testimony had transformed Verna from an astute, intelligent businesswoman into a depressed, lovesick, and neurotic woman desperate to marry him. She even suggested a suicide pact. Verna was either an excellent actress, or eleven witnesses were mistaken or lying when they said she was perfectly normal on November 5 and 6. The general was gambling that twelve middle-aged men would believe that a woman who had successfully managed employees for five years would commit suicide because one of them declared his love. In 1937, and with no women on the jury, it was worth a chance.

As Kinsolving walked to the front of the courtroom where Henry Denhardt sat calmly waiting and watching him, he knew that he faced a formidable witness. Kinsolving took the offensive, attacking quickly with his questions, hammering at Denhardt's story, and hoping to catch him off guard. He attacked the claim that Verna was suicidal on November 6. But according to Denhardt, when they were out in public, Verna's demeanor was normal. It was only when they were alone together that she showed her depression.

"She only exhibited that depression to you?" Kinsolving asked.

"She didn't have much to say, but attended to her business quietly, and we were quiet together a good deal of the time, because I knew her state of mind."[411]

Kinsolving asked him to tell the jury where he went after he separated from Verna on the afternoon of November 6. Denhardt's first stop was to get a shave at a hotel several blocks away. Afterward, he walked several more blocks to return to the Pendennis Club and "loafed in there awhile."[412] Denhardt was at the Pendennis Club around two thirty, reading the newspaper and talking with acquaintances. After approximately thirty minutes, he walked another block and returned to the Seelbach, but he wasn't sure how long he stayed.

"Oh, I go in there and meet my friends from over the state, and I don't time myself as to the length of time I stay," he said.[413] But he did not stay at the Seelbach. He walked a half block to the Kentucky Hotel and was unsure of the time he arrived there.

"Did you register at the Kentucky Hotel that afternoon?"

"I did."

"Did you get a room at that hotel?" asked Kinsolving carefully.

"I did."

Denhardt testified that he was in the room for forty-five minutes to an hour. Kinsolving did not ask him why he rented a hotel room, and Denhardt did not elaborate. Three of the four places he visited that afternoon were hotels. The Seelbach and the Kentucky Hotel were within a half block of one another, yet he left the Seelbach to rent a room at the Kentucky. It doesn't seem likely that Verna was with him. Ballard Clarke saw her between four fifteen and four thirty; Verna was on her way to meet Denhardt at the parking lot and he was nowhere in sight. If they were together in the hotel and left the room separately, surely in a city as large as Louisville, they would have felt confident to walk two blocks together to leave for the afternoon.

Kinsolving probed very carefully around the subject of the rented room. So carefully, in fact, that he failed to ask a crucial question. Why was a sick man doing so much walking and visiting that afternoon? If Denhardt really was sick and had rented a room to rest, he probably would have volunteered that information. Several times during his testimony, he commented that on November 6 he was sick from a cold. Denhardt's movements that afternoon were suspicious, and his testimony did nothing but deepen the mystery. Doc Garr would later claim that Denhardt had an accomplice on the night of November 6.[414] If he did, the rented room would have offered a perfect opportunity to finalize plans. Whatever Denhardt's reason for renting the room, it was for something important to him. The night before, he stayed at a hotel in LaGrange. It would be unusual for the normally frugal general who had not even paid his attorneys to rent two hotel rooms within twenty-four hours.

Denhardt claimed that Verna was depressed and suicidal, but she was driving his car when they left Louisville. Kinsolving quizzed Denhardt why he did not insist that Verna go home, especially since he knew her daughters were waiting for her. But Denhardt emphatically denied knowing Frances and Mary Pryor were waiting, and insisted that it was Verna who wanted to continue the drive.

"And you didn't insist on her going in?" asked Kinsolving skeptically.

"No."

"Went on out to Browning's filling station."

"That's right."

"Your car became disabled."

"Yes."

"She got out, with her mental distress, and went to get aid."

"That's right."[415]

On cross-examination, Denhardt's replies were brief, obviously unplanned. He was becoming irritated at Kinsolving, but remained calm. Denhardt also claimed that he did not hear Verna ask George Baker where the nearest telephone could be found.

"What was the matter with you?" Kinsolving asked in disbelief. "You were sitting right in the car where she was."

"I didn't say she said it."

"She was at the car there."

"She was at the car and I was in the car."[416]

Kinsolving also attacked Denhardt's testimony of Verna's

sudden disappearance from Baker's driveway. "You didn't become apprehensive from the times she told you during the day that she was going to destroy herself?" he asked.

"I had no thought that she would kill herself."[417]

He also asked Denhardt why he did not attempt to stop the Shepherd car for help. Denhardt assumed they would not stop at night for a stranger.

"Mrs. Taylor had, a few minutes before, got out in the road and stopped Hundley at the intersection in the night, hadn't she?"

"Objection. He's arguing with the witness," said Rodes Myers. Judge Marshall agreed.[418] Kinsolving had made his point for the jury's benefit. Denhardt claimed that Verna was despondent and suicidal, but he was not alarmed enough by her disappearance to flag the Shepherd car for help. Kinsolving also pointed out that Denhardt told George Baker the story that Verna had gone to look for her glove.

"I said she might have done that," said Denhardt testily.

"You told him that she had, didn't you?"

"I did not."

"You didn't tell him she had gone for any personal reason."

"Well, I didn't want to discuss that."[419]

Denhardt also readily admitted telling George Baker that Verna was the finest woman he ever knew even before her body was found. "That is exactly what I said, and I still say it," he said.[420]

Kinsolving hammered hard hoping to shake Denhardt's composure. But Kinsolving himself was becoming frustrated by a calm, shrewd witness who always had a ready explanation. Several times, Judge Marshall warned Kinsolving about arguing with the witness. Denhardt admitted that when Verna's body was found, he did not get into the ditch to check on her.

"You didn't know whether she was dead at that time," said Kinsolving.

"Oh yes, yes."

"How did you know she was dead?"

"Mr. Hundley's lantern revealed the fact that she was dead. I knew when I saw her that she was dead . . . her mouth open, lying on her back with her head back."

"You didn't go down to the body?"

"No, sir."

"Or feel her pulse?"

"No."[421]

He also admitted that after Hundley left for LaGrange to seek help, he walked back to his car with Shaver, leaving Verna's body alone in the ditch. He once again pled his sickness.

"Why didn't you stay with the body?"

"I told you I was sick, Mr. Kinsolving."

"You did it because you felt better up there at the car than you did 610 feet away?" asked Kinsolving in a loud voice.

"Objection!"

"Sustained."[422]

During his direct examination by Rodes Myers, Denhardt did his best to introduce emotion into the loss of his fiancée. His testimony was often maudlin, with long and dramatic answers. But when he faced Kinsolving and had to reply to questions he had not seen ahead of time, Denhardt was different.

Kinsolving struggled and became irritated with Denhardt as a witness, but he worked hard to show his coldness and emotional detachment. He gave the jury some questions to ponder. Would they have acted in the same way if they heard a gunshot and their "suicidal" fiancée was missing in the darkness? Would they have stood and waited while a battery was installed knowing their fiancée could be injured? Would they have left her body alone and unguarded in a ditch on a dark highway?

Ultimately, the only people who could say that General Denhardt lied that day were Verna Garr Taylor, Chester Woolfolk, and Denhardt's attorneys. Denhardt had found a clever way to present his current version of the truth to the jury, but they would never know it was a sham.

During cross-examination, Kinsolving challenged nearly everything the general had to say, but he did not quiz Denhardt about the truth of his allegations against Woolfolk. If the prosecutor knew that there was more to the story of Verna and Woolfolk than Denhardt was telling the jury, he let it pass. Kinsolving was not only the prosecutor, he was also a friend of the Garr family and Roy trained his hunting dogs. If he probed too deeply, he would risk opening a painful door that no one wanted him to enter. At this point, Kinsolving probably believed it did not matter. There was enough evidence of the general's guilt to convict him without publicly embarrassing Verna's family and damaging her reputation.

Chapter 25

THE DEFENSE RESTS

General Denhardt's expert witnesses were compelling and their credentials were impeccable. It was no surprise that their opinions were the direct opposite of Kinsolving's experts. The defense team also conducted a ballistics test using a hog's carcass, Denhardt's revolver, and pieces of Verna's dress and slip. They also fired the revolver to compare the wounds at set distances. The crowd stared as a hog's carcass was wheeled into the courtroom during the testimony of Denhardt's first expert, Major Seth Wiard. Wiard, an instructor in firearms identification for the Institute of Criminal Science in Washington DC, gave his opinion that Verna died from a contact shot. It was not the first loud gunshot that killed her, but the second shot. The sound was different because she held the gun pressed against her body.

Wiard held up Denhardt's brass-finished fountain pen pistol for the jury to see. The pistol was typically loaded with a .38 caliber tear gas cartridge that would cause a muzzle flash and a pronounced smell of gas from fifteen to twenty feet away. A blank .38 cartridge would cause an even louder report and more flame and smoke from the muzzle. A cartridge loaded with a live .38 bullet could be disastrous. It had the potential to break the gun or severely injure the hand of the shooter. If Denhardt fired the pistol and used a tear gas cartridge or a blank cartridge, Wiard believed that Baker should have either smelled the discharged gas or heard a louder shot.

In March, Wiard fired two test shots using Denhardt's .45 caliber revolver. The next witness, R. O. Sherberg, performed a paraffin test on his hands. Sherberg, the defense expert on the paraffin test, was there to challenge the testimony of F. C. Buckmaster and John Messmer. His task was to raise more doubt in the minds of an already confused jury. Sherberg's work at the Coroner's Office of Cook County, Illinois, focused on toxicology and chemistry. Sherberg claimed that he had performed at least fifty paraffin tests, but in his opinion, the test was unreliable. In one experiment, he performed a paraffin test on a lab assistant who had handled guns for six months without firing a shot. His result was a heavy positive test. Another subject who lit six matches had a paraffin test with a strong positive reaction.

The test Sherberg performed on Major Wiard after he fired Denhardt's revolver was negative. Sherberg's own test was negative after firing the gun and washing his hands with the same soap used by Smith Keightley to clean Verna's hands. In March, Sherberg visited Denhardt's farm with Wiard. He asked Wiard to wash his hands, light a match, and walk out of Denhardt's room handling the doorknob. Sherberg testified that Wiard's paraffin test was positive after lighting the match. He thought Verna's paraffin test was meaningless. "In my opinion, I think the test has no value after washing the hands, and under those conditions, I would say it meant nothing."[423]

"Thank you, Mr. Sherberg," said Otte as he walked back to the table.

Sherberg's testimony was another blow to the two paraffin tests. The courtroom and Sherberg waited expectantly for a rousing cross-examination from the prosecution, but it never came.

"Any questions of this witness, Mr. Kinsolving?"

"No questions, Your Honor."

Henry Denhardt was briefly recalled. He told the jury that during the weekend before his paraffin test on Monday afternoon, he had washed his hands a number of times and bathed twice. There was no electricity in his house and he used kerosene lanterns for light in the evenings. Denhardt used ordinary kitchen matches to light the lanterns. His testimony provided even more reasonable doubt for the jury to consider.

Dr. Roy L. Carter, a physician for thirty-nine years and the coroner of Jefferson County, Kentucky, for sixteen years, estimated that he had examined the bodies of over a thousand homicide or suicide victims. In his opinion, Verna died instantly from the gunshot and fell to the ground. Otte asked him if blood would have "squirted" from Verna's wounds, either in the front or the back.

"There would have been none squirted out. The blood would have filled up the cavity of the chest, and if she were lying on her face some might have run out this anterior wound, or if she were lying on her back, some would have run out the wound in the back."[424]

Carter's opinion actually supported the testimony of Keightley, Ricketts, and Messmer who noticed no bloodstains on the outside front of Verna's dress. The testimony of both the defense and prosecution witnesses apparently closed the door to the possibility of blood spatter on Denhardt's overcoat. But Kinsolving would maintain that there was blood on the coat because Denhardt moved Verna from the road. Kinsolving had no questions on cross-examination.

General Denhardt shared his large farmhouse with the Cole family, and four members of the family were called to testify about the fountain pen pistol. Mary Cole, daughter of farm manager John Cole, gave the most compelling testimony. Mary Cole had lived on Denhardt's farm for two years, and she recalled that he moved his personal effects there from Frankfort in March or

April, 1936. Mary told the jury that after she heard the gun had become important in the case against Denhardt, she searched for it upstairs.

"Where did you find it?" asked Rodes Myers.

"Upstairs in the storage room on the second floor. It was in a brown envelope in a big box."[425]

Mary knew that she found the gun on January 30 because she noted the day on a calendar. She was also present when Messmer performed the general's paraffin test.

"Did you notice anything or any mark on any of his fingers?" asked Myers.

"Yes, sir. Right there on this forefinger."

"You are pointing to the right index finger?"

"Yes, sir. It was a cut place."

"About how long was it?"

"About a quarter of an inch."[426]

Myers nodded and said, "Thank you, Miss Cole."

"Any questions, Mr. Kinsolving?"

The presence of a cut on Denhardt's finger was a surprise, and Kinsolving quickly started his cross-examination. There was urgency in Kinsolving's voice when he asked, "Was it bandaged? Was that cut bandaged?"

"No, sir."

"You never saw it on there until those men came there that day?"

"No."

"You still live on the Denhardt farm?"

"Yes, sir."

"Still live in that house?"

"Yes, sir."[427]

The Cole family members all testified that although they were close to Denhardt on a number of occasions, they never saw him carrying the fountain pen pistol. While Denhardt was their landlord, and the Coles had much to lose if they crossed him, their testimony was consistent and believable. Kinsolving's theory of the second shot was interesting, but he was never able to prove that the fountain pen pistol left the general's farm.

Myers called Denhardt's longtime friend, Dr. A. T. McCormack as his next witness. McCormack was the Kentucky State health commissioner and secretary of the State Board of Health. He was sixty-four years old and had known Henry Denhardt since they were small children. McCormack had been the physician for the entire Denhardt family from 1896 until 1918. Dr. McCormack was out of town when Verna Taylor died, but saw the newspaper headlines when he returned on Sunday, November 8. He immediately drove to the general's farm to check on his friend.

"He was very restless when I got there. He was in bed, but he was very restless and [got up and] moved about the room, talking, and he hit his finger against some piece of furniture . . . I forget what it was . . . and as he did it, as it came up, several drops of blood came down from that finger; and every now and then, as he would go around, talking and making gestures, like he does, he would throw his finger down and a drop or two of blood would come off that finger."[428]

McCormack examined the finger and noticed a small jagged cut. For the majority of people, such a small cut would be of little consequence, but according to McCormack, Denhardt was a "bleeder." If he cut himself shaving, he could bleed for thirty minutes to an hour. He once inoculated him with an antitoxin for diphtheria and the general bled freely from the small puncture wound. A nosebleed would have to be cauterized. McCormack treated the finger while he was there on Sunday. On Tuesday, he returned with J. F. Blackerby, another mutual friend. Denhardt was in bed when they arrived, and McCormack asked to see his cut finger. He washed and treated it again before they left the farm.

J. F. Blackerby, director of the Kentucky Bureau of Vital Statistics, had been friends with Henry Denhardt for thirty years. He verified that he saw McCormack treat the cut on Denhardt's finger. On cross-examination, Kinsolving asked him where the cut was located.

"It was on either the index or middle finger, I think, of the right hand. I couldn't be positive. I just—"

"Where on that finger was it located?" Kinsolving probed.

"Well, I wouldn't be able to say. It was somewhere on the finger toward the end of it."

"You don't recall which finger it was?"

"I don't recall which it was."[429]

The final defense witness was the most distinguished of all the experts who appeared at the Denhardt trial. Dr. Alexander S. Wiener of Brooklyn, New York, was widely respected as an authority on serology and blood grouping. Wiener was a graduate of Cornell University and the Long Island College of Medicine. He was head of the Blood Transfusion Division at the Jewish Hospital of Brooklyn. Wiener claimed to be very familiar with blood spatter and the possible size and shape of blood droplets.

In early 1937, he visited Kentucky to determine General Denhardt's blood type. His objective was to compare the stains on Denhardt's overcoat with the blood on Verna's dress and slip. He collected blood from Denhardt's thumb for testing.

He said, "I found that when I punctured General Denhardt's finger the blood came quite freely, because the skin was soft and thin."[430]

Dr. Wiener was the only witness who made a diagram of the bloodstains on the overcoat. Otte motioned for Myers to step forward and don the general's overcoat. Myers stood in front of the jury as Dr. Wiener left the witness chair to point out the bloodstains.

"Dr. Wiener, from the spots of blood that you saw on the

coat, how much blood would it take to make those spots, in your opinion?" asked Otte.

"I would say if you take an eyedropper, about half a dropper full could easily make all the spots that I have seen."

"How would that compare with an ordinary teaspoon?" asked Otte.

"It would be about one eighth of a teaspoon."[431]

In Wiener's opinion, the bloodstains on the coat were drops that could have come from the dripping of a finger or hand. Otte described the cut on Denhardt's finger and asked if it could produce enough blood to make the droplets Wiener diagrammed on the overcoat.

"A small cut of the character just described could bleed sufficiently to make all the stains which I saw when I examined the coat."[432]

Wiener also believed that if Denhardt had moved Verna's body off the highway as Kinsolving claimed, there would have been smears of blood on the front of the coat and sleeves. As Dr. Wiener slowly made his way out of the crowded courtroom, John Berry rose to his feet. "Your Honor, the defense rests."

The trial was nearly over, and Kinsolving had to make a quick decision. Which witnesses should he recall to testify in rebuttal? Many of them had been in court listening to the testimony, so his choice was limited. Kinsolving's witnesses had never mentioned the cut on the finger. He decided to call Coroner Ricketts in rebuttal. When he was recalled to the witness chair, Ricketts denied seeing a cut.

"His hands were perfectly sound. There wasn't a scratch on them, because I stood there and watched Mr. Messmer take the test the whole time he was there. There wasn't a mark of any kind."

"Was there any abrasion or scratch or wound on his face?" asked Kinsolving.

"No, sir."[433]

Kinsolving also tried to recall Mary Pryor but met a solid wall of objections. She had been in the courtroom for most of the trial and listened to Denhardt's testimony. Marshall agreed with the objections and lectured Kinsolving.

"I warned you several days ago to keep your witnesses out of the courtroom."

"Well, we did."

"You don't seem to have kept this witness out," said Marshall.[434]

Eventually, Marshall compromised and allowed Mary Pryor to testify outside the jury's hearing. Kinsolving asked if Verna was able to eat breakfast with her on the morning of November 6.

"Yes, Mother did."

"State, please, what she ate."

"She had bacon and eggs and toast and tea and oatmeal, and I think there was some preserves."[435]

It was the perfect rebuttal to Denhardt's claim that Verna was upset and nervous when he picked her up. Verna ate the large breakfast of a busy woman with places to go and business to conduct. It would not be unusual if she were unable to eat lunch and only drink a cup of tea a few hours later, as Denhardt claimed. Unfortunately, the jury did not hear the testimony, and the trial ended with Mary Pryor's description of her last breakfast with her mother.

Late in the afternoon of Friday, April 30, Kinsolving and John Berry formally announced that they were finished, and with a bang of his gavel and a stern warning to the jury, Judge Marshall declared that the attorneys would begin their closing arguments on Monday.

Chapter 26

A VERDICT IN NEW CASTLE

It had rained nearly every day of the trial, and Monday, May 3, was no exception. The rain-soaked crowd began arriving at five a.m., their heavy boots and shoes leaving a trail of mud across the tiled floor of the courthouse and up the iron stairs to the second floor. Judge Marshall would not tap his gavel to begin until nine o'clock, but by seven fifteen, twelve hundred spectators packed the courtroom. Those who could not shove their way into the courtroom wandered the upstairs and downstairs hallways. Reporters arriving at the usual time found the path to the press table blocked. When they were finally able to elbow their way through the mob, they were trapped at the table. No one wanted to miss the "speeches" of the attorneys. It was an event nearly as anticipated as General Denhardt's testimony.

Just before nine, twelve weary men filed into court and took their places in the jury box. A Chicago reporter claimed in one of his articles that the original jury was so exhausted they had to be excused and a second jury impaneled. That was blatantly untrue. The reporter spun a wild story of riding with the sheriff around Henry County to find fresh men to refill the jury box. He spiced his tale with country simpletons and illiterate farmers unable to serve because they couldn't read or write. It was fiction, but the story made a splash in the Associated Press where sensationalism and newspaper sales in the 1930s were often more important than the facts.[436]

Judge Marshall banged his gavel to bring the mob to order. On one side of the room, Frances, Mary Pryor, and the Garr brothers sat tense and silent near their attorneys, waiting for the day to begin. Verna's family had endured nearly two weeks of agonizing testimony and grisly trial exhibits. They had travelled a painful road to see justice done in a court of law.

Across the room at the defense table, Henry Denhardt looked pale and sick as he waited with his attorneys. The closing arguments were the final chance for Denhardt's legal team to convince the jury that they should give him his freedom. The twelve men solemnly looking back at him from the jury box had several legal options. They could find him innocent, or send him to the electric chair, imprison him for what remained of his life, or convict him of voluntary or involuntary manslaughter. As the noise in the courtroom subsided into whispers, and six attorneys rifled through their notes preparing to present final arguments, the odds were against Henry Denhardt, and he knew it.

The attorneys would make their closing arguments by alternating from the defense to the prosecution. Kinsolving would have the last word in the case and make the final plea to the jury. Rodes Myers opened for the defense, and from the beginning, he attacked John Messmer, accusing him of either being careless with exhibits or deliberately tampering with them.

"He's so anxious to make a name for himself that he is willing to send an innocent man to the electric chair!" shouted Myers. "It's all politics and Messmer that are responsible for the indictment against General Denhardt!"[437]

Messmer sat quietly, but glared at Myers and grew red in the face during the scathing attack. It was a difficult moment for a man who devoted so much time and energy to the case, and only received his usual pay from the City of Louisville.

Ballard Clarke was just as loud and fervent in his address to the jury. He referred to Denhardt as a "Gay Lothario," and Verna as a "sweet lovely person" that he had known since she was a "girl in pigtails."

"If he killed her, he killed her in cold blood!" shouted Clarke.[438] He appealed to the jury as one Kentucky man to another to send Denhardt to the electric chair. "It's either murder or suicide, and we all know Verna didn't kill herself."[439] Clarke became so impassioned, waving his arms and pacing back and forth, that some of the spectators laughed.

"Wait just a minute, Mr. Clarke," said Judge Marshall with fire in his eyes. "I will not warn you again," he said pointing at the crowd. "The next time I hear laughter or any outburst, I will clear this courtroom!" Marshall had not kept order for nearly two weeks to see it slip away at the end. After a short pause for effect, he turned and said, "You may continue, Mr. Clarke."

Clarke eventually ended his emotional speech by pointing at Denhardt and shouting, "Give him the death he deserves!"[440]

Clarke Otte spoke to the jurors in a calm, measured voice. He reviewed the evidence and testimony of witnesses on both sides and moved theatrically across the courtroom holding up Verna's bloodstained garments in front of the jury box. Otte waved the general's revolver, repeatedly jamming it against his breast and pulling the trigger with a resounding click in front of the spellbound spectators. He lashed out at John Messmer and criticized his lack of scientific training. "My friends, a little knowledge is a dangerous thing!"[441] He also attacked Clarence Roberts, Kinsolving's original fountain pen witness, and accused him of lying. "The man who got him to come into court and tell that story should be hunted out, and I hope and pray the young boy will mend his ways and step aside from the path of sin!" said Otte sanctimoniously.[442] After nearly three hours of argument, Otte finally closed: "I ask you to acquit this man and send him home where he belongs!"

For eight long hours, the attorneys shouted and pointed, one side pleading for death, the other for acquittal. Each side attacked the other's evidence as flimsy and fraudulent. By the end of the day, only three attorneys had given their closing arguments, and Judge Marshall dismissed court to start again in the morning.

The next day, Wirt Turner opened for the state with a speech of one hometown man talking to a jury of home folks. He stood close to the jury box, speaking in a quiet voice and ridiculing the idea that Verna would kill herself. Turner appealed to the jurors' "plain country commonsense," and reviewed Denhardt's suspicious behavior on November 6.[443] He also defended John Messmer, and accused the defense attorneys of staging an attack against his credibility. "If Captain Kinsolving thought for a minute that John Messmer was falsifying evidence, he would prosecute him as vigorously as he has Henry Denhardt!"[444] He asked them to remember Verna's two motherless daughters and "Treat him as you would a man who made an orphan of your children!"[445]

John Berry's closing arguments were eloquent and passionate. "Are you going to send a man to the electric chair because he didn't help push a car or make a dramatic demonstration?" he asked the jury.[446] He insisted that General Denhardt spoke honestly and truthfully, and his actions on the night of November 6 were sensible and logical. Verna Garr Taylor committed suicide not because of one concern, but because of an accumulation of worries.

"I don't know why Mrs. Taylor killed herself. But I do know that in the closet of every heart are skeletons to follow and to haunt. I know that from my own experience, and you know it from yours. You haven't told all that's in your heart; I haven't told all that's in mine, and I'm not going to."[447]

Berry also declared that if Ballard Clarke testified to everything he knew, he "could have told of a problem no decent man would discuss, no court would admit, no decent set of men would listen to."[448] Berry did not elaborate, but he probably skated as close as anyone would come during the trial to revealing the relationship between Verna and Woolfolk.

The dramatic comment must have raised eyebrows in the courtroom, and left the jury puzzled and wondering what salacious details the attorneys were hiding. The *Oldham Era* was more cautious in its coverage. The newspaper noted that Berry accused Kinsolving and Ballard Clarke of knowing something "that had made Mrs. Taylor moody just before her death."[449]

Berry told the jury that Verna dropped the keys and flashlight while she wrestled with the revolver. She either fired a first shot to test the gun or accidentally tripped it. Her heels made prints in the mud as she staggered backward with the revolver. She spun it upside down so that the butt and trigger faced upward, pressed it against her breast, and fired. When she collapsed, her body tumbled into the ditch. The heel of her shoe caught in the mud as she fell, and it rolled down the embankment with her body. There was no explanation of how the shoe ended up between her arm and her body. There was also no explanation of why her body was not lying at the base of the embankment, but at least eight feet from the road.[450] At the end of his argument, Berry became so emotional that he began to weep. Denhardt's stoic façade crumbled, and he too began crying. Berry tearfully ended by asking the jurors to remember the love letters the couple had exchanged.

The general's tears were still wet on his face when Kinsolving took the floor to make his closing argument. His was the final argument, one last chance to convince the jury, and he began his speech slowly with a history lesson. "You know this case you are here to decide may have as much bearing on the state of Kentucky and Henry County as the first shot fired in the Revolution had on the nation."[451]

He meticulously reviewed the facts and emphasized Denhardt's delay in checking on Verna after hearing the gunshot. He told the jury that Verna had no reason to commit suicide, and that Denhardt made up his story about Chester Woolfolk. He asked them to consider why Denhardt had parked on the court square in LaGrange on the night of November 5, and theorized that he killed Verna in a fit of jealous anger. According to Kinsolving, Denhardt shot Verna on the highway, lifted her body by the shoulders and dragged her into the ditch. The course of the bullet was upward because she was falling backward at the time she was hit, and the heel prints stepping backward were proof. The spots of blood on the general's overcoat came from Verna's body as he moved her off the highway. Kinsolving's story made no more sense than Berry's version of events, and it was obvious that none of the attorneys really knew how Verna died. But it all made for an eloquent, dramatic argument, and people on the sidewalk outside could hear him shouting as he asked the jury to send Denhardt to the electric chair.

In a quieter voice, Kinsolving said, "I believe Verna Garr Taylor's spirit is in this courtroom, and I believe that if that spirit could talk, it would say every word this defendant said about their conversation was a lie."[452]

He scoffed at the idea that Verna committed suicide and told the jury that the only thing to support it was the general's own statement. "He admits she offered to give his ring back that day. I tell you, he killed her in anger when she told him she was going to break off with him."[453]

He finally declared, "In my opinion, the evidence in this case justifies a verdict of guilty, and if you give him the death sentence, you won't give him any more than he deserves!"[454] With those words still ringing in the courtroom, Kinsolving turned and walked back to his seat at the prosecution's table.

For courtroom antics, theatrics, suspense, and melodrama, there was nothing to equal the closing arguments of the Denhardt trial. The crowd expected accusations, finger-pointing, and impassioned pleas worthy of revival preachers, and they were not disappointed. After two days of final arguments, the trial officially ended on May 4 at 5:25 p.m.

Judge Marshall warned the jury not to discuss the case or form any opinions outside the jury room; they could return a verdict whenever they were ready. He placed Denhardt in the custody of the local jailer, and gave him the option of placing Denhardt under guard at the hotel. "No sir, I believe I will take the prisoner over to the jail," he replied. J. D. Simpson wisely did not want the issue of special treatment for a prisoner raised when he ran for reelection. He escorted Denhardt to the Henry County Jail where he would remain until the jury returned its verdict.

A local reporter captured the moment. "When the jury retired, the spectators poured from the courtroom. Attorneys grabbed their briefcases and hats and pushed for the exits, eager for a breath of fresh air. Outside, the tension that had held the spectators spellbound relaxed. Men and women laughed and smiled. Restaurants and cafes were packed. The streets were lively with chatter. Automobiles started up. The sharp cry of a farmer to a dozing horse was heard."[455]

But there was no relief in the tension for the Garr brothers, Mary Pryor and Frances, or for Denhardt and his brother and sister. It was a time to wait, and no one could predict how long the jury would take. The men of the jury filed out of the courtroom, ate dinner, and started to work. They asked to see all of the exhibits presented during the trial: Verna's bloody dress and slip and the tattered fragments marked with powder stains from test shots; the side of a hog filled with bullet holes; pieces of bullet-riddled pork floating in Mason jars; Denhardt's gun and the empty shells it contained when Verna's body was found; Denhardt's overcoat; the Sparkograph pictures; Verna's diamond engagement ring; and the brown jar containing pieces of Verna's flesh. The jury room windows had no curtains, and people passing by on the street could watch the jury huddled at a long table beneath two bare electric bulbs. They sent word at eleven that they would retire for the night and continue work in the morning.

Early the next day, they were back in the room with the long table and suspended light bulbs, discussing and deliberating. Late in the morning, there was a sudden flurry in the courthouse and rumors began flying as the jury filed back into the courtroom. Everyone in the hallway quickly ran into the courtroom to grab a seat.

"Gentlemen," asked the judge, "have you reached a verdict?"

"Why no, sir," replied the foreman, looking surprised.

"Then what are you doing in here?" demanded Marshall.

"Somebody told us to come in, that you wanted to see us."

Judge Marshall looked as perplexed as the jury. "No one can tell you to go anywhere and see anybody, not even me. You don't come into this courtroom again unless you have a verdict or can't agree."

Mumbling "Yes, sir," they filed out of the courtroom looking puzzled, and were escorted by the sheriff back to the jury room.[456]

A reporter noted, "All day a murmur of voices drifted through a plain, brown-painted door on the second floor of the tree-hemmed old courthouse here. A young blond deputy sheriff sat with his legs propped across the hallway, on guard."[457]

Hours slowly passed and the jury continued to argue Denhardt's fate. Shortly after dinner, they shoved the hog's carcass into the hall. Tillie Baldwin, court stenographer and official custodian of exhibits and trial records, was at a loss as to what to do with it. After asking for legal opinions around the courthouse, Denhardt's attorneys took the decaying carcass away.

Verna's hometown waited anxiously for word from New Castle. "All day Wednesday, people in LaGrange awaited the word that a verdict had been reached but none came. By many it was thought that the jury would report its findings on Thursday."[458]

As time continued to pass with no verdict, the family and their team of attorneys grew more uneasy. Perhaps the jury was divided or hopelessly deadlocked, and in a death case, the failure for all to agree would mean no verdict, a hung jury. After the excruciating days of the trial, the thought of going through it all again was unbearable. As Verna's family waited and watched the hours pass, Denhardt spent the time in his cell, occasionally looking out of the barred windows at the crowd waiting on the street and courthouse lawn. Bertha waited too, either visiting with him, or sitting for long hours at the courthouse. By the time the jury had been deliberating eighteen hours, rumors were flying in New Castle that they were deadlocked.

On Thursday morning, May 6, Judge Marshall was barely seated in the courtroom when the twelve men filed in and formed a circle in front of him. Marshall ordered the courthouse bell to be rung. The clanging could be heard up and down the streets of New Castle and everyone came running.

The jailer ushered in General Denhardt. "His face was gray beneath two days of beard. His collar was crumpled, his necktie knotted loosely," wrote one reporter. "But he showed no nervousness as he chewed gum steadily and stared about the room with wide-open eyes."[459]

Judge Marshall announced to the rapidly filling courtroom that the jury had something to report. He warned everyone that there were to be no demonstrations when the jury made their announcement. Marshall asked if they had reached a verdict.

"No, Your Honor," replied the foreman. "We have considered the case and are unable to get one."[460]

The judge polled the jury and each of the twelve men nodded somberly as they were called. He asked if there was any hope of reaching a decision and the men shook their heads. They were hopelessly deadlocked. The judge could do nothing but thank the jury for their work and consideration of the evidence, and reluctantly discharge them.

Denhardt, seated next to John Berry at the defense table, smiled broadly. "A great victory," he exulted, "a great victory!"[461] Berry interrupted by warning him that he would have to return to jail until his bond could be set. Denhardt would still require bond until there was a second trial.

The reporters were watching for the Garr brothers to enter the courtroom, and they arrived shortly after the verdict was announced. But Jack and Roy Garr had already heard the news outside, and as they entered the room, one reporter noticed that "Roy's ruddy face was paler than usual, his mouth grim."[462] They stood silent and numb, watching Denhardt celebrate with his attorneys. Their only hope for justice was to go through another trial.

Judge Marshall had warned the jury not to disclose publicly how they stood on Denhardt's guilt or innocence, but as usual in a small town, word passed quickly. The *Henry County Local* reported, "The *Local* has learned that the first ballot, according to information, resulted in one juror insisting on the electric chair, four for life imprisonment and seven for acquittal. On later ballots, the jurors were five for life imprisonment and seven for acquittal, according to reports current as coming from the jurors."[463]

On April 23, the prosecution had marched into court with a case that looked like a sure conviction for murder. But a scrappy, argumentative, and thoroughly prepared defense team had managed to pull their client from the jaws of death. It was an astounding result, and disappointing for a family who had relied on the legal system. But ultimately, the evidence was too confusing and conflicting for the jury to determine that Denhardt was guilty beyond a reasonable doubt.

H. B. Kinsolving looked pale and fatigued. He refused to

speak with the reporters, shaking his head and waving them away. The thought of going through another trial was too painful, too overwhelming. He saw the stunned looks of disappointment on the faces of Verna's family, and placed his hand gently on Roy's shoulder. "We'll get him next time," he said quietly. They would return to fight another day in September, but they had lost their best chance for a guilty verdict. The hostility against the general was at a fever pitch when the trial began, but the mistrial had somewhat subdued the calls for blood. By September when circuit court convened again in New Castle, the hostility might subside even more. If they hoped to get a conviction the second time, they would need damning new evidence against Denhardt or proof that he lied under oath.

The reporters hanging on every word and nuance noticed that Denhardt's blustering confidence was quickly returning.

"Apparently, after today's developments, General Denhardt felt out of the woods. 'The best thing that could have happened,' he declared after the jury reported. 'If the first hangs, they all hang.'"[464] He beamed as he posed for photographs. But the reporters also noticed that Denhardt showed the strain of the past months; he had aged visibly since November 6. He walked unsteadily down the iron stairway with his attorneys holding his elbows for support. Both Henry and Bertha Denhardt looked frail and elderly as they clutched one another and walked toward a waiting car that would take them home to Bowling Green.

Dr. McCormack renewed his friend's $25,000 bond, and the general was temporarily free until September, relieved and exultant with the end of his trial. But his journey home that night to Bowling Green was perilous. Mrs. Rodes Myers was driving her husband, the general, and Bertha when they were involved in a head-on collision at a narrow bridge. No one was injured, but both cars sustained considerable damage. Friends picked up the group, and they continued the long ride home.

The general and Bertha would stay temporarily at their brother's home in Bowling Green until they could move into their own house. In May, the September term of the Henry County Circuit Court seemed far away. But the summer of 1937 would pass quickly for General Denhardt, and he would find once again that he was never far from the headlines.

Chapter 27

THE STRANGE DEATH OF
PATRICIA WILSON

It had been nearly a year since Henry Denhardt knocked on Verna Garr Taylor's front door to ask about a house for rent. By the time he returned to Bowling Green after his trial for her murder, the reputation he had spent a lifetime pursuing had vanished. He was no longer "General Denhardt, distinguished statesman and war hero." He was now "General Denhardt, murder suspect," and regardless of how much he chose to ignore it, he lived under a cloud of suspicion. Bertha and Jesse Denhardt and his closest friends remained firm in their support. But the extended Denhardt family was divided on his guilt or innocence, and did not know what to make of the situation.[465]

Denhardt also continued to live in fear of the Garr brothers and even considered wearing a bulletproof vest. Rodes Myers later wrote, "Then he decided he was letting his imagination run away with him and that he would not wear armor; still he had been ever watchful against attack."[466] Denhardt probably also feared more bad publicity if word spread that he was wearing body armor on the streets of his hometown.

General Denhardt had convinced himself that his mistrial was a great victory and a vindication. He either believed that the majority of people agreed with him or chose to ignore the truth. After the trial, the rumblings against Denhardt and speculation about what happened in New Castle became an angry undercurrent. Gossip circulated that members of the jury had been bribed.[467] To the general public, it appeared that Denhardt had escaped justice because he was a man with political connections and wealth, capable of retaining the best defense attorneys and expert witnesses. While a suspicion of the wealthy and powerful during the lean Depression years may have fueled the notion, it was also no secret that Denhardt had evaded the legal system in 1935 with Governor Laffoon's pardon. Public sympathy had always been with Verna's family.

In Bowling Green, Denhardt soon found that everyday life was haunted by reminders of Verna Garr Taylor's death. One day while he was at the local post office reaching up to retrieve mail from his box, an elderly woman—small, but outspoken—recognized him and bluntly asked, "Now, didn't you kill that woman?" The general, taken by surprise, muttered "Goddamned old woman," and quickly retreated for the door.[468] Teenagers made prank calls to his house. Elizabeth Ann Barrickman Smiser was a seventeen-year-old freshman at Bowling Green Business College when she called the general's house one night on a dare from her friends. "Why did you kill that beautiful woman from Oldham County?" she asked when he answered the telephone. He demanded to know who was calling, and she quickly hung up the phone.[469]

The general's life was spiraling out of control before he met Verna Taylor. By May 1937, it was in a shambles beyond repair, but Denhardt attempted to pull his life back together that summer. The first item on his agenda was to settle the issue of legal fees. Henry Denhardt owed his life to the tenacity of John Berry, Clarke Otte, and Rodes Myers, but by early summer, he had still not paid them. His strained relationship with Clarke Otte during the trial had continued to deteriorate and the two were not speaking. During the months of May, June, and July, letters flew back and forth between John Berry in New Castle, and Denhardt in Bowling Green, quibbling over the legal fees and Denhardt's fury at Otte.

Two weeks after his trial ended, Denhardt wrote to Berry, "After the trial was over, and when everyone was saying that there would not be another trial Otte again urged that the fee be fixed at once before I could get the idea, which is prevalent everywhere and openly talked by all lawyers in the state, that there would be no other trial." He also criticized Otte's performance at the trial. "Of course we all know that Otte did none of the things he boasted he would do in my case." But by the end of the letter, Denhardt reluctantly agreed "to use as much cash as possible and secure the balance by note secured by mortgage which will be bankable, the fee agreed on several days before the commencement of the trial to-wit: $3,000. While I consider this a very large fee, it will be paid or secured. This is a larger fee than was ever paid to any one man in a murder trial in this part of the state. It is three times larger, I am informed, than was ever paid any one lawyer in your county."[470]

In the letter, Denhardt was once again full of his old bluster and bravado, referring to mysterious third parties to support his belief that there would not be another trial.

In his reply letter, Berry admitted, "There was talk about fees, and I probably participated in it as much as anybody because it has been my observation that lawyers require fees to be paid in advance, or to be adequately secured." He wrote that he did not require this in Denhardt's case because he was more concerned with his defense than anything else at the time. Berry wrote, "Of course I know that all of the time you have protested that my fee was too large regardless of what figure was suggested." Before the trial, Berry asked for $5,000, but the general insisted it was too much. Berry countered with $3,500. Denhardt agreed to pay him $3,000, but wrote a check for $500, which Berry refused, as credit toward the $3,000. If the general agreed to pay $3,000, he wanted payment in full for his services.[471]

Berry also made it clear that his work on Denhardt's case, and his failure to pay led to a decline of revenue in his office. He was required to borrow to make ends meet. "As to your financial circumstances, I have not gone to the trouble to make an investigation. I have had another aim and end in view, but I know that you and members of your family together are easily in position to pay my fee in full."[472]

In his reply letter, Denhardt wryly noted, "May I again say that it is not at all customary to pay legal fees in advance here, unless in the case of a regular criminal and I do hope I have not fallen to that degree."[473]

John Berry had earned every penny of the fee he requested. But the letters and negotiations continued between the two. The general suggested arbitration, but did not want to travel to New Castle to negotiate the fees. "I do not want to go into your judicial district because the party of whom I have been warned against so frequently will feel absolutely free to take my life anywhere in that district. Unless I have to go to court there, I believe it is best that I remain away."[474]

Denhardt suggested a meeting in Bardstown or Frankfort, but noted that because of a nervous condition, his doctor "advised that I refrain from actively participating in any conferences unless absolutely necessary."[475] Denhardt designated two attorneys to work out the details of a settlement on his behalf.

By early July, Denhardt was still negotiating fees and using his letters as a forum to belittle Otte. "Regarding a settlement with Mr. Otte, I have come to the point where I will be no longer annoyed by his high-pressure methods. I have paid him approximately $1,500. I regard his services to me as not only not helpful but as being a hindrance in my case." He continued, "Instead of me owing him I think he owes me."[476]

But while Henry Denhardt quibbled about what he was willing to pay and exchanged businesslike—but not unfriendly—letters with Berry, another front was opening. In early July, Denhardt was once again in the headlines, accused of murdering another woman.

The Seelbach Hotel is one of Louisville's grandest old landmarks. Since 1905, the four-diamond hotel has hosted a number of distinguished, and not-so-distinguished guests, including gangster Al Capone. F. Scott Fitzgerald supposedly was inspired to base a scene in *The Great Gatsby* on the elegant old hotel. On November 6, Verna Garr Taylor and Henry Denhardt also briefly spent time there over lunch during their fateful day trip to Louisville. But one of the Seelbach's enduring legends is of the "Lady in Blue," a spirit who supposedly haunts the hotel where she tragically died, and is occasionally spotted by staff members or guests. The "Lady in Blue" was Patricia Wilson, and in early July, Henry Denhardt was accused of her murder.[477]

In a petition filed by Edward Langan, public administrator of Jefferson County on behalf of Wilson's sister, Denhardt was accused of assaulting and beating Wilson, causing her to fall to her death in an elevator shaft of the hotel. The murder allegedly took place on the night of July 14 or in the early morning hours of July 15, 1936, and the wrongful death action requested $75,000.[478]

Little is known about Patricia Wilson, but during the investigation of her death by the Louisville Police Department, she was quickly dismissed as a "party girl," a woman attracted by the wealthy and powerful men who frequented the Seelbach Hotel.[479]

The petition did not elaborate on Denhardt's relationship with Wilson, but he vehemently denied any involvement in her death. When *Louisville Courier-Journal* reporter John Herchenroeder contacted the general for a statement, Denhardt laughed off the lawsuit, claiming he had been on his farm in Oldham County on the evening Patricia Wilson died.[480] As expected, the *Bowling Green Times-Journal* was indignant and outspoken in his defense: "There is no limit to the extent those behind the persecution of General Denhardt will go to libel, slander, defame and if possible to destroy him."[481]

Denhardt was casual with the reporters who asked him for a comment, but he was secretly concerned. For months, he had weighed the possibility of selling his Oldham County farm, but refused, fearing a wrongful death lawsuit in civil court by Verna's family. This legal action from a completely different direction took him by surprise, and in late July, he responded furiously by filing a countersuit. Denhardt, as usual, accused his unnamed political opponents. He also blamed the Garr brothers and their attorneys for the lawsuit, believing that when they failed to convict him, "they moved into Jefferson County and maliciously, unlawfully, and wickedly filed the suit in connection with the hotel death."[482] Denhardt asked for $150,000 in damages, $100,000 for the conspiracy against him and $50,000 for slander.

Always faithful, John Berry and Rodes Myers filed his countersuit. Denhardt had barely settled his dispute over trial fees with John Berry. In late July, the general enclosed a check made out to Berry in one of his lengthy letters. "I am enclosing herewith my check for $2,090.88, which in accordance with our agreement recently made at Bardstown is in full payment for all your services in my case in connection with the murder charge of Mrs. Verna Garr Taylor to the conclusion thereof, and furthermore covers all your expenses up to this date.[483] With his check and letter, Denhardt dismissed the death of the woman he "desperately loved" as a businesslike reference for services rendered.

As for the strange death of Patricia Wilson, his charge that the Garr family and their attorneys were involved in a conspiracy against him was fantastic and unsupported. The outcome of the lawsuit and countersuit was never resolved. The quickly approaching fate of General Denhardt would leave the questions surrounding his involvement and possible relationship with Patricia Wilson unanswered.

As the general fought back on this new legal front, he was also preoccupied with reinstatement to the command of the Seventy-Fifth Brigade of the Kentucky National Guard. Denhardt blamed Major Joseph M. Kelly for suspending him from his duties as a brigadier general. Kelly was both assistant adjutant general of Kentucky, and the executive officer of the Kentucky National Guard. Denhardt claimed that Major Kelly visited him when he was a prisoner at the Jefferson County Jail, and demanded his resignation from the Guard. Denhardt refused, declaring that he was innocent of the charges against him. Kelly threatened to have him undergo a physical fitness examination. Denhardt was so concerned with the possibility of a fitness examination that he asked a state senator and Rodes Myers as a state representative to approach Governor A. B. Chandler for help.

For Denhardt to throw himself on the mercy of his old political enemy indicates how desperate he was not to lose his military status. In the end, Chandler came to his aid. He instructed Major Kelly that he did not want politics injected into the Kentucky National Guard, and according to Denhardt, "Major Kelly for a time desisted from his efforts to embarrass me."[484] But Kelly instructed the paymaster to deduct Denhardt's pay for the days he was in jail. The general was furious. In a lengthy letter, Denhardt profusely thanked the governor for his help and launched into a tirade against Major Kelly. Denhardt indicated that their problems began in 1931 when he, rather than Kelly, was appointed adjutant general. In the letter, he made a legal and military argument why he should retain his position and be paid. He reviewed his illustrious military record for Chandler's benefit, bragging that "Governor Morrow was good enough to say of me that he regarded me the best soldier produced from civil life during the war."[485] The dispute ended with Denhardt once again with the rank of brigadier general and back in command of the Seventy-Fifth Brigade. In August, he reported for guard duty at Fort Knox and was once more at the head of his troops.

If Henry Denhardt believed there would not be another murder trial against him in Henry County, his lawyers knew otherwise, and they were steadily becoming more alarmed as summer passed. The time set for the second trial was quickly approaching, and Denhardt was still at odds with Clarke Otte. While he continued the feud, and downplayed Otte's role in the trial, Berry and Myers knew how important Otte was to the case. In a letter to Rodes Myers in mid-August, John Berry mentioned that Kinsolving had called on him and expressed his enthusiasm over the start of another trial. Berry was very concerned by the visit.

"If you will pardon some frank suggestions, which will not set well with General Denhardt when you tell him of them, I should like to observe that we had better make up our minds that this case is going to be tried in September, and prepare for that ordeal; that General Denhardt should refrain from his cocky interviews about the trial, even if he is to participate prominently in the mock warfare at Fort Knox; and that he make peace with Clarke Otte upon some basis . . ."

Berry's letter noted that with Denhardt's life at stake, Otte had the necessary expertise, and that "you and I, are not equal to the job of taking care of his part of the defense when the responsibility for that has been assumed and born [*sic*] by him all of the time." Berry urged Myers to reason with the general and make him understand that regardless of what he believed, there was going to be another trial.[486]

Denhardt remained nonchalant and unconcerned. In mid-August, the *New York Times* caught up with Denhardt during mock war maneuvers at Fort Knox. "'I don't think they'll hold another trial in September. They don't have enough evidence,' the general said as he mopped his head. 'I didn't do it,' he added."[487]

By early September, Berry's legal alarms were ringing, and he wrote another worried letter to Rodes Myers. "As the September term of the Henry Circuit Court approaches, I find myself more and more concerned about the prospects of the trial of the charge against General Denhardt, and particularly his apparent indifference to the fact."

He once again expressed concern over the continuing feud between Denhardt and Otte. "I had hoped that long before this the relationship between General Denhardt and Otte would be repaired and that a conference would be held by all of us. Here it is just a short time before the term of Court, with all to do that must be done in behalf of his defense."

Berry had been sick from hay fever and asthma, and claimed he was in no shape to be hurried and rushed. He once again urged Myers to impress on Denhardt the seriousness of the situation and the necessity of making peace with Clarke Otte, "but if he does not, it is his party and not mine." Berry copied Denhardt, and asked Rodes Myers to hand deliver the letter.[488]

Denhardt finally heard Berry's pleas to settle the feud with Otte. On September 11, he wrote Berry that he had offered Otte a settlement. The general could not resist one final tirade against Otte. "Otte has done nothing but cause trouble since the time he was firmly fixed as one of my counsel. Had he spent one-fourth of the time representing me instead of talking fees and encouraging others to charge me fees, I certainly would have been acquitted."[489] In the letter, he also ordered Berry to issue subpoenas for the September trial, "especially on Bookie, the laundry people, Mrs. Lee, Ricketts, and others who are close to the prosecution. This at least will give them something to think about."[490]

Berry suggested a conference to resolve the differences between Denhardt and Otte, and the attorneys agreed to meet in Shelbyville, Kentucky, on September 20, the night before the second trial. Denhardt was in high spirits as the trial date approached, confident he would win, and looking forward to ending his legal troubles.

But the general was right all along when he said he would not be retried. The end of his murder case was not waiting for him in New Castle, but in the small town of Shelbyville. In Shelbyville, a full harvest moon, three grieving brothers, and the general's fate would be waiting for him on Main Street in front of the old Armstrong Hotel.

Part III

SHELBYVILLE

"This is the first time I ever heard anyone claim
self-defense when they shot the victim in the back as he was
running like the devil to get away from them."

—

Kentucky Attorney General Hubert Meredith
September 25, 1937

Chapter 28

THE GARR BROTHERS, SEPTEMBER 20, 1937

During the hot summer months of 1937, ugly rumors, threats, and accusations flew back and forth between LaGrange, Bowling Green, and Louisville. In Bowling Green, the general was so afraid of the Garr brothers that he considered wearing body armor. In LaGrange, well-meaning friends warned Roy Garr that Denhardt would kill him if he had the opportunity. One of the men who warned Roy was George Blaydes, son of Dr. H. B. Blaydes. George Blaydes was not only a friend of the Garr brothers, he was also a private investigator who worked in Louisville with John Messmer.[491]

Roy would later claim, "Well, I feared him, I knew he killed my sister, and I knew any time he would kill us any opportunity that he got. I knew he was a killer."[492] Doc Garr, too, was warned that Denhardt was a dangerous man to cross. Friends told him, "You be careful, Doc, be careful; you know you swore out a warrant for him, he has got it in for you."[493]

In July, the situation became even more intense when Denhardt publicly accused the family and their attorneys of trumping up the Patricia Wilson lawsuit. The wild rumors spread until the situation was ready to explode at the least provocation. There was a witches' brew of strong emotions between the parties—frustration, anger, suspicion, and hatred—but the overwhelming emotion driving both sides was fear. It was the key ingredient for another tragedy.

Two persistent rumors brought the Garr brothers to the opening day of the Henry County Circuit Court docket on September 20. The first concerned the old issue of venue. The brothers had heard that Denhardt would try once again to move the trial, and they were determined to keep it in Henry County.

"I wanted to fight that," said Roy. "I wanted it held right there in New Castle where she was killed, where he killed her."[494]

The second rumor spreading in Oldham and Henry Counties was more disturbing to Verna's family—Denhardt supposedly planned to introduce new evidence that would tarnish Verna's reputation. If so, he either intended to give more details about the rental of the hotel room on the afternoon of November 6, or talk about Verna's relationship with Woolfolk.

During the trial, Kinsolving had not explored the mysterious rental of the hotel room. Why he touched on the topic of the room but did not ask the all-important question remains one of the mysteries of the case. Perhaps he feared what Denhardt might say. But in not asking the question, Kinsolving left open the possibility that Verna was with Denhardt, and that there was a physical relationship between the two.[495]

However, it is more likely that Denhardt planned to reveal additional details about Verna and Woolfolk. His letter of September 11 ordered John Berry to send subpoenas to Bookie Taylor and the laundry employees, and included the ominous comment, "This will give them something to think about." The choice of witnesses was a veiled threat to Verna's family. If they insisted on a second trial, they would suffer the consequences. The general intended to take the gloves off this time, and the trial was going to be ugly.

On the morning of September 20, Roy wanted to talk with Kinsolving about both rumors, especially the one involving his sister's reputation. He also wanted to discuss potential new trial witnesses.

Kinsolving was busy in court that morning, and the Garr brothers waited for a chance to catch him between clients and motions. But an hour passed, and when Roy finally saw Kinsolving in the corridor, he was too busy to say more than a few words. There was no time to continue to wait. Roy's wife had a doctor's appointment, and he left to drive her to Louisville. Jack, who had driven from Cincinnati early that morning, left for his mother's house. Doc tarried in the courthouse for a short time, but finally left New Castle on a veterinary call to treat a cow. The brothers would reunite around seven o'clock that evening when Roy stopped by his mother's house on his way to Shelbyville.

Kinsolving heard the news about the Shelbyville defense meeting at the courthouse that morning. It must have taken him by surprise because he stopped by the clerk's office to use the telephone to call Wirt Turner. He also mentioned the meeting to a reporter from Cincinnati. While the exact place and time may have been unknown that morning, it was an easy assumption that if Denhardt and Myers were traveling to Shelbyville, they would stay at the Armstrong Hotel. It was the most likely place for them to spend the night, and to have a conference.[496]

Late that afternoon, two reporters, curious about the news of a defense conference, quizzed John Berry. Berry confirmed the meeting in Shelbyville and the reporters agreed there would be no public statement. But the news had already spread. It was no secret that Denhardt would be in Shelbyville that evening.[497]

The town of Shelbyville, Kentucky, seat of Shelby County, was sixteen miles south of LaGrange, and fifteen miles northwest of New Castle. It was a busy agricultural town in a county known for sleek saddlebred horses, purebred cattle, and a thriving dairy industry that supplied the continuous demand in nearby Louisville. In 1937, burley tobacco was the major crop. On Saturdays, people drove to town from surrounding communities such as Clay Village, Bagdad, and Finchville to spend their hard-earned money, visit the bank, or meet with their attorneys. Shelbyville was home to both H. B. Kinsolving and Judge Charles Marshall. The Main Street business district was lined on both sides with impressive three- and four-story brick buildings, and the Armstrong Hotel was one of the largest. The hotel had been a landmark on Main Street since 1859, and did a steady business among out-of-town guests visiting Shelbyville.

On September 20, 1937, a perfect day of sunshine and turquoise skies just before the fall equinox, Henry Denhardt and Rodes Myers left Bowling Green in the afternoon. After a long, dusty drive, they arrived at the Armstrong Hotel around seven. Louisville would have been the preferred safe place to spend the night, but Shelbyville was an easier drive to New Castle. The two men registered, and checked into a double room on the third floor while they waited for John Berry and Clarke Otte to arrive for the conference. Otte, Berry, Myers, and General Denhardt ate a pleasant and amicable dinner in the hotel dining room, and the general and Otte were once more on speaking terms. The attorneys knew that if the defense hoped to win an acquittal this time, they needed to present a unified front in the courtroom.

By afternoon, news of the meeting at the Armstrong Hotel had reached John Messmer in Louisville. Since the end of the trial, Messmer had also received warnings from well-meaning friends to be careful; Denhardt would get him if he had the chance. He had heard the whispered gossip that Denhardt and his attorneys intended to slur the reputation of Verna Taylor in the second trial. For Messmer, the meeting in Shelbyville presented a golden opportunity, and he telephoned Kinsolving on the afternoon of September 20 with a plan. He wanted to plant a Dictaphone in the room next to the conference to listen in on the conversation. Messmer still fumed from being used as the scapegoat during the first trial, and he was concerned about the rumors of threats. The listening device would be the perfect opportunity to discover what was said about him during the meeting, and whether there were plans afoot to slur Verna's reputation.

Kinsolving later said, "I unequivocally told Messmer I could have nothing to do with it."[498] While Kinsolving wisely did not agree to the scheme, he also did not tell Messmer not to plant the Dictaphone. Messmer decided to go forward with his plan, and telephoned detective George Blaydes with the assignment around six p.m.

Blaydes arrived in Shelbyville between eight-thirty and nine o'clock, and registered at the Armstrong Hotel under the assumed name of T. C. Anderson of Fort Wayne, Indiana. He was assigned the room next to General Denhardt, and heard the voices of the attorneys before he set up his equipment. By the time the Dictaphone was in place, and the short wire attached to his headset, the conference was over and the attorneys were leaving the room. Blaydes was not sure whether all of them had left, and he continued listening, hoping to hear more conversation. His equipment not only picked up sounds from Denhardt's room, it also amplified noises from the street below. He waited patiently, hoping to hear something he could report to John Messmer.

Next door to Blaydes, the attorneys finished their conference around nine forty-five p.m. John Berry was still suffering from asthma and allergies, and the attorneys decided to use his illness to ask Judge Marshall for a continuance. Earlier that day, Berry had obtained a letter from a Louisville doctor that he would attach to his motion to continue Denhardt's case. The doctor wrote that Berry's illness might cause him to "break down and collapse" during a stressful and lengthy trial.[499] Under the circumstances, there was a good chance that Marshall would postpone the trial.

Otte and Denhardt made peace that evening, and it was Otte

who spoke the final words of the meeting when he rose to his feet and shook hands with Denhardt. "General, I'll see you tomorrow morning in New Castle." They agreed to meet in Berry's law offices and walk together to the courthouse. The dinner and meeting had been a success; they were united once again and ready for the second trial.

Denhardt walked Otte and Berry outside to the curb in front of the hotel. He watched the taillights of Otte's car merge into the traffic on Main Street and speed west toward Louisville. But Denhardt lingered under the streetlights beside John Berry's car, continuing to talk with him as the minutes passed until Berry finally said his goodbyes and turned his car toward New Castle.

It was a beautiful evening and a large harvest moon glowed in the sky over Main Street, illuminating the sidewalk and the darkened storefronts. There were people walking from the motion picture show and others headed for the local pool hall. Denhardt suggested to Rodes Myers that they walk to a nearby restaurant for a beer before turning in for the night. Myers agreed, and the two strolled at a leisurely pace east on Main Street toward the restaurant two blocks from the hotel.

Earlier that evening in LaGrange, Roy Garr had stopped by his mother's house on his way to visit Kinsolving, and Doc and Jack agreed to ride with him. They left LaGrange around eight o'clock. Jack was unarmed, but Roy and Doc had their pistols. When they arrived at Kinsolving's house, Jack and Doc waited in the car while Roy knocked at the door. Roy talked with Kinsolving for twenty to thirty minutes, and when he returned, the brothers decided to visit Ryon Blakemore in Shelbyville. Blakemore owned and operated Blakemore's Grocery next to the Armstrong Hotel. He was a lifelong friend of Roy Garr and related to him through Verna's marriage to Rowan Barclay Taylor.

Doc parked his automobile on Main Street, and the three

brothers went into the store to visit. They discussed bird dogs, hunting, and local gossip with a group of men hanging out in the store. Blakemore arrived twenty minutes later, and Roy talked with him about the latest developments in the second trial. It was ten o'clock when they finally left the store, and Doc was anxious to get started on the forty-minute drive home. He was driving with Roy beside him and Jack in the back seat. As they were leaving, Roy suddenly decided he should confirm that Blakemore would be at the trial the next morning.

"Him and Jack kinda fussed and said, 'You have always got somebody else to see, you can't get home,' or something like that," Doc later recalled.[500] But Doc stopped the car on Sixth Street, a narrow street parallel to the Armstrong Hotel. He climbed out of the car to walk to the grocery with Roy, and Jack waited in the back seat of the automobile.

Two blocks away, Denhardt and Myers finished their beers and began the short walk back to the hotel for the night. The general was in good spirits, and Myers later recalled him saying as they walked, "Well, Rodes, I feel better in mind and body then I did at this time before the last trial. I have a hunch we'll come out of it this time all right."[501]

The men passed a city patrolman as they slowly approached the corner of Sixth and Main Streets. They stepped off the curb and had reached the middle of Main Street when Rodes Myers recognized two tall, broad-shouldered men in the moonlight, walking near a car parked on Sixth Street.

"There are the Garr brothers!" shouted Myers.

It all happened very quickly.

Panicked, the general ran for his life, zigzagging military style toward the entrance of the hotel. "He was going into a slow run, or as fast maybe as he could run, in the direction of the hotel," said Myers.[502] It was a fatal error in judgment. Rather than walking another direction and throwing his hands in the air, Denhardt charged toward the hotel door in the direction of the Garr brothers.

"He come right quartering towards me," said Roy.[503] "I looked up and the first thing I saw was Denhardt, the next thing I saw going for his hip, right hip pocket and by God I went for mine pretty fast, and when I got my gun I shot twice, I was scared and I saw him and it scared me. I saw that dead sister of mine when I saw him, I went to shooting. I emptied my gun before I quit shooting."[504]

Doc saw Denhardt make a motion like he was preparing to draw a gun and he also opened fire. He later said, "I knew I had to do something; I thought my time had come."[505] The brothers continued to fire wildly as Denhardt staggered toward the hotel doorway.

Jack was unarmed and sitting in the parked automobile. "I heard somebody say the name of Garr in kind of a loud voice, and so I naturally looked up, my name being Garr. I saw Denhardt and Mr. Myers standing in the middle of the street, or in the street . . . I saw then some kind of motion by Mr. Denhardt, you couldn't see it very plain, looked like he crouched over just a little bit, some particular motion, peculiar motion."[506]

Jack jumped out of the car and ran toward his brothers who were pursuing Denhardt. The corner of the hotel building briefly hid Denhardt from their view, but the brothers ran behind him firing their pistols. For a moment, it appeared that four men were all running in the same direction—toward the hotel doorway—until the one in the lead suddenly collapsed.

When Denhardt made his last mad dash, Myers turned to run in the other direction. He stopped in shock when he glanced back and saw Denhardt lying in the hotel doorway. "Well, after I had stopped out in the center of the street and saw this last shot fired at General Denhardt, Doctor Garr had turned in my direction with a gun in his hand and I threw up my hands and turned and faced him and I said, 'Doc, for God's sake, don't shoot me.' He said, 'You son of a bitch, you defended the son of a bitch that killed my sister.' I said, 'Doc for God's sake, don't do that,' and Roy Garr came and grabbed his arm."[507]

Doc slowly lowered his gun, and Rodes Myers escaped with his life that night. Roy ordered Myers to go inside the hotel and he quickly obeyed, stepping over his friend's body and the rapidly spreading pool of blood in the doorway. Doc, Roy, and Jack walked to Blakemore's Grocery for help but the door was locked. "Come on," said Roy, "let's go to jail or hunt the law."[508]

The sound of gunshots brought people running from all directions. Upstairs in the hotel, George Blaydes was still listening on his Dictaphone when he heard the sudden explosion of gunfire on the street. He threw down his equipment and ran downstairs to see what had happened.

The first person to reach the general's body was Harry Flood, proprietor of the hotel. Flood was at the poolroom several hundred feet away when he heard six or seven gunshots explode nearby. One of the men shouted that something had happened at the hotel, and Flood quickly ran out the door and down the street. His son, Howard was on duty by himself in the hotel lobby. When Flood reached the front of the hotel, he saw Denhardt's body sprawled in the doorway and yelled for someone to call a doctor. He later said, "Well, at first I ran up and looked at him, I didn't know, I reached under him, when I raised him up . . . I was trying to feel his heart to see if he had any heartbeat, the blood ran out in my hand. I thought then he was dead. I just turned him a little bit out of the door."[509] Young Howard Flood stood staring in shock behind the hotel cigar counter.

Dr. A. C. Weakley arrived at the scene minutes after the shooting. He elbowed a path through the gathering crowd and moved toward the body in the hotel doorway. Weakley squatted beside Denhardt, and saw two bullet holes in his back and one in the back of his skull. There were no signs of life, and there was nothing he could do. The general was dead, a handkerchief still clutched in his hand.

Night patrolman Jeptha Tracy was a block away when he heard gunshots from the direction of the Armstrong Hotel. Tracy ran for the hotel, and when he arrived, the Garr brothers walked up to him and surrendered peacefully.

"I told him I shot this man and here was my gun," said Roy. "I told him Denhardt went for his gun, for his right hip, and I went for mine, when I recognized him and saw what he was doing."[510]

Roy tried to explain that Jack was unarmed, but the officer insisted he come with them. The brothers were escorted to the nearby Shelby County Jail. When they arrived, Doc Garr said, "I've got a pistol too," and pulled a large .45 caliber Colt pistol out of his pants to hand to Tracy.[511]

Word spread so quickly that the brothers had scarcely reached the jail before a shocked and disheveled Kinsolving ran in the door. Ballard Clarke arrived a short time later. It was quickly decided that Clarke would represent the Garr brothers, and he spoke with reporters gathering outside the jail.

"I told them not to see anyone or to talk to anyone," he informed a reporter, "but if they are willing to see you, it is all right with me."[512]

"It may be all right with them, but it ain't all right with me," said the jailer, slamming the door on the reporter.[513]

The *Louisville Times* commented, "Despite reports and rumors of threats of violence, the slaying, coming as it did on the eve of the trial, was a shock. Telegraph and telephone wires began to hum and the news soon spread over the state and, by radio, to other states."[514]

Before the news could reach the Denhardt family in Bowling Green, Rodes Myers telephoned Bertha to tell her what had

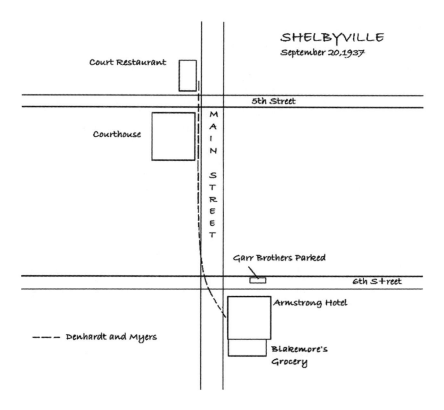

happened. Bertha was waiting to hear if Judge Marshall would grant the continuance before she made the trip to be at her brother's side during the trial. Clarke Otte had reached his home in Louisville when he heard the news, and John Berry was already in New Castle. They both turned their cars around and sped back to Shelbyville where they met Rodes Myers at the Shannon Funeral Home. The three attorneys were talking together when Dr. McCormack rushed in the door.

Dr. McCormack performed one last service for his lifelong friend that night. He assisted the coroner, Dr. F. L. Lapsley in the official examination of Denhardt's body. Lapsley determined that one bullet entered the upper right arm, another entered behind Denhardt's left ear, and a third struck the left side of the back three or four inches below the spine. The doctors recovered the bullet from Denhardt's skull, and Lapsley believed it was the fatal shot. The other two shots passed through the body without striking a vital organ; they were not recovered.[515] Denhardt had no weapons on him. A letter from his ex-wife was tucked in his pocket, and Myers took the letter with him to return it to Elizabeth Denhardt.

Lapsley prepared the death certificate; for the cause of death, he simply wrote "murdered." The certificate stated that Denhardt was divorced, but named Elizabeth Denhardt as his wife. His business or occupation was "attorney-at-law."[516]

The amazing events of the night of September 20, 1937, ended with the Garr brothers locked in the Shelby County Jail, the general lying dead at Shannon's Funeral Home, and the normally quiet town of Shelbyville in an uproar. By the light of the full moon, everything had changed and turned upside down. As commonwealth attorney, Kinsolving was now in the impossible position of prosecuting his friends. Ballard Clarke represented the Garrs as murder suspects and Rodes Myers was the key witness for the prosecution. Denhardt's violent death at the hands of the Garr brothers was an astounding end to what had once been a distinguished life.

That night, the town of Shelbyville replaced New Castle as the hub in the wheel of the continuing Taylor-Denhardt tragedy.

Chapter 29

WHEN THE ROLL IS CALLED UP YONDER

On Tuesday, September 21, a trial that would never be held was on the Henry County Circuit Court docket. H. B. Kinsolving had one remaining item of business, a legal formality in court to have the case against Denhardt dismissed by Judge Marshall. It was generally believed that Kinsolving's evidence would have been stronger in the second trial. Denhardt's nurse would have testified that he told her the blood on his overcoat came from cattle he dehorned. A woman from the Community Laundry was ready to testify that she heard Denhardt threaten Verna's life two days before she died. Kinsolving and the LaGrange town marshall had also learned that, several days before the first trial, Denhardt supposedly threatened to "kill a negro" with his fountain pen pistol. One newspaper reported, "Mr. Kinsolving had spent considerable time in the past months working on the prosecution's case, associates revealed."[517]

But after all the hours of investigation, preparation, and anxiety, the gunshots fired that Monday night ended the murder case against Denhardt forever. It was time for Kinsolving to put it all behind and leave the tragic death of Verna Garr Taylor for the history books. On Tuesday morning, he made his final appearance in the familiar setting of the second-floor courtroom in New

Castle. When Judge Marshall called the case against Denhardt, Kinsolving walked to the front of the courtroom and asked the judge to dismiss the charges.

"If it please Your Honor," Kinsolving said in a low but audible voice, "I wish to call the attention of the court to the death of the defendant last night."

"Dismissed," replied Judge Marshall before Kinsolving could continue.[518]

Reporters later asked the judge for a comment on the general's death, and he judiciously remarked, "It was a terrible tragedy."[519]

Early the same morning, Mary Pryor and Frances drove to Shelbyville and were admitted to the dreary cellblock. They were dismayed at both the sight of their beloved uncles behind bars and the news coverage that linked their family name with the word *murderer*. But with Denhardt's death, a chapter in their lives had closed. They would never have to see him again and no longer have to worry whether he would be acquitted of their mother's murder.

Their uncles had spent a restless night. Roy had recently injured his foot falling from a horse, and a doctor was called to the jail to treat him. Outside the barred windows, hundreds of people passed on the street hoping for a glimpse of the brothers. The men hung a blanket from the window to screen them from curious stares. They had been served with murder warrants, but their arraignment was postponed until Friday. It would give Rodes Myers time to attend the general's funeral before he returned to Shelbyville as the lead witness at the examining trial.

On Tuesday, the Garrs were subdued and quiet, and only Jack seemed to be in a jovial mood. When asked if they would pose for photographers, they declined. "At least not until we have time to shave," quipped Jack.[520]

Out-of-state reporters had been calling for information, and the telephones at the jail had been ringing all night. Telegrams of support for the Garr brothers began to arrive along with baskets of food. It was as if royalty had been jailed in Shelbyville. Late on Tuesday afternoon, the Garrs agreed to pose for the photographers gathered outside the jail. A number of them were from outside Kentucky and already in the area to cover the second trial, but their focus now was on an even more sensational news story. Though the brothers agreed to have their photographs made, they refused to make any statements about what had happened the night before. The three men posed solemnly in front of the flashing bulbs, looking weary and uncomfortable with all the attention. They held their jacket lapels and stood straight and unsmiling, staring into the cameras. Doc was gaunt and solemn with his small, clipped mustache; Roy was round-faced and burly; Jack, the handsomest of the trio, sported his fashionable pencil-thin mustache. They looked like members of a Wild West posse who had captured the bad man and agreed to pose afterwards. The photograph was featured in *Life* magazine, and close-up photographs of the brothers appeared in *Newsweek*.[521]

Outside the jail, Main Street teemed with people walking slowly by the Armstrong Hotel and poking their fingers into the stray bullet holes that pitted the walls of nearby buildings. One bullet had even lodged in the wall of the hotel lobby. It was an amazing event for the small town of Shelbyville, and everyone wanted to hear what the Garr brothers would have to say, but they remained silent.

When the reporters shifted their focus to Rodes Myers and bombarded him for interviews, he gladly obliged. Early Tuesday morning, he was awakened at the hotel by a transatlantic telephone call from London, England, and "conversed with the British press about details of the slaying, and then elaborated on what happened as he and the General crossed Sixth and Main Streets in the bright moonlight."[522] Myers described himself as "living on velvet" after his narrow escape from death.[523]

Britain's *London Daily Herald* had covered the case since Verna's death, and blatantly referred to Denhardt's murder as an "honour slaying." "The brothers, reviving the Kentucky 'feud' law, are said to have shot him down rather than risk his acquittal, or his escape from the death penalty."[524]

Myers granted a number of interviews, but on Tuesday afternoon, it was time for him to leave Shelbyville and return the general's body to his family. Driving Denhardt's car, he led the hearse bearing his friend's embalmed body home to Bowling Green.

With the death of Henry Denhardt, only two of the five bright and ambitious children of William and Margaret Geiger Denhardt remained alive. The younger William had died in 1921 after a short illness, and a sister, Minnie Denhardt Moss, died in 1935. The sad task fell to Jesse and Bertha to make funeral arrangements for their youngest brother.

The Denhardts of Bowling Green were as respectable and well liked in their community as the Garrs and Taylors of LaGrange. But while the older Denhardt siblings were conventional, community-minded, and uncontroversial, their youngest brother was stormy and mercurial. Unlike the rest of his quiet, respectable family, trouble seemed to follow Henry Denhardt, and his overbearing manner did nothing to discourage it. The general had made many enemies over the years, and storms followed wherever he went, but no one could have predicted such a violent and disgraceful end to his life. In Bowling Green, grief-stricken Bertha and Jesse Denhardt made arrangements for two funerals. One would be a private service for close friends and family, the other an elaborate military funeral. When Rodes Myers arrived in town followed by the hearse, Denhardt's body was taken for private viewing to the home he had shared with Bertha during the summer.

On Thursday morning, family and friends gathered at the house for a private service. A family friend stood near the piano and plaintively sang an old hymn that was the general's favorite, "When the Roll is Called Up Yonder."

> When the trumpet of the Lord shall sound, and time shall be no more,
>> And the morning breaks eternal bright and fair;
>> When the saved of earth shall gather over on the other shore,
>> And the roll is called up yonder, I'll be there.
>> When the roll is called up yonder,
>> When the roll is called up yonder,
>> When the roll is called up yonder,
>> When the roll is called up yonder, I'll be there.

The *Courier-Journal* reported on the service and quoted some of Rev. Dr. George W. Cheek's brief message: "We are not here to speculate where the soul of this man may be today. That is a secret between him and God. Our concern is with our friends who are left. I shall say nothing of the manner of his death. But in the name of Jesus, who also was slain by his enemies, I beg the friends here with us to remember the words spoken from the cross: 'Father, forgive them, for they know not what they do.' The little group of perhaps fifty persons sat on the wide porch, in the kitchen, and in the hall. Only the quiet, uncontrolled weeping of the dead man's sister broke the silence."[525]

At the conclusion of the private service, Denhardt's body, formally dressed in full military uniform, was moved to the Denhardt Armory, named for him during more illustrious days. A flag on the armory roof flew at half-staff as the general lay in state. Conspicuous among the attendees were a large group of state and national politicians. Two former Kentucky governors attended: Governor Fields in whose administration Denhardt served as lieutenant governor, and Governor Ruby Laffoon, under whose orders he "invaded" Harlan as adjutant general. There were state senators, a United States senator, congressmen, and judges. Rodes Myers, Clarke Otte, and John Berry were among those who served as pallbearers or honorary pallbearers.

There had been a dance at the armory the night before, and the second-floor auditorium was hastily prepared for the funeral. White ribbons adorned rows of chairs, and massed flowers covered the auditorium stage. The general's flag-draped coffin was open for viewing, and reporters snapped photographs as people filed past. The general looked composed and serene, his hands crossed over his torso. His mouth held just the trace of a smile that seemed to say, "I died with my secret; now you'll never know."

The *Courier-Journal* reporter described the scene: "Later the chairs filled with women in bright cottons who fanned themselves and talked in undertones; with a sprinkling of veterans and shirt-sleeved Negroes and wide-eyed children who tiptoed past the coffin with held breath, then fairly ran for the back of the hall."[526]

Two members of the local National Guard units stood as sentries at the casket. Eight were designated for guard duty and rotated every fifteen minutes. Approximately one hundred guardsmen participated in the rites. The services included a review of Denhardt's life, remarks by the chaplain of the 149th Infantry, and music by the 149th Infantry band.

After the funeral, the military units formed on the street in front of the armory. The infantry band stepped out first in the funeral procession playing a Chopin dirge. The hearse bearing Denhardt's body followed them through the thronged and dusty streets of Bowling Green. They marched through the gates of Fairview Cemetery to the Denhardt plot near the front, and formed ranks with their weapons beside an open grave prepared for the general. Raising their rifles, they fired three volleys over the grave as a tribute. The irony of the final salute of gunfire was not lost on one reporter covering the event. "Three volleys of gunfire over an open grave fittingly ended the last journey today of Brig. Gen. Henry H. Denhardt, Warren County's stormiest citizen."[527]

In Fairview Cemetery, the general would rest with his parents, brother William, and sister Minnie near the large impressive stone that marked the family plot with the name "Denhardt."

When Denhardt's brother, William "Will" Denhardt died in 1921, there was a genuine outpouring of sadness and grief among the people of his hometown. A friend who wrote a eulogy for the *Bowling Green Times-Journal* declared, "Every employee in his office down to the newsboy knew "Mr. Will" for a gentleman and loved and respected him. Hundreds of friends throughout the city were shocked and grieved as there passed from lip to lip the fatal message 'Will Denhardt is dead.'"[528]

The death of Henry Denhardt did not evoke the same outpouring of grief. Reporters covering the event noted that the people outside his family and close associates watched the funeral spectacle with apathy and curiosity.

"Bowling Green did not conspicuously mourn the passing of its most widely known citizen. Clerks and shopkeepers stood in their doorways to watch the cortege file by. A luncheon club startled the official mourners grouped in the lobby of the Helm Hotel by a burst of hearty laughter and singing at the opening of their meeting. Men and women filed by the coffin speculating in conversational tones on the invisible bullet holes. On street corners and at restaurant tables, men discussed the Garr brothers with interest and conjecture but with no active condemnation."[529]

The *Chicago Daily Times* reported that "one survey by newspapermen covering the funeral, indeed showed widespread feeling that the general 'got what he deserved.'"[530]

For months, the reporters had been relentless in their articles about Denhardt, and they continued to be merciless after his death. In response, Bertha and Jesse Denhardt issued a lengthy statement in the Bowling Green newspaper as co-owners and publishers: "Shaken and hurt and distraught as we were by the news of his murder, we could not have conceived the possibility that the metropolitan newspapers of this and other states would have pursued his honored remains into the very grave by the publication of posthumous stories that carry their malice and falsity in every line."[531] In their statement, Bertha and Jesse Denhardt made it very clear that regardless of what was said and published, they supported and believed in their brother. "We have known, honored and loved him longer than has anyone else and have understood him better."[532] They reviewed Denhardt's younger life, and his decision to become a lawyer. "As our father had been a shoemaker by trade, so our older brother apprenticed himself and became a typesetter, then printer and publisher. Our younger brother Henry was cast in a more ambitious mould [*sic*]. With the help of the rest of us he went through college and was graduated in the law."[533] They continued with a review of his distinguished service in the military, and his life as a lieutenant governor and state adjutant general:

> During the last administration, he was adjutant general. This administration was almost one continuous warfare and his loyal soul knew but one command, his governor. Following the defeat of his faction in the primary, in which he had done his part with all the energy and bitterness that Kentuckians have accustomed themselves to in any party warfare, he supported his party through his newspaper in the general election and had retired to his farm as had many a soldier and statesman before him, hoping to be secure in the increase of his flocks and the bounty from his lands. This hoped-for utopia was destroyed by a tragedy in which he was unwillingly and unwittingly a part. His innocence of any criminal part in the events of that fateful night were beyond a doubt proven by the unquestioned testimony of two simple, honest men, Mr. Baker, a farmer, and Mr. Hundley, a barber.[534]

The Denhardt siblings believed their brother and rested their faith in his innocence on George Baker's excited statement. They also adopted the general's position that had he been anyone else, the case against him would never have gone to the grand jury. It was "a persistent group which had always desired to destroy him and which finally brought him to a brutal death."[535] But they refused to become involved in a murder trial against the Garr brothers and provide an attorney to aid in their prosecution. They declared that they would leave it to the legal system to dispense justice in what they called "an obviously cold-blooded murder."[536] They relied on the court to enforce the law properly, and if it failed to do so, there would remain a stain upon the dignity of the state of Kentucky that would "degrade" it in the eyes of the nation. "We have no intention of participating in another 'Roman holiday' such as disgraced the previous trials. We believe faithfully that when it was written 'Vengeance is mine, saith the Lord' that the Lord meant what he wrote."[537]

The article was an obituary, a family response to Denhardt's murder, and a condemnation of the press. It was stirring, but ultimately the spin of a grieving family showing public support for their deceased brother. While Bertha and Jesse openly supported Denhardt and gave him an ostentatious public funeral, the rest of the state viewed his death quite differently. Some questioned whether the flag over the capitol in Frankfort should be lowered to half-staff in tribute, customary in the death of a former state official. Lieutenant Governor Keen Johnson, acting as governor while Chandler vacationed in Mexico, settled the issue. The flag was lowered to half-staff for Denhardt on the day of his funeral.

Major Joseph Kelly, Denhardt's old enemy, responded to an inquiry about the proper courtesies to be extended at the death of a brigadier general. "Accordingly all of these honors were tendered to General Denhardt in Bowling Green, where his command had its headquarters. In addition, on the day of General Denhardt's funeral, the flag was lowered at half-mast on the State Capitol Building at Frankfort, between the hours of one o'clock and sundown."[538]

True to their published statement, Bertha and Jesse Denhardt did not hire an attorney and stayed away from the chaotic scene in Shelbyville. Like the Garrs and Taylors in April, they placed their faith in the legal system to see that justice was done. The Denhardt family, and the rest of the country waited to see what would happen when the Garr brothers were tried for murder.

Chapter 30

PUBLIC SENTIMENT

On Wednesday, two days after Denhardt's death, Ballard Clarke requested bond for the Garr brothers. He argued fervently to County Judge Harry Walters that there were Oldham County men ready and willing to pay the bond regardless of the cost. But Walters denied his request. The brothers were officially charged with willful murder, and they would have to remain in jail until the court heard their stories at the examining trial. The news was disappointing to Roy, Doc, and Jack, who spent the long days receiving visitors, and reading the letters and telegrams that continued to pour in from all over the nation. On Wednesday, their bail was denied, but the brothers also received some very good news. Attorney Ralph Gilbert announced he would join in their defense.

Ralph Waldo Emerson Gilbert was the man everyone wanted on their side. He had practiced law in Shelbyville since 1901, and been a Shelby County judge, two-term member of Congress, and a former state representative. He was currently a state senator and the Senate floor leader for Governor Chandler. Gilbert also had a reputation as a formidable attorney. Henry Denhardt had tried to hire him for his defense team in November 1936, but Gilbert declined. In the Garr brother's case, both the prosecution and the defense wanted Gilbert on their side, but he made a popular decision when he chose to defend the brothers.

A Chicago newspaper was quick to point out that with Gilbert defending the brothers it appeared state politics was entering the murder case. "Gilbert is Gov. A. B. ("Happy") Chandler's floor leader in the state senate. Denhardt was Chandler's bitterest enemy. Thus the picture is one dramatic in the extreme—"Happy" Chandler's floor leader to defend the Garr brothers . . ."[539] It was, of course, an exaggeration. Denhardt and Chandler had been on different political sides in the past, but it was Chandler who came to Denhardt's rescue and helped him resume his military command. Ralph Gilbert joined the Garrs' defense team with John K. Todd, a Shelbyville attorney with forty years of experience; George L. Willis Jr., a thirty-nine-year-old Shelbyville attorney with a general practice; and Ballard Clarke. The brothers asked for a speedy trial and it looked like they would get their wish. Plans were made to try them during the Shelby County Circuit Court term set to begin on October 4.

Kinsolving was facing a tangled personal and legal web. Roy, Doc, and Jack Garr were his friends, and Roy trained his hunting dogs. He was now in the impossible position of prosecuting them for killing Denhardt, the man he had prosecuted for killing their sister. Kinsolving was adamant that a substitute prosecutor would have to be found. On Thursday, as the general was buried in Bowling Green, Kinsolving travelled to Frankfort to meet with Kentucky Attorney General Hubert Meredith and ask for his help. As attorney general, fifty-seven-year-old Hubert Meredith was also Kentucky's chief prosecutor, and served as chairman of an advisory council that supervised all state prosecutors. Kinsolving asked for Meredith's office to step into the gap left when he resigned from the case, and Meredith agreed. He issued a public statement that he would replace Kinsolving on the case and personally prosecute the Garr brothers. Meredith entered the fray believing that Denhardt's murder was a planned ambush, and he was determined to send the brothers to prison or the electric chair. But he would soon realize that he was an out-of-town, "foreign" attorney stepping into a buzz saw powered by public sentiment. The sympathies of the public and press had always been on the side of the Garr and Taylor families. The slaying of Denhardt did not change their view, and ironically, although the victim in this case, Denhardt would soon be on trial again.

Ballard Clarke assumed the role of spokesman for the brothers. On Thursday, he described them as "ready and rarin' to go," eager to move forward with the examining trial.[540]

"'They did not know that General Denhardt was in Shelbyville,' Mr. Clarke declared. 'Think of all the chances they've had to kill him if they had wanted to. They did not come over here with any idea of that kind in their minds.'"[541]

By mid-week, rumors were flying that the Garr brothers would plead self-defense. When quizzed about the rumors, Clarke replied, "Men don't kill each other for nothing."[542]

Ballard Clarke was accessible to the reporters, and eager to make statements on his clients' behalf. He was nearly as talkative as Rodes Myers, who was quoted a number of times retelling his dramatic story. But not everyone appreciated Myers's public assurances that Denhardt was an innocent man. Shortly after the shooting, Myers reported that he was receiving threatening letters.

The *Courier-Journal* reported, "Three of the letters are anonymous and apparently from the same person, he said. They were mailed on September 21 and are postmarked from Train 94 or 98, Chicago & Alton Railroad. 'Looks like you've gone far enough in Denhardt case if you're smart you'll drop it. DO YOU GET THIS.'"[543]

Another read: "Everyone of any intelligenc [*sic*] know who read your Dash Dash in the newspapers that it is an infamous lie and know that YOU know it. If you had sense enough to keep your mouth sut [*sic*] you might come out better in the long run YOU telling people that Denhardt did not kill the widow you know you are liar and the most people of the state know it . . ."[544]

Another "long and abusive" letter was postmarked from Lebanon, Kentucky, and written by a man who described himself as a veterinarian. The writer included the sentiment: "Sincerely hope Garr brothers will get you and Berry both before this is over. We need more Garr brothers."[545]

The letters were poorly written, but the sentiments were very clear and Myers took them seriously. He was also concerned about threats overheard by friends in Shelbyville. One friend warned him that he had heard someone say Myers "would be dealt with the same as Denhardt, but only nobody would know this time who was responsible."[546] During the investigation of the letters, Myers revealed that it was not the first time he had received threats. During the Denhardt trial, he received a threatening phone call, but "O. C. Dewey, chief of the Louisville bureau of the F.B.I. did not reveal who made the call."[547]

The Garr brothers had suddenly become folk heroes, abruptly and unwillingly thrust into the spotlight in Kentucky and across the nation. They were popularly viewed as common men who performed an uncommon deed when they avenged the murder of their sister and defended her reputation. The letters, threats, and outpouring of public support made it obvious that when Myers returned to testify, he would be walking into a hornet's nest.

On Thursday, the brothers attended a legal conference at George Willis's law office. It was the first time they had been outside since Monday night, and they were reported to be in a good frame of mind and ready for Friday's arraignment and examining trial. A huge crowd was expected in town on Friday. Most of the businesses in LaGrange would be closed so that the locals could drive to Shelbyville and support the brothers.[548]

Judge Walters wisely decided they would need a larger venue

and announced that he would move the hearing to the circuit courtroom in the Shelby County Courthouse. Subpoenas had been issued for witnesses, and everything was in readiness for the latest courtroom drama as Friday, September 24, dawned in Shelbyville.

The two-story, stone Shelby County Courthouse, with its large Corinthian columns and a portico bearing an elaborate stone carving of the scales of justice, was an imposing presence on Main Street. Sweeping stairs climbed to an impressive entrance of double doors that led into a marble-floored hallway. The fortress-like stone jail with its long, narrow windows was located at the rear of the courthouse. The courthouse and jail were a short walk east from where Denhardt died in front of the Armstrong Hotel. Early on Friday morning, a large mob of people climbed the stone stairs and pressed through the front doors of the courthouse. The second-floor courtroom filled early for the scheduled ten o'clock appearance of the Garr brothers. There was a large, supportive crowd of relatives, friends, and neighbors from Oldham County. Mary Pryor and Frances sat near the defense table with their aunt, Juanita Holmes, who had traveled from New York to be with her brothers and nieces.

Rodes Myers made a dramatic arrival accompanied by two state policemen. Myers feared for his life and asked the head of the state police to provide him with armed protection. He would testify as the prosecution's lead witness against the brothers, but he intended to leave Shelbyville immediately afterward.

The Garr brothers arrived in the courtroom together, shaking hands with friends, smiling and waving at people in the crowd who loudly wished them well: "Go get 'em, Roy!" "Keep your heads up, boys!" "We're with y'all!"

Spectators filled the courtroom to capacity, crowded the aisles, and pressed close to the judge's bench. For the next six hours, the crowd would listen intently, spellbound by the witness accounts of the night General Denhardt died. It would be the first time they would hear Doc, Roy, and Jack's version of why they killed him. County Judge Harry Walters entered and took his seat, tapping his gavel. The prosecution would draw first blood. Hubert Meredith called Rodes Myers as his first witness.

Myers was grave and solemn as he took his oath and seat in the witness chair, and his armed guards stood nearby. He described the events of September 20—his arrival with Denhardt at the Armstrong Hotel; the dinner with Otte and Berry in the hotel dining room; the conference between the attorneys in the hotel room; and the stroll to the restaurant for a beer with Denhardt. He recalled the shock of seeing the brothers, shouting, "There are the Garr boys!" and watching as Denhardt suddenly broke into a run. Myers said he saw Roy stand near Denhardt's feet as he lay helpless in the doorway. He heard him say, "You son of a bitch, you killed my sister," and saw him fire a final shot into Denhardt.[549]

"You know of any cause or reason he gave either of them upon that occasion for shooting him?" asked Meredith.

"I do not, sir."

"Did he address any remark to them, or say anything to them?"

"I never heard him say a word."[550]

At this point, a very satisfied Hubert Meredith said, "There is the witness, gentlemen." Ralph Gilbert had no questions and Dr. Lapsley was called as a witness. When asked about his findings, Lapsley was given permission to read his autopsy report into the record. Lapsley confirmed that all three bullets struck the general from the rear.

The next witness was Dr. A. C. Weakley who arrived at the scene shortly after Denhardt was shot. He noted the same bullet wounds described by Lapsley, but gave the opinion that Denhardt died from the shot that entered his brain just behind the left ear. He also believed that the wounds were caused by the same .38 caliber gun.

Meredith called night patrolman Jeptha Tracy to the witness stand. Tracy had been a Shelbyville patrolman for ten years, and on the night of September 20, he was making his usual rounds on the quiet city streets. He heard the gunshots and ran to the hotel. When he arrived, no one was near Denhardt's body. Tracy saw three men walking toward Blakemore's Grocery and he followed them.

"Well, when I got down there, Roy come out the door and he handed me a gun."

"What did he say?" asked Meredith.

"He said, 'I am the man that done the shooting.'"

"What kind of gun did he hand you?"

"He had a .38, nickel-plated, Smith and Wesson hammerless."[551]

Tracy examined the gun and all five chambers were empty. He escorted the three brothers to the jail, and when they arrived, Doc Garr handed him a pistol that was sticking in his belt. Doc's gun appeared to have been recently fired.

Rodes Myers's story that he saw Roy fire the final shot into Denhardt's brain was damaging and had to be addressed. On cross-examination, Gilbert asked hotel proprietor Harry Flood to describe the shots he heard, and whether they were fired rapidly, in quick succession.

"Well now, the way I heard them, they seemed to be about two shots, and then, right after that, seemed to be like six or seven shots, but the two shots separately, four or five more, I couldn't tell exactly."

"I will ask you this direct question," said Gilbert carefully. "Was there a number of shots fired and then an interval and then one shot?"

"And one shot?"

"Yes."

"I didn't hear that."[552]

Gilbert had made his point and moved next into questions

about the day Denhardt and Myers arrived in Shelbyville. He asked Flood if he received any calls at the hotel that day asking whether Denhardt had a reservation.

"No, sir, that is a misrepresentation of the reporters down there, because there was not, because I checked on that."[553]

Flood also recalled that when he walked to the poolroom before the shooting, he did not see an automobile parked on Sixth Street. The Garr brothers were evidently not parked and waiting in their car for Denhardt to return to the hotel.

"Your Honor, the prosecution has no further witnesses," said Meredith.

Everything was going well in Meredith's case against the brothers. The testimony was overwhelming that Roy and Doc shot Denhardt in the back as he ran for his life. Myers testified that Roy stood over the general, cursed him, and fired a final shot. Meredith felt confident in his case as Gilbert and the defense team prepared to call the Garr brothers to testify. The crowd in the courtroom had thinned as the noon hour and lunchtime approached. Throughout the morning, the Garr brothers sat stoically and "scarcely noticed the witnesses and appeared to pay little attention to the testimony."[554] But the opportunity to give their version of the events of September 20 was rapidly approaching. When the lunch recess ended, Roy, Doc, and Jack would each take the witness stand for the first time.

Chapter 31

MURDER OR SELF-DEFENSE?

Roy was the first brother called by Ralph Gilbert to testify. As word spread on the streets outside, people rushed into the courthouse, jamming into every inch of available space in the courtroom.

During his examining trial and murder trial in New Castle, Henry Denhardt had faced a hostile courtroom crowd. In contrast, the people who crowded into the Shelby County courtroom for the Garr trial were curious, but also sympathetic, respectful, and supportive. Roy Garr faced family, friends, neighbors, and the townspeople of Shelbyville and LaGrange.

He also faced the local and out-of-state reporters who followed the case closely, but did not condemn the Garrs. Their articles were not filled with the negative, insulting, and sometimes outlandish personal comments they had used to describe Henry Denhardt: "He is a bulbous man, General Denhardt, the stocky type become padded and somewhat saggy from the flesh pots. . . . His once square jaws are now loose flaps of skin over soft flesh. . . . His eyes are so pale as to be scarcely discernable, even at a short distance. The Denhardt ears are out of proportion . . . they are small, almost lobeless, womanish."[555]

Overall, the Garr brothers fared well in the newspapers. As a witness during Denhardt's trial, Roy was frustrated by the constant objections of the attorneys, and his inability to say what he had come to say. But this time, he was the defendant, and everyone in the courtroom was waiting to hear his story. It was clearly Roy Garr's moment, and the crowd loved him.

Roy recalled that he first met Henry Denhardt at Verna's home in early summer, 1936. Later, when Denhardt was prosecuted for her murder, he attended the trial every day and was active in the investigation.

"Had you, or anyone at your request called up to learn the whereabouts of General Denhardt?" asked Ralph Gilbert.

"No, sir, I never even thought about calling . . ."[556]

On the night of Denhardt's shooting, Roy stopped at H. B. Kinsolving's home to talk about the trial set to start the next day. Roy said that they discussed the rumor that Denhardt would attempt to besmirch Verna's character during the second trial. They also discussed potential new trial witnesses.

"Well, one of them was Mrs. Webster that wanted to go on as a witness and say that she heard Denhardt threaten to kill Verna, that if she didn't do it, whatever it was Mrs. Webster overheard, he told her he would kill her."[557]

"Did you know that he, or any of his attorneys were in Shelbyville?"

"No, sir, I hadn't given him or his attorneys any thought about being there."

"Either of your brothers know he was in Shelbyville?"

"Not to my knowledge."[558]

Roy described the events leading up to the shooting and the chaotic scene on Main Street. His voice broke as he spoke of seeing Verna just before he started shooting. He remembered watching Denhardt tumble to the ground in the doorway, turning to look for his brothers, and seeing them standing in the street.

"Did you ever go up to General Denhardt's body and place a pistol near him and shoot him in the head or anywhere else?"

"No, sir, I did not."

"Did you ever shoot him or approach his body after he fell in the door?"

"I did not."[559]

Gilbert returned his questioning to the point where Roy heard someone say, "There are the Garr boys!" Roy thought his head was down when he heard the words, but he looked up quickly.

"It scared me, and scared me when I saw old Denhardt reaching for his hip pocket."[560]

Gilbert asked Roy why he was armed that night. Roy replied that after the scene at the Eminence diner, and hearing of Denhardt's threats, he typically carried a gun when he was anywhere around LaGrange or Louisville.

On cross-examination, Meredith asked Roy if he was not angered that new evidence reflecting on his sister's character would probably be introduced at the trial.

"No sir, it worried me, but I knew nobody would believe anything against her."[561]

"Didn't you feel outraged, Mr. Garr, at the thought that such evidence might be introduced?" he asked Roy.

"No, sir, because I knew we had evidence to send him to the electric chair this time. I knew that."

"But did you feel outraged?" Meredith continued.

"Why sure."

"At the idea he would attempt such a thing after you thought he killed your sister?"

"I naturally would be, why naturally I would be."[562]

Meredith also questioned Roy about the lunchtime scene in the Eminence diner.

"Don't you know he kept his face to you because he was afraid you might shoot him, isn't that correct, now?"

"No, sir, we didn't have a gun or pocket knife or nothing."

"There was nothing to keep him from shooting you then if he wanted to, was there?"

"I suppose not, but he sure did act like he was going to."

"You construed that to mean he was trying to kill you because he backed away from you and left immediately?"

"Sure."[563]

Meredith asked Roy about his fateful decision to return to Blakemore's Grocery after the brothers had already visited and left.

"You knew when you were there you wanted him to attend the trial."

"That was just an afterthought. I asked Doc—"

"When did that afterthought occur, before or after the killing?"[564]

"Objection!" shouted Ralph Gilbert, jumping to his feet. The courtroom buzzed with excitement. Judge Walters banged his gavel and called for order. "Now . . . Mr. Garr, please respond to the question."

"After I left I just thought, wonder if I told Blake to be sure and be there in the morning."[565]

Meredith entered the case at the last minute, and it was obvious that he was not familiar with landmarks in town. He asked Roy, "What street is the hotel on? I am a stranger here."[566]

If he did not know the prominent location of the Armstrong Hotel, he could not visualize where the Garr brothers parked on Sixth Street. As his cross-examination continued, Meredith asked Roy questions that anyone familiar with the area would already have known. He even asked him the width of Main Street, and Roy told him he had no idea. Meredith also asked if Denhardt's back was to him when he first spotted him on the street.

"He was facing me just like you are," replied Roy.

"Didn't he turn and run like a turkey the minute he saw you?"

"No, sir, he threw his hand on that hip."

"And didn't he turn and run from you, and you pursued him and shot him three times in the back when he wasn't doing anything on this earth to you, isn't that the truth of it?"

"I know he kept that hand in his hip pocket, and I went to shooting, I really went to shooting, too."[567]

Meredith had done his best to rattle and confuse Roy, but he was a calm and very believable witness. Roy testified that he did not like Denhardt; knew he killed Verna; did not know Denhardt was in Shelbyville; and believed Denhardt had a gun in his pocket. When it was finally over, he left behind the impression of an honest man confronted with a confusing, threatening situation on a shadowy street where he made a split-second decision based on fear. Meredith finally shook his head, said, "No more questions," and stared at the floor as he walked back to the table.

Gilbert asked the youngest brother, thirty-seven-year-old Jack Garr to come to the front of the courtroom and take the witness chair.

"Did you come to Shelbyville expecting to have any trouble?" Gilbert asked.

"Not a bit in this world, no, sir."

"Were you armed?"

"No, sir."[568]

Jack's account of the events leading up to the shooting did not vary from Roy's testimony. He recalled that Roy decided he had to go back to Blakemore's Grocery to be certain his friend would be at the trial. He listened from the back seat as Doc and Roy argued good naturedly about Roy having so much business that they would never get home. But Doc stopped near the corner of Sixth Street so Roy could run back inside and speak with Blakemore. Doc climbed out of the driver's seat to go with him.

"Had you seen General Denhardt at that time?"

"No, sir."

"Did you know he was in Shelbyville at that time?"

"No, sir."

"Did you, or to your knowledge, either of your brothers, call here and ascertain if he was here, or expecting to be here?"

"No, sir."[569]

Jack stayed behind with the car, and as his brothers walked toward Blakemore's, he heard someone say the name "Garr" in a loud voice. By the time he reached them, several shots had already been fired. He recalled seeing Denhardt's body lying in the hotel doorway. Myers had turned to run another direction and was standing in the middle of Main Street. None of them approached Denhardt's lifeless body in the doorway.

Ralph Gilbert nodded at Meredith and said, "You may ask the witness." He walked back to the defense table.

Meredith was certain the Garrs had planned Denhardt's murder, and that they had more than one motive to kill him. They believed he killed their sister and they wanted to avenge her death. They were concerned that if Denhardt was tried again, he would slur Verna's character. But Roy and Jack were convincing witnesses, and the testimony of Jack mirrored the account offered by Roy. Meredith knew he had his hands full as he approached Jack Garr for cross-examination. He asked him why Doc got out of the car with Roy if he did not believe it was necessary to tell Blakemore to be at the trial.

"Did it take both of them to tell him that?" asked Meredith.

"Well, I don't know that."

"What did Doc go for?"

"Just to go with him," Jack replied.

"Doc said it wasn't necessary to go, and yet he went with him?"

"Yes, sir."

"Don't you know, Mr. Garr, that you had seen General Denhardt and knew he was here and parked there to get a chance to contact him?"

"No, sir."[570]

At the end of Jack's testimony, Meredith had done his best, but he could not find any weaknesses to exploit. Only one brother remained for him to challenge. If any of the brothers would crack under the pressure of cross-examination, it would be Doc Garr.

Ballard Clarke, Doc's friend and attorney, questioned him. Doc readily admitted to continuing mental problems from his service in the war.

"I will ask you if following your service in the army you suffered a nervous breakdown at any time thereafter?"

"Well, yes, I did. I had a slight breakdown."[571]

After Denhardt's spring trial, Doc continued his veterinary work in Oldham and the adjoining counties. He had not seen Denhardt or had any contact with him since the end of the trial.

"Had you boys ever been to Shelbyville before?" asked Clarke.

"Yes, we have."

"Much or little?"

"A right smart."

"Did you ever come over to see Captain Kinsolving and Ryon Blakemore before in connection with this case?"

"Yes, sir."

"You and your brothers were assisting at that time, still interested in the prosecution of this man who was charged with the death of your sister?"

"Very much so, yes, sir."[572]

Doc also denied any knowledge that Denhardt and his attorneys were in Shelbyville. He admitted that he feared Denhardt and was aware of his reputation with a gun.

"I have always heard of him as being a dangerous man, heard of him, he draws pistols on people frequently and like of that."[573]

When the shooting started, Doc saw Rodes Myers in the street, and ran to cover him in case he had a gun.

"Did your brother, Jack, have a pistol with him that night?"

"No, sir, he did not."

"Did you or your brother, Roy Garr, go up into the door of the hotel and shoot Henry Denhardt as he lay there in the door?"

"I did not."

"Did your brother, Roy Garr?"

"If he did, I didn't see him and I was taking pretty close watch on him," said Doc.[574]

Doc said they were very upset after the shooting and walked to Blakemore's Grocery to see if the door was open. But the store was closed and the door locked.

"Turned around and started up the street and Roy said, 'We had better see the law, I guess,' and I said, 'Well, Jack wasn't in it,' just that way, and I told the officer after Roy gave him his pistol, I started talking to him, telling him that Jack wasn't in it. He said, 'Well, he was with you, he can go along, too.' I said, 'All right.'"[575]

Roy immediately surrendered his weapon, but Doc kept his gun until they reached the jail. When the jailer asked him if he was armed, Doc pulled out his pistol and handed it to him.

Meredith had one last opportunity to crack the Garr brothers that day, and he started his cross-examination of Doc where Ballard Clarke had left off on direct.

"Had no desire to, did you?" said Meredith sarcastically.

"Well, I didn't especially love him."

"Had no desire to hurt him, did you?"

"No, I—"

"And so you thought he killed your sister, is that right?"

"I thought he killed my sister."[576]

Doc said he was armed that night because he would be in Shelbyville after dark, the trial was getting ready to start, and he wanted to protect himself. In the past, it had never been his practice to carry a firearm, but after hearing the rumors of threats made by Denhardt, he was alarmed enough to keep his pistol close. But he denied that he had any intention of shooting Denhardt. The brothers did not discuss whether they were carrying weapons; Doc did not know Roy had a gun, and he assumed Roy did not know he had a pistol. Doc usually carried his pistol in the glove compartment of his car, but placed it in his pocket when the brothers were visiting in Blakemore's Grocery. Meredith hammered Doc about the pistol. How did he know Jack was unarmed, but did not know whether Roy had a gun? Doc replied that Jack did not own a pistol.

"Well, now, why did you put your pistol in your pocket when you went into Blakemore's?"

"Well, I generally want to be safe. I didn't feel safe anytime."[577]

The gun remained in the glove compartment of his car throughout the day until he walked into Blakemore's Grocery that evening. Meredith asked him why he felt it necessary to carry the gun into the store if he was among friends and did not expect Denhardt to be there.

"Might not have been in there, but might have been out when I come out."[578]

Meredith's continued probing about Doc's gun raised an interesting question. If the brothers were visiting friends in Blakemore's, and had no inkling that Denhardt was in Shelbyville, why did they feel it necessary to carry guns into the store? For the first time, and with the most vulnerable of the brothers, Meredith began to raise questions about their intentions that night. He asked another interesting question. If Doc did not feel it was necessary to accompany Roy into Kinsolving's house earlier that evening, why did he think it was necessary to accompany him into Blakemore's Grocery the second time?

"Just to be going, just two brothers going over there. That is all," replied Doc.

"Did you think he could have made that final request?"

"Yes, sir. I could get out and walk around, too. I know people in Shelbyville. May see people I knew."

"You didn't go out to see anybody you knew, did you?"

"No, sir."[579]

Meredith was unable to shake him. Doc held to his story that he got out of the car because Roy asked him to go, and because he just wanted to go along with him. Meredith also queried Doc about where he parked the automobile on Sixth Street. He would not give up on the possibility that the brothers deliberately parked their car on a shadowy side street when they could have parked on Main Street. Doc testified that there were cars along the street in front of the hotel, and they would have to park a distance away. He also gave the excuse that there was a hill, "and if your brakes are not so good, it is dangerous to park your car there."[580] When Meredith asked him if there was anything wrong with his brakes, Doc replied, "Not necessarily when I don't park on a hill. I would rather not, might forget to put a brake on."[581]

As a witness, Doc was very calm, and always had a ready, if somewhat odd reply to Meredith's questions. At times, he appeared to be toying with the prosecutor, and he was a difficult witness on cross-examination. Meredith asked him where Jack was when the shooting stopped. Doc shrugged his shoulders and said, "He was around there somewhere."[582]

Meredith managed to make a point that the .45 Colt pistol was quite large, and would not have been easy to conceal or carry in a pocket. Doc testified that he usually carried it under his vest. But on the night of Denhardt's shooting, he had tucked the gun in his pants where it was readily accessible. When Meredith finally signaled that he was finished with Doc Garr, the testimony of the three brothers was complete. Roy and Jack were solid, convincing witnesses, and it was impossible for the prosecutor to crack their testimony. Meredith had come close to making inroads with Doc's testimony, but ultimately he stood up under the pressure. When Doc left the witness chair and returned to the table to sit with his brothers, only two witnesses remained.

Gilbert called H. B. Kinsolving to corroborate Roy's testimony that he met with him on the night of September 20. Kinsolving also disclosed that during the afternoon, Sergeant Messmer telephoned with news about the planned conference between Denhardt and his attorneys in Shelbyville. Messmer spoke with him about a scheme to place a Dictaphone next to the hotel room where the meeting was planned. To the best of his knowledge, the Garr brothers knew nothing about the scheme. When he spoke with Roy that evening, Kinsolving did not reveal any of his conversation with Messmer. He denied telling Roy that Denhardt was in Shelbyville. When Gilbert was finished, Meredith shook his head, "No questions, Your Honor."

Kinsolving emphatically denied telling Roy that Denhardt was in Shelbyville. But the Garr brothers were his friends, and it is hard to believe that he would not warn them to be careful or stay out of town. Denhardt was usually armed, and if the Garr brothers were not, it could have been deadly for them.

After six hours, the examining trial was drawing to a close and the final witness, former sheriff John Dawson Buckner was called to testify. Buckner was leaving the Shelby Theater on Main Street with his wife when he heard two shots ring out close together. He turned and saw what he thought was a group of four men running. Initially, he believed the shots were fired from an automobile approaching the hotel on Main Street. He saw Denhardt fall in the doorway, but did not see Rodes Myers holding his hands in the air. Buckner's testimony offered little more than the earlier witnesses who were present, heard the gunfire, and saw a confusing melee under the streetlights. When Buckner was dismissed, the only issue remaining was whether the Garr brothers would return to their homes on bond or stay in jail. The attorneys stood to argue their positions for and against bond, and the crowd waited anxiously.

"Throughout the long, hot day the crowd had sat tense and absorbed by the testimony of the three brothers, who related in unhurried, almost deadly calm manner how their path chanced to cross that of General Denhardt here Monday night and how two of them fired at him when he reached for his hip pocket," the *Courier-Journal* reported.[583]

At the end of the day, they listened as Ralph Gilbert declared, "Mr. Myers told it in a way it could not have possibly happened. I do not accuse him of perjury, but in his excitement, he confused the situation. There was not a series of shots and a pause and then that one lone shot."

He argued vehemently in favor of granting bond to the brothers. "Here are three citizens of an adjoining county who stand high in their community. Whether or not General Denhardt killed their sister in cold blood, the facts are she was in his presence and only in his presence when she came to a horrible death. Here are three virile, manly brothers, whose standing and reputation for right-doing is such that folks who know them have come in great numbers."[584]

Hubert Meredith argued just as vehemently against bond, determined to persuade the judge that the general's murder was planned. "Now the shoe's on the other foot. They took the law into their own hands and now they come in here with this old flimsy about reaching for his pocket. If ever there was a plain case of premeditated murder, this is it."[585]

Gilbert countered. "If these boys had been ambushing, waiting for Denhardt, they would have seen him first, not him seeing them first and running toward them. Why, two members of the general's counsel are the crack pistol shots of this state."[586]

The arguments for and against bail raged back and forth between Gilbert and Meredith, with Meredith arguing "not to turn these men loose because of maudlin sentiment," and Gilbert claiming that Denhardt was known to be overbearing and did not stop for anyone if he wanted to carry out his objective.[587]

Meredith scorned the possibility of a chance encounter in

Shelbyville. "We know why this killing occurred. The judge knows. Everybody knew before they came here. They killed Denhardt because they believed he killed their sister."[588]

The spectators crowding into the aisles and almost onto the judge's bench hung on every word and silently pulled for the judge to grant bail to the brothers. When the attorneys finally nodded that they were finished, Judge Walters thanked them and warned the courtroom that when he gave his decision, there were to be no demonstrations. But when Walters announced that he would grant the brothers' bond, the spectators exploded in "fervid, sustained hand-clapping that utterly deluged the thirty-year-old courthouse. Yells, unbridled, went up in various parts of the courtroom and hundreds of neighbors and friends crowded to the table where sat the three brothers, Roy Garr, Dr. E. S. Garr and Jack Garr."[589]

Mary Pryor and Frances rushed to the table to hug and kiss their uncles. There was wild excitement in the courthouse, and it left no doubt where the community stood on the murder of Henry Denhardt.

Six men filed into Judge Walter's office to sign bonds of twenty thousand dollars each for Roy and Doc Garr, and ten thousand dollars for Jack. For the first time, the Garr brothers spoke with the press.

"I'm awful happy to go home. This is the way I had hoped it would be," said Roy.[590]

A reporter wrote that "Dr. E. S. Garr, the frail veterinarian said, 'I feel like a million dollars. I feel better than I have in the last ten months. I'm going home to see mother.'"[591]

Jack Garr told the press that he planned to return home to Ohio and said, "I feel like they do. I feel like those people did in that courtroom and they know the difference between right and wrong."[592]

The Garr brothers left Shelby County as free men that night. Of course, it was only temporary because County Attorney Coleman Wright declared that he would ask a grand jury for indictments on October 4. But on the night of the examining trial, they left the dismal Shelby County Jail behind and returned home. They would be back in another week when a grand jury would decide whether to indict them for willful murder.

Chapter 32

A SEARCH FOR COURAGEOUS AND FAIR-MINDED MEN

On October 4, a familiar figure dressed in black robes entered the Shelby County courtroom and moved a brass spittoon within striking distance of the judge's bench. Judge Charles Marshall was the circuit judge for Shelby County. If the twelve men standing uneasily in front of him returned an indictment, he would preside over the trial against the Garr brothers. Eleven of the jurors were farmers, and one man operated a store and served as postmaster in nearby Simpsonville.[593]

There were a number of cases on the docket for the grand jury to consider that day, but only one had drawn the large number of reporters to Marshall's courtroom. He calmly surveyed the twelve men, and turned his attention to the printed form on his desk. *"Commonwealth of Kentucky vs. E. S. Garr, Roy Garr, and Jack Garr"* was typed at the top in bold letters. It was a strange reversal of circumstances. For nearly two weeks in late April and early May, Marshall had watched the three brothers from where they sat facing him near Kinsolving's table. The defendant in that trial was now the victim, and the three brothers were charged with willful murder, the same charge returned against General Denhardt in January. It carried a penalty of death or life in prison. Once again, the eyes of Kentucky and the nation were on his courtroom, and

Judge Marshall felt the solemnity of the moment as he turned a stern eye toward his grand jurors and formally addressed them.

"This is a democratic form of government and should be held as such by all people," he said. "Bureaucracy is controlled by a group of citizens, but democracy is managed by all the people. The followers of bureaucracy are continually seeking to undermine the government and destroy its aims. We are governed by a constitution which every citizen should read and study; it is flexible to reach everyone's condition." Marshall warned of the spread of "fascism, communism, and Hitlerism," and his concern that "unless the people wake up, these forms of government are liable to spread."[594] He told the grand jurors that they must be fair and impartial and return indictments if an offense was committed. He said that if they failed in their duty, "they really were guilty of treasonable acts against the government."[595] At the end of his speech, he was satisfied that he had thoroughly warned and admonished them.

Marshall watched as the men of the grand jury filed out of the courtroom to begin their work. During the first afternoon, they called several witnesses including Patrolman Jeptha Tracy, Harry Flood, Coroner Lapsley, and John Dawson Buckner. Attorneys, reporters, and spectators watched intently as each witness disappeared into the jury room and left a short time later. By the time the jurors finished for the day, it was late afternoon. They left the courthouse to return to their homes.

The next morning, there was a brief sensation when Rodes Myers arrived by taxi from Louisville. Myers was the final witness and testified for nearly an hour before quickly leaving Shelbyville. Later that afternoon, the atmosphere was tense and expectant as the jurors filed into the courtroom. They reported indictments in two other cases, but there was no word on an indictment against the Garr brothers. The attorneys for both sides waited as the hours slowly passed.

At one point, County Attorney Coleman Wright intercepted a mysterious postcard addressed to the foreman. It read, "I think the Garr brothers did justice; they ought to go free."[596] Evidently, the postcard also expressed the sentiments of some of the grand jurors. Once again, they finished for the day and left for their homes. It was beginning to appear that something very unusual was happening; the grand jury was deadlocked.

That evening, Ballard Clarke walked to the Armstrong Hotel and knocked at the door of the room where Roy and Jack Garr were waiting. Clarke explained the odd situation to the brothers. If the grand jury failed to return an indictment, the case could be called again in the future with another grand jury. The brothers wanted speedy justice. They did not want to be left waiting for another grand jury. Clarke decided there might be a way to give the grand jury a nudge if Judge Marshall, Hubert Meredith, and Coleman Wright all agreed to his plan.

The next day, while Roy and Jack waited for news in the hotel lobby, the grand jury members argued and paced the floor of the jury room. Nine of the twelve jurors had to agree for an indictment, but they were deadlocked. Ballard Clarke approached Judge Marshall with his plan. He asked the judge if it would be possible to send a note to the grand jury. Judge Marshall paused and rubbed his chin as he considered the unusual request. He finally agreed to the note if the prosecution had no objections.

The *Oldham Era* reported, "In a statement made public shortly after the conference Clarke said, 'We requested the county attorney to insist that the grand jury return some indictment or dismiss the case.' Clarke said he and other members of the defense believed the grand jury had ample time to form some definite opinion and that the Garr brothers did not want the case continued to a later grand jury."[597]

Coleman Wright returned to the jury room with a handwritten message from Ballard Clarke. Within the hour, the foreman suddenly appeared at the door and whispered to a guard, "Please have Mr. Wright come in immediately before they change their minds."[598] A short time later, the jury trooped into the courtroom and lined up beside the judge's bench. The foreman handed a copy of the joint indictment to Judge Marshall, and Marshall solemnly announced, "Gentlemen, this indictment charges willful murder against Roy Garr, Dr. E. S. Garr, and Jack Garr.[599] When he looked at the jurors and asked if the paper he held was a true bill, each man nodded his assent. Judge Marshall announced that the brothers would be formally arraigned before him the next morning.

It was late Wednesday afternoon when Roy and Jack received news of the indictment and scheduled arraignment. But only two brothers were present to hear the news. Doc was not with them, and his appearance at the examining trial would be his final involvement in the case. Verna's death, Denhardt's trial, and Doc's participation in Denhardt's murder had sent his frail mental condition into a tailspin from which he would never really recover. As his brothers waited for word from the courtroom, Doc was in LaGrange, sedated and under the medical care of Dr. Blaydes. At nine o'clock on Thursday morning, Roy and Jack walked into court for their formal arraignment, and Doc's absence raised a storm of argument from Hubert Meredith that his bond should be forfeited. In response, Ballard Clarke filed an affidavit from Dr. Blaydes with the court.

"The affidavit from Dr. Blaydes set out that Dr. Garr had suffered 'mental disorders' over a period of years and had been hospitalized," the *Courier-Journal* reported. "It stated Dr. Garr was of 'a highly nervous temperament, easily excitable and at the present time is a person of unsound mind; that he is irrational and has hallucinations and illusions and is now confined to his home near LaGrange, under influence of opiates.' Further, the physician's affidavit said it was impossible to determine the result of Dr. Garr's present mental condition and that it might be necessary to confine him to an institution."[600]

Meredith stubbornly argued that Doc's bond should be forfeited, and that the brothers were not eligible for bond because they were indicted for willful murder. "They shot a man three times in the back while he was running from them. It is our humble judgment that the evidence is strong and the presumption is very great," Meredith declared.[601]

Judge Marshall nodded. He asked the attorneys to wait while he read the transcript from the examining trial, and two hours later, he returned with his decision. The *Oldham Era* reported, "Before announcing he would grant bond, Judge Marshall said: 'The facts as shown in the record of the examining trial indicate that there may be a less charge than willful murder against the defendants. There is indication that they were in such a state of mind that they committed this act in sudden heat and passion. These questions are to be tried by a jury.'"[602] Marshall also pointed out that Jack's only connection to the murder was his presence at the scene. Over Meredith's strenuous objections, he granted the brothers bond. But Marshall agreed with Meredith that under Kentucky law, there was nothing to do but forfeit Doc's bond, and with his current mental state, there was no guarantee that he could ever be tried. Marshall entered an order setting Doc's trial for February 1, 1938, and issued a warrant for his future appearance which was mailed to the Oldham County Sheriff's office. Although Marshall agreed that the law required Doc's current bond would have to be forfeited, his bondsmen would not have to make a reply unless he failed to appear in February.[603]

Ballard Clarke requested that the judge set the earliest trial date possible. Marshall nodded, and Meredith did not object when the start of the trial was set for Monday, October 18. The murder trial against the Garr brothers would begin within a week of their arraignment, and less than a month after Denhardt's death.

On the morning of the trial, there was hope that a jury could be selected from two panels of twenty-four jurors that had already been summoned for duty. But when Meredith questioned the first panel of potential jurors, seven men immediately stood aside because they had formed opinions on the case. Another prospective juror asked to be excused because of a physical condition. Eventually, the panels were exhausted, and only seven men were tentatively seated. Marshall ordered Sheriff Barnes to bring in one hundred additional jurors by the next morning and ordered him to find men younger than sixty years of age, and not to ask women to be jurors.

"Mr. Sheriff, you go out and find one hundred men who know their own minds. I command that."[604] With an imperious wave of his hand, the judge sent Sheriff Barnes on his quest. When he released his seven jurors for the evening, Judge Marshall told them they could go to their homes, but they were not to discuss the case with anyone. "I want an absolutely fair and honest trial in this case by courageous and fair-minded men," said the judge.[605]

The next morning, the search for a jury continued when one hundred potential jurors appeared in court, and the attorneys once more began questioning the men. Jack and Roy Garr, neatly dressed in dark blue suits, sat easily at the defense table, talking with attorneys and friends as the tedious process continued. By the time court recessed for lunch, nine jurors had been accepted.

"The entire morning was consumed, and not until seventy-two of the panel of one hundred men brought into court by Sheriff Forest Barnes, Jr., had been exhausted and the defense and prosecution had used most of their peremptory challenges was the jury finally selected," the *Courier-Journal* reported.[606]

There were ten farmers, a retired merchant, and an operator of a truck line who was served by the sheriff as he sat in his truck. The newspaper also noted, "There was also a good deal of conversation, particularly by out-of-state newspapermen, when it developed that one of the jurors, Mr. Brooks, had figured in the fatal shooting in 1931 of a man who had raided his hen house."[607] Curtis Brooks and his neighbor had pursued the chicken thief in a car. When the thief shot at them, Brooks returned fire with a shotgun, killing the thief, but he was eventually acquitted of manslaughter. At the time Brooks was selected for jury duty, Hubert Meredith did not know about the case, but later claimed he would not have challenged the selection of Brooks as a juror.

On Tuesday afternoon when the jury for the Garr case was finally selected and sworn, Judge Marshall addressed the twelve jurors. "This is a serious trial where two men's lives, liberty, and reputation are at stake. It is one of the highest duties that falls to a citizen of this country to determine the guilt or innocence of a fellow citizen."[608]

Coleman Wright rose to his feet and solemnly read the formal indictments charging the three Garr brothers with willful murder, noting that Dr. E. S. Garr was unable to be in court because of mental illness. In response to the judge's query about the defendants' plea, Ralph Gilbert responded with a firm "not guilty," and the trial was finally set to begin.

After all of the supportive telegrams and letters, the public demonstration at the examining trial, the problems in obtaining an indictment and seating a jury, Hubert Meredith and his co-counsel Coleman Wright knew that it would be difficult to convict any of the Garr brothers. But late in the afternoon of October 19, they began their futile quest by calling Rodes Myers to the witness chair.

Chapter 33

A TYPICAL DR. JEKYLL AND MR. HYDE

It was mid-October, Indian summer in Kentucky. The temperatures stayed cool in the evening and morning, but soared higher with the sun during the day. Inside the Shelby County courtroom, the press of people made the room even warmer, and the women in dresses and hats fanned furiously with stiff cardboard fans that advertised local churches, funeral homes, and businesses. A table next to Hubert Meredith and Coleman Wright was reserved for local and out-of-state reporters. Roy and Jack Garr sat at a table on the opposite side of the courtroom with their attorneys, ready to begin the final battle.

The case had begun with three brothers, but only Roy would face the jury's decision. Jack was unarmed the night Denhardt died, and during the trial the charges against him would be dismissed. As for Doc Garr, it would be months before he was to be tried. Rodes Myers took his oath to tell the truth and the largest courtroom crowd in Shelby County history waited expectantly. "All seemed ready for the greatest and perhaps final chapter in a great Kentucky drama," the local newspaper reported.[609]

As Myers gave his account of the night Denhardt died, Coleman Wright wheeled into the courtroom a large blackboard covered with a diagram of Main Street and the intersecting streets. Myers stepped down from the witness chair and used a ruler to point out the route he walked with Denhardt toward the Armstrong Hotel. It was the second time he had told his story in a courtroom, and once again, he held to his version that he witnessed Roy deliver one final shot into Denhardt's head.

George Willis cross-examined Myers. Using the diagram on the blackboard, he was able to show that when Denhardt and Myers crossed Main Street approximately fifteen feet east of the hotel doorway, they were directly in the path of the Garr brothers on Sixth Street. Willis also asked him whether Denhardt was holding anything in his hand as they walked toward the hotel. "No, I didn't see anything," Myers answered.[610]

On the afternoon of the first day, Meredith and Wright called five witnesses from the examining trial. They also called funeral director Everett Hall who carried a large box into the courtroom. During his testimony, he removed Denhardt's bloody blue serge coat, shirt, and underwear, all riddled with bullet holes. At Meredith's request, he held them up for the jury to see. Hall testified that he found a handkerchief, key ring, letter, and a coin purse in the hip pockets of Denhardt's trousers.

The final witness of October 19 was Shelbyville City Patrolman Jeptha Tracy. On cross-examination, George Willis asked him if he saw anything in Denhardt's dead hand. "He had a handkerchief in his hand; it was in his right hand," answered Tracy.[611] Myers had testified that there was nothing in Denhardt's hand as they walked toward the hotel. Tracy testified that upon surrendering, Roy said, "Denhardt reached for his pocket and I beat him to it."[612] With his cross-examination of Tracy, Willis was able to imply that as Denhardt ran across the street he must have reached for his pocket to retrieve the handkerchief.

On Wednesday, the first full day of trial, the exasperated spectators and reporters waited impatiently while the attorneys spent half of the morning session in Judge Marshall's chambers arguing the admissibility of evidence. Throughout the trial, there would be more long delays while the attorneys argued and Judge Marshall made his decisions. A reporter later complained, "The pleasure and entertainment of those who have thronged the Circuit Court room for the four days the Garr bros. have been on trial have been marred by the almost unprecedented amount of time the court has listened to argument of attorneys in chambers. Half the jury's time has hung heavy on their hands as they have set [*sic*] idle in the jury box."[613]

Throughout the rest of Wednesday morning and early afternoon when the attorneys were not arguing in Marshall's chambers, Meredith continued to call his witnesses. None of them offered anything new or definitive in his quest to convict the brothers. Accounts of the gunfire they heard conflicted with Rodes Myers's testimony. Witnesses remembered hearing two shots followed by a pause, and then a fusillade of five shots together. No one heard a final, single gunshot. Young Howard Flood who was behind the cigar counter of the hotel and facing the front door did not see anyone approach Denhardt's body after he fell.

Meredith asked John Berry if he told anyone about the conference with Denhardt in Shelbyville. Berry admitted that late in the afternoon of September 20, he mentioned to two reporters that Denhardt would be in Shelbyville for a conference that evening. When Kinsolving telephoned him with the news that Denhardt was dead, Berry drove back to Shelbyville. He stopped by the Armstrong Hotel and spotted investigator George Blaydes in the hotel lobby. But Judge Marshall would not allow Berry to testify about what he saw Blaydes carrying. It wasn't pertinent to the case.

By the time Meredith and Wright completed their roster of witnesses, the people in the crowd who had also attended the examining trial had heard most of it before. They were ready to hear Ralph Gilbert's case, but before the first defense witness could be called, there was another lengthy debate between the attorneys in Judge Marshall's chambers. This time, the arguments were about the testimony of the next two witnesses, John Messmer and private detective George Blaydes. How much could Blaydes reveal about what he had overheard on his spy equipment that night? Would the testimony really be pertinent to the trial? How far could Messmer go in testifying to what he knew of the general's reputation?

A reporter from the Shelbyville newspaper complained, "More and much time was lost in further discussion in the judge's chambers of points of law, raised by the commonwealth who seems to have had a bad day from start to finish."[614]

When the attorneys filed back into the courtroom, Ralph Gilbert called Police Sergeant John Messmer into court to take his oath as a witness. Other than Roy Garr and Sheriff Walter Briggs, Messmer was the only witness to testify at both Denhardt's trial and the Garr brothers' trial. Gilbert asked him if he knew Denhardt as "a man of overbearing and violent temper" and there were more objections from Meredith and another discussion behind closed doors.[615] When they finally returned, Messmer testified that he knew General Denhardt as an "overbearing" man. He also denied telling the Garrs that Denhardt would be in Shelbyville or about the plan to eavesdrop on the conference.

George Blaydes told his story of how he received the assignment to plant a Dictaphone from Messmer, and how he had registered at the Armstrong Hotel under an assumed name. Both Messmer and Blaydes claimed that they learned about the conference from reporters in Louisville on the afternoon of September 20. Both testified that they did not tell the Garr brothers that Denhardt was in Shelbyville. Messmer, Blaydes, and Kinsolving had personal friendships with the Garr brothers, and all three knew that Denhardt would be in Shelbyville for the conference. But they emphatically denied telling the brothers about the conference or warning them to stay away from Shelbyville.

Roy Garr was called as a witness in his own defense on October 20. The *Shelby Sentinel* reported on his testimony, saying his answers were "so convincingly like those at the examining trial as to stamp him an exceptionally fine witness."[616]

Once again, Meredith did his best to unsettle Roy during cross-examination, but he held firm to his version of the events. "Once or twice during the long ordeal he showed some indication of fatigue, but never any sign of either fear or evasion," according to the local newspaper.[617] Roy denied that he knew anything about the plan to eavesdrop on the conference. He repeated his original story that he believed Denhardt had a gun.

The *Courier-Journal* reported his testimony. "I knew Denhardt was a killer. He had a reputation for never having gone without a pistol. I went wild when I saw him go for his gun. I just don't remember what happened. I saw him fall."[618]

When Roy was dismissed, Meredith saw his best chance for a conviction step down from the witness chair with him. Wednesday was a frustrating day for Meredith and it did not improve after Judge Marshall tapped his gavel and dismissed court. When Meredith returned to Coleman Wright's office that evening, he discovered that a thief had stolen his coat and the papers he had left in the pockets. Thoroughly discouraged, Meredith returned to Frankfort by bus Wednesday night without his overcoat.

Jack Garr was the first witness called on Thursday morning and, according to news reports, he was as cool and calm under fire as his brother. "His confirmation of all that his older brother had said was in the same calm, quiet but unshakable tones and manner that have characterized both the witnesses and their attorney's conduct of this trial."[619]

Meredith asked, "Didn't Roy kill Denhardt because of his sister's death?"

"I think not," Jack coolly answered.

When Meredith continued to quiz Jack why Roy killed Denhardt, he replied, "Because he was in fear of his life."[620]

Thursday, October 21, was the final full day of testimony, and it was the most memorable day of the trial. Ralph Gilbert set out to convince the jury that the brothers had good reason to fear Henry Denhardt, and he began by calling Birdie Bennett, Verna's former housekeeper. Bennett took her seat in the witness chair, dignified and wearing her best hat and dress with a fur piece thrown over her shoulders. The jurors leaned forward to catch every word. Bennett told the story of the argument she overheard between Denhardt and Verna in late October 1936. Bennett said that Denhardt was furious at Verna's brothers. "He said, I'm going to get them all three and especially that damn big-headed Roy Garr. I will shoot him down like a rat."[621]

Gilbert's next witness, Gussie Brawner of LaGrange, was also employed by Verna. In December 1936, she made a brief visit to Denhardt's farm to locate a relative. While she was there, she overheard Denhardt say, "If it had not been for those damn brothers and for those damn brats of girls of Mrs. Taylor's, we would have been married and this trouble would never have happened. If I'd of killed those damn Garr boys and the girls, that's what they'd deserved."[622] Afterward, she repeated the story to Bookie Taylor, Verna's brother-in-law. Gilbert called Taylor as his next witness and he confirmed Brawner had told him about the threatening statement.

The most damning and sensational testimony against Henry Denhardt that day was given by a group of his military associates. During Denhardt's murder trial, Kinsolving subpoenaed Lieutenant Edwin B. Topmiller, but the lieutenant was never called as a witness. Topmiller, however, was not on Kinsolving's witness list to testify to the general's dark side, but because he gave Denhardt the fountain pen gun. Somehow, Gilbert and his team had learned that there were military men who had interesting views to offer about Denhardt and they subpoenaed them for the Garr brothers' trial.

Brigadier General Ellerbe Carter testified. Carter had not only served with Henry Denhardt, he had also been his political opponent. In 1928, Denhardt lost the Kentucky gubernatorial primary to Carter. Gilbert asked him about Denhardt's reputation for being "overbearing, quarrelsome, and dangerous," and Carter did not mince words when he answered.[623] "I knew him as one of the most violent, unscrupulous, domineering and brutal men I've ever known in my life."[624]

"Objection!" shouted Meredith, jumping to his feet.

"Sustained. The jury will disregard that comment," said Judge Marshall.

Gilbert continued by asking if he knew whether Denhardt typically carried a gun. Carter responded that Denhardt had carried one on his person or in his car since 1931. On cross-examination by Meredith, Carter denied that there had ever been a military rivalry between the two men.

"Were your feelings toward him kind or unkind?"

"Mixed," Carter said with a shrug.[625]

The second military witness was First Lieutenant Franklyn L. Ullrich of the Kentucky National Guard, a former aide-de-camp to Denhardt. When Gilbert asked him about Denhardt's reputation, he was forthright and critical. "In my opinion, he was a man power drunk. He was a very officious, domineering type of man."[626]

Ullrich also confirmed that Denhardt always had a gun in his briefcase, desk, or pocket. Another witness, Major Joseph M. Kelly, executive officer of the Kentucky National Guard, was assistant adjutant general during the years that Denhardt served as state adjutant general. The two men had been at odds in the past. Denhardt's death created a vacancy and an opportunity for

Major Kelly to become brigadier general of the Seventy-Fifth Infantry Brigade.[627] Kelly's appearance at the trial gave him another opportunity. He would have the final word on his stormy relationship with Henry Denhardt. Kelly described Denhardt as a "typical Dr. Jekyll and Mr. Hyde and added 'he was cruel and inhuman. He threatened my life and—'"[628]

"Objection!" shouted Meredith before Kelly could continue.

The large crowd was amazed by what they had heard. The courtroom was swept by a wave of whispers and low voices as men and women turned to speak to each other. Judge Marshall banged his gavel in irritation and threatened to clear the room. "If you think I won't do it, just try again," he bellowed in a voice that carried the length of the room and out into the hallway.[629]

Meredith cautiously probed Kelly about his feelings for Denhardt and he replied, "I had no reason to have unkind feelings for General Denhardt; I pitied him."[630]

Denhardt's military associates were subpoenaed and their appearance was involuntary, but they were surprisingly outspoken in their criticism of a fellow officer. The men had worked closely with Denhardt, and their testimony revealed a side of him that stayed hidden during his murder trial. If they had been called as witnesses in April, they might have been less opinionated. But with Denhardt dead, there was nothing to fear, and they freely offered their opinions for the Shelbyville court.

During the trial, it quickly became apparent why Ralph Gilbert was the man both sides wanted on their team. He was thorough, meticulous, and left no stone unturned in his defense of the brothers. Gilbert probably could have ridden the wave of public sentiment and won an acquittal for Roy Garr, but he was not the kind of lawyer to take that risk. Gilbert even called five physicians to testify to the mental state of Roy Garr just before and during the shooting. Roy's testimony that he feared Denhardt; that he saw Verna or a vision of her just before he started shooting;

and that he believed Denhardt was going to slur her character all raised questions about his mental state. Dr. Milton Board of Louisville described Roy's state of mind at the time of the shooting as "impulsive, emotional insanity. The inhibitor, the governor, was gone."[631] Whether he was rational after the shooting had no bearing on his mental state at the time he pulled the trigger. All of the physicians confirmed that Roy was temporarily unable to control his actions due to his emotional state.

Gilbert also continued to call witness after witness who testified that Denhardt was a dangerous man who typically carried a gun. Throughout Thursday afternoon, Hubert Meredith listened helplessly as the victim in his case was portrayed as gun-toting, violent, overbearing, and menacing. The character and reputation of Denhardt was on trial, and this time he was unable to defend himself. Gilbert called other witnesses to show the jury that the Garr brothers were men of high morals and character. LaGrange Methodist minister W. B. Garriott, Judge W. P. Yancey, and Oldham County Sheriff Walter Briggs all testified to the brothers' excellent reputations in the community.

Friday morning, as hundreds of people filed into the courtroom and took their seats, there was a sudden commotion in the crowd. Those already seated jumped to their feet, and others pointed excitedly at an elegant, well-dressed couple who paraded unhurriedly into the courtroom. People gaped and stared at D. W. Griffith, famed Hollywood actor and director, and his very beautiful and youthful wife, actress Evelyn Baldwin. Griffith had been born in Oldham County and retired from Hollywood to a home on Verna's street in LaGrange. He did not personally know the Garr family, but had come to see the final act in the real-life drama that had gripped his home state for nearly a year. The director and his wife took seats of honor near the defense table with the Garr brothers.

A law school class from the University of Louisville also

crowded into the courtroom that day to see justice in action. Mrs. Ralph Gilbert, wife of the defense attorney, was the lone female student in a class of young men who watched D. W. Griffith, and especially his beautiful wife, enter and take their seats.[632]

—

When he had tapped his gavel and called the unruly crowd to order, Judge Marshall began the day by dismissing Jack as a defendant. It came as no surprise, and there were no demonstrations in the courtroom. Judge Marshall instructed the foreman of the jury to sign Jack's dismissal order and read the formal language into the record of the trial: "We the jury find the defendant, Jack Garr, not guilty." Jack was pleased to be dismissed, but insisted that he would stay in the courtroom by Roy's side until the jury brought in its verdict.

Ralph Gilbert, Ballard Clarke, George Willis, and John Todd had hastily assembled a defense for the brothers in less than a month, and the number of witnesses called and the thoroughness of their case was amazing. By noon on Friday, the prosecution was buried under an avalanche of witness testimony that supported the Garr brothers' fear of Henry Denhardt. When it was finally over, Gilbert announced, "The defense rests, Your Honor." All that remained were Judge Marshall's instructions to the jury and the attorneys' closing arguments.

Before he adjourned court for the lunch recess, Judge Marshall read the formal instructions. The jury could find Roy Garr guilty of willful murder, voluntary manslaughter, or they could acquit him. The judge instructed the jury to bring in a verdict of acquittal if they found that Roy was temporarily insane.

Ballard Clarke was the first attorney to give his closing argument after the lunch recess. For an hour, he methodically reviewed all of the important points of the defense's case. He emphasized the testimony against Denhardt's reputation and character. At the end, he delivered the most memorable line of all the closing arguments: "I say to you that you have a right to shoot a mad dog if it attacks you. The fact that he turns his back to you makes no difference . . . I ask you to find Roy Garr not guilty, and when you do, you will receive the plaudits of not only the citizens of Shelby County and Kentucky, but of the nation."[633]

County Attorney Coleman Wright followed and reviewed the facts of the case from the state's point of view. Speaking in a quiet conversational tone, he asked the jury to find Roy guilty of willful murder. "Roy Garr has committed a great crime. He took the life of a man. It is your duty to apply the law. Forget race, creed, color, and feeling and do your duty."[634]

Late in the afternoon, Ralph Gilbert walked to the front of the courtroom to deliver his closing argument. Gilbert declared that the night Roy shot Denhardt, he "had the law of God and man on his side."[635] He asked the jurors to find him innocent and do it quickly. "Don't stay out there, but come right back with the verdict!"[636] A man in the courtroom was so overcome that he suddenly began yelling loudly. Judge Marshall furiously banged his gavel and called for one of the deputies to move quickly. "Arrest that man!" he ordered. Everyone watched as the deputy sheriff securely clasped the man by the arm and led him out of the courtroom. Judge Marshall gave a satisfied nod and said, "A couple of hours in jail might make him realize he was disorderly in the courtroom."[637]

Gilbert, Wright, and Clarke finished by four o'clock, and Judge Marshall called a recess until seven. When court resumed, it would be Meredith's turn for one last impassioned plea to convict Roy Garr. Most of the crowd in the courtroom waited patiently as the hours passed, unwilling to brave the rain outside or lose their seats.

Just before seven o'clock, they watched as Meredith left the table and walked resolutely to the front of the courtroom. He had been ill throughout a day that had started before dawn. But he was determined not to go down without a fight, and for the next two hours, his blistering arguments in favor of Roy's conviction held the full attention of the courtroom. Meredith could concede that the general ran in the direction of the brothers, and perhaps he did make a movement toward his hip pocket for a handkerchief. But at the point where Roy rounded the brick corner of the hotel and knew that Denhardt was not returning fire, yet continued to shoot at his back, it became an execution. Regardless of the witnesses who testified to Denhardt's violent and dangerous personality and his penchant to carry a gun, "He got what he deserved" was not a defense under the law. Meredith finally looked intently at the twelve men in the jury box and said, "When you come back with your verdict, we'll know which side of the question you're on, whether you are on the side of law and order or whether you believe a man can take the law into his own hands. . . . I've been called old fashioned and a mossback, but I believe that all of us will someday face a judge who will try the case according to the evidence and not flimsy defenses. I don't care whether you give him the death penalty or life imprisonment, but I believe Roy Garr should be convicted!"[638]

It was an excellent, well-argued speech, and at the end, Meredith had done all he could to convince the jury that Roy was guilty. He was the final actor to take the stage in the drama that began on a dark highway in Henry County on November 6, 1936, and ended in Shelbyville's courtroom on October 22, 1937. It was just after nine when the jury filed out to begin their deliberations. Hubert Meredith packed his briefcase, and walked slowly down Main Street to catch a bus back to the state capital. But he left Shelbyville too soon. His bus had scarcely reached nearby Frankfort when the jury suddenly reappeared in the courtroom.

Chapter 34

AFTER THE SHOUTING DIED

Many involved with the case expected the jury to spend a short time discussing the facts, reviewing the exhibits, and then retire for the evening and start fresh the next morning. But the men of this jury were ready to finish the job and go home for the night. An hour and fifteen minutes after leaving the courtroom, and after only one ballot, they were back in court with a verdict.

Despite Marshall's warning to the crowd to restrain themselves, the words "We find Roy Garr not guilty" set off a wild demonstration of clapping, cheering, and rebel yells.[639] The clamor spread through the hallways of the courthouse, down the marble stairs, and into Main Street where hundreds of townspeople joined in the exuberant celebration.

Judge Marshall desperately pounded the bench with his gavel, trying to get control of the uproar in his courtroom. A local reporter captured the moment. "After excitement had subsided and some measure of order had been restored, Judge Marshall polled each juror and each in turn answered 'not guilty.' The enthusiastic throng cheered each response."[640] After the judge polled the last juror, the crowd rushed the table to congratulate the brothers and their attorneys. There was such a press of people that deputies had to force a passage through the mob for Roy, Jack, and their nieces to exit the courtroom. It was a spectacular and joyous ending to what one writer called the "blood-stained romance" of Verna Garr Taylor and General Henry Denhardt.[641] Fifteen days short of the first anniversary of Verna's death, it all ended in Shelbyville with celebration and congratulations to the Garr brothers and their defense team. A reporter asked Coleman Wright if he would dismiss the indictment against Doc Garr in light of what had happened. He replied with resignation, "What would you do? If we couldn't convict Roy, we certainly couldn't convict Dr. Garr."[642]

In an interview after the verdict, Roy commented, "I'm happy that it's all over. I want to go home now and forget it all."[643] But while life would eventually return to some semblance of normalcy for the family, they would never be able to forget it all. The wounds left from the tragedy would never completely heal.

Immediately after the trial, the brothers were often requested as public speakers, but declined the invitations. In late October, they disappointed the members of the Methodist Ladies Aid Society in Shelbyville when they refused an invitation to dine as guests of honor.[644] Everyone wanted to hear from Roy Garr, the man who defended the honor of his sister by killing her murderer. Hundreds of congratulatory letters to the brothers poured into Shelbyville and LaGrange from all over the country.

Family members tell the story of a Garr relative who was stopped for speeding in New York. The trooper asked to see her driver's license and noticed that her last name was "Garr" and she was from Kentucky. He asked if she was related to the Garr brothers. When she admitted that she was a relative, he told her to continue driving and walked away without issuing a speeding ticket.[645]

Roy and Jack Garr did not want to be heroes. They did not enjoy the adulation, and only wished to move forward with their lives and put the events behind them. It was not always easy. Their tragic family story was told and retold in popular detective magazines. *Front Page Detective* and *True Detective* both ran articles with titles guaranteed to capture the interest of the reading public—"Kentucky's Bloody Denhardt Feud," and "The Truth about General Denhardt, Kentucky's Bizarre Love Drama."[646] The detective magazines certainly skewed the facts to make a more titillating story. The tragedy was even set to music in true Kentucky fashion. Inaccurate, but entertaining, *The Ballad of Soldier Henry* by George A. "Doc" Hendon Jr., was popular and circulated soon after Denhardt's murder.[647]

> The harvest moon was shinin'
> On the streets of Shelbyville
> When General Henry Denhardt met his fate
> The Garr boys was a waitin'
> They was out to shoot to kill,
> Death and General Denhardt had a date.
>
> Oh, sad the fate of Soldier Henry
> In the town of Shelbyville
> His military record clean.
> He lies beneath the sod
> His soul has flown to God,
> And he's buried in Bowling Green.
>
> Now pretty Verna Garr
> Lies a moldin' in her grave
> In LaGrange just sixteen miles away.
> The folks for miles around
> Claim the general shot her down
> Because she wouldn't let him have his way.
>
> The Garrs said he's killed their sister
> On State Highway 61
> Though he'd been tried by twelve men good and true,
> They knew they couldn't rest

Till they seen justice done,
So they done what the jury failed to do.

Little did the general fear
As he sipped his glass of beer
With lawyer Otte brought from Louisville
That before an hour had fled
He'd be layin' cold and dead
With Verna's secret locked within him still.

As the general reached the doorway
Of the old Armstrong Hotel
He stumbled and he fell upon his face;
Roy Garr rushed up beside him,
Smoking pistol in his hand,
And seen that he'd passed on to God the case.

"Don't shoot me, I'm a lawyer,"
Cried attorney Rodes K. Myers,
As he raised his hands and pleaded for his life,
His frantic cries were heeded
By Dr. E. S. Garr,
Who spared him for his children and his wife.

Now ladies, don't you worry,
If you have a brother good,
That you will meet poor Verna's fate,
Your loving ones around you
Will protect your womanhood
While the law is what it is
In this here state.

As time passed, the furor finally began to die and the saga that
had captured the imagination of a nation for nearly a year faded

from the headlines; Americans became more concerned with the news of an approaching war. Jack returned to life in Ohio with his wife, Margaret, and their infant daughter. Roy returned to Bettie and his farm outside LaGrange. The brothers continued to train their bird dogs and live quiet lives.

But Doc Garr's life could never return to normal, and his mental and physical health continued to decline. In February 1938, Hubert Meredith asked the court to dismiss the charges against him. There were only a few lawyers and court officials on hand when Meredith made his motion and Judge Marshall dismissed the case.

"The proceedings in court took only a few minutes," the *Oldham Era* reported. "Attorney General Meredith told the court that in view of acquittal last October of Roy and Jack Garr he saw no reason to continue the prosecution and would ask that the murder charge be dropped since it would be impossible to secure conviction. Coleman Wright, county attorney of Shelby County, concurred in this opinion and Judge Marshall approved the dismissal order."[648]

Doc Garr was in and out of the veteran's hospital as a voluntary patient throughout 1938. In December of that year, the Denhardt case suddenly flashed into the headlines again when Doc announced that while Denhardt was involved in Verna's murder, he was not the shooter. Doc believed that Verna had somehow learned something on Denhardt that could be "deadly damaging."[649] It had the potential to destroy both Denhardt and a colleague. On the night Verna died, Doc believed that Denhardt had at least one accomplice. Denhardt took Verna's purse from the death scene because there was a letter inside that incriminated the man who actually shot her. Denhardt "entered into a plot with the writer of that letter to get sister out of the way, to stop any chance she might expose them," according to Doc in an interview he gave with the *Louisville Times*.[650] Doc said he had material evidence that would prove his case. He also claimed that three attempts had been made on his own life since the end of the trial. Like Verna, he knew too much.

The Kentucky Attorney General's office received Doc's letter but declined to investigate. Hubert Meredith said, "There is not sufficient evidence for me to authorize any action."[651] Considering Doc's mental state, it was easy for Meredith to dismiss the allegations as fantastic.

Jack Garr was contacted at his home near Cincinnati for a comment on the letter. "There's not a thing in the world to it. Denhardt really did it. We knew it all the time."[652]

Roy was in Brownsville, Tennessee, with his hunting dogs and was not asked to comment, but there is no doubt his response would have been much the same.

"I'll see that the truth about Verna's death is known if I die for it," said Doc. "And when the real story breaks, it will blow the top off the courthouse."[653] A month and eighteen days later, Doc was dead from peritonitis after surgery for an ulcerated stomach. Roy and Jack rushed to the hospital, but arrived too late to say goodbye to their brother. He was given a military funeral and was buried in Louisville at Cave Hill Cemetery. The conspiracy theory about Verna's murder died with him.

Old-timers in LaGrange tell stories of Roy's later years and how he would drive his horse and buggy into town for a drink. When it was time to go home, he would climb into his buggy, slap the horse's rump, and settle back to doze as the horse travelled the familiar route home. He often said that the general's ghost rode beside him on some of those dark nights.[654] The story may only be local legend, but it is true that Roy was haunted by the night of September 20, 1937, for the rest of his life. He died in 1962 at age seventy-one, and his obituary in the *Oldham Era* made no mention of his involvement in the death of General Denhardt and the murder trial in Shelby County. His brother Jack followed in 1963 at age sixty-three; he is buried in Cincinnati, Ohio.

Henry Denhardt did not leave behind any children, and the legacy he worked a lifetime to attain was destroyed by the allegations of his involvement in the murder of Verna Garr Taylor. It is interesting to speculate whether his historical role in early twentieth-century Kentucky politics would be more prominent had he not died under a cloud of suspicion.

As a lieutenant governor, Denhardt was a progressive democrat who supported free education and textbooks for Kentucky's schoolchildren. He advocated making Mammoth Cave a national park years before it became a reality in 1941. During the 1920s, Denhardt organized a highway patrol that evolved into the Kentucky State Police in 1948. At one time, he was certainly a capable man, but by the mid-1930s, he had become so threatening and erratic that Ballard Clarke referred to him as a "mad dog," and his military associates called him a "Dr. Jekyll and Mr. Hyde." Their comments raise the question whether, by the last years of his life, Denhardt was suffering from a form of dementia or a mental disease related to his lengthy alcohol abuse.

Denhardt died with debts unpaid from his murder trial. Even "Brother Wright," who took the measurements at the death scene, had not been paid by September. Dr. McCormack, one of the executors of the general's estate, wrote John Berry in November 1937, "I am really quite humiliated in not being able to send checks immediately to all of them, but the whole thing is in such a tangle that I haven't been able to find any more blood in the turnip than had already been squeezed out of it, apparently."[655] McCormack did not indicate whether "all of them" included the expert witnesses whose testimony was so valuable during Denhardt's trial.

Shortly after the general's funeral, the family considered moving his remains to Arlington National Cemetery, but at some point, they decided to leave him buried in his hometown. It is quite possible that Bertha could not bear the thought of him so far away. As the years passed, she faithfully visited the cemetery and left flowers for her younger brother. Denhardt's grave marker in Bowling Green's Fairview Cemetery has a weathered bronze front that details his illustrious military service. The graves of his immediate family surround him. The Armstrong Hotel burned in 1944, and a historic marker on busy Main Street in Shelbyville marks the site of the former hotel and Denhardt's death.

Chester Woolfolk is remembered as a slim, unassuming, and bashful young man who played the saxophone beautifully and smoked Camel cigarettes.[656] But the jury is still out on the question of his true relationship with Verna. The fact that he was never called as a witness, even to rebut the general's testimony, is suspicious. It's very possible that Kinsolving and his team knew Woolfolk had something to say that Verna's family did not want made public.

In 1985, an article in the *Courier-Journal Magazine* looked back at the Denhardt case and explored the mystery of Chester Woolfolk and his possible role in Verna's life. By then, Rodes Myers had been dead for twenty-five years. The author of the article wrote that Philip Ardery, a renowned attorney and author, claimed that Myers had told him Denhardt was innocent. According to Ardery, Myers said that Denhardt lied on the witness stand to protect Verna's reputation. "Myers said Denhardt told him that Verna admitted having an affair with another man, that she had broken it off but that the man had threatened to kill both her and Denhardt if she insisted on marrying Denhardt and that the man had followed them to Louisville that day and shadowed them on their return."[657]

The same story had actually been around for quite a long time. In late 1937, one of the popular detective magazines spun a wild tale of a gathering of friends at Denhardt's home just after the trial ended. "As a Southern gentleman," Denhardt had told his friends, "I took a chance on the noose rather than tell the whole truth. That is to say, gentlemen, I couldn't bring myself to expose just why Verna shot herself."[658] The story went on to allege that on November 6, a tearful and suicidal Verna Taylor confessed to Denhardt that she had an ongoing relationship with Chester Woolfolk.

The original source for the story of the affair is Denhardt. There is no doubt he believed Verna and Woolfolk were romantically involved. There is also no evidence that anyone ever considered Woolfolk a suspect in Verna's murder. As a young man, he was described as somewhat backward, easily embarrassed, and quick to blush. The glowing descriptions of Verna, of her steady reputation at work and in the community indicate that it would be far out of character for her to have a clandestine love affair. But stranger things have happened, and it's not impossible that in the early years after her husband's death, Verna turned to the young man for comfort and something more than friendship. While the details of how Verna died are hazy, the relationship with Woolfolk is the key to her murder.

Verna's death deeply affected Woolfolk, and family and extended family members noticed the change in his demeanor and personality. "After her death, he hardly spoke a word to anybody; crossed to the other side of the street if he saw a relative or friend approaching," according to one writer.[659] He joined the Air Force during the war years, and when he returned to LaGrange, he remembered the lessons learned from his beautiful employer and opened the town's first dry cleaning business. He eventually became a wealthy man. Woolfolk was in his fifties before he finally married.

John Messmer's reputation survived the Denhardt trial and he continued his work as chief of the Louisville Police Department

Crime Laboratory. In 1938, he was awarded the pistol that killed Denhardt as a prize for his private firearms collection. Messmer, a World War I veteran, returned to military life and enlisted in the army in December 1942. He served during the war years as a post intelligence officer in charge of criminal investigations. In September 1945, he suffered a massive heart attack at Fort Knox where he was stationed. Captain John Messmer was forty-eight when he died; he is buried in Louisville's Cave Hill Cemetery.

The Cole family continued to live on the farm after Denhardt's death and John Cole managed it for the new owner as he had for Denhardt. The family always believed in Denhardt's innocence, and John Cole once remarked to his grandson that Denhardt was one of the most honest men he had ever encountered. When Denhardt told him he did not kill Verna, Cole believed it based on his experience and history with Denhardt. The grandson remembered Denhardt as a large, stocky man who was always kind to the numerous Cole children on his property.[660]

Mary Pryor and Frances remained in Oldham County and raised their families, and between them, they had five grandchildren who never had the opportunity to meet their remarkable grandmother. The sisters chose to move forward and live their lives quietly in grace and dignity, never dwelling on the past sadness, but resiliently moving toward the future. Like their mother, they relied on their strong religious faith to get them through the hard times. As the years passed, family members recall that they wore out the bindings of their Bibles.

Occasionally, a local newspaper or magazine would publish an article about their mother's murder and Denhardt's trial and death. Typical of their generation, Frances and Mary Pryor remained silent about private family affairs. They did not appreciate the continued news coverage of what had happened to their family in 1936 and 1937. The painful memories of those years were best left in the past where they belonged.

In the years after her mother's death, however, Frances would visit the *Louisville Courier-Journal* archives and pore over the old news articles from the case. Whatever she was searching for, she never found the answers to her questions.

In her later years, Mary Pryor lived in her grandparents' house across the narrow street from Verna's home on Fourth Avenue. She would spend hours by the second-story window in her chair, staring across the street, perhaps remembering happier times spent in the house with her mother and sister before life changed so abruptly on November 6, 1936. She once mysteriously remarked to the new owner of her childhood home that the house held secrets, but declined to elaborate.

Mary Pryor died in 1999, and her younger sister, Frances Herndon Taylor Yager followed in 2009, at age eighty-eight. The Community Laundry was sold several years after Verna's death and later burned to the ground. Today, there are new apartments in the area of LaGrange once known as "the bottom" where the busy Community Laundry stood.

The only landmark remaining from the night of November 6, 1936, is the Bakers' small, white clapboard farmhouse. Browning's Service Station has been replaced by a modern convenience plaza that serves travelers exiting from nearby Interstate 71, and the Pendleton Schoolhouse is long gone. But George and Nettie's house and driveway and the barn and outbuildings near the house are deserted but standing. The side porch and window where George Baker saw Denhardt walking in his driveway is there in a house that is now ramshackle and abandoned. There are also traces of the old roadbed that run east from the corner of the Baker yard and follow the highway toward the intersection where the Browning Service Station once stood. But there is nothing to mark the place where Verna Garr Taylor's body was found on that dark night so many years ago. She is remembered in local legend as a beautiful woman in black whose restless spirit walks Highway 146 just beyond the old Baker house.

After the acquittal of the Garr brothers, the Denhardt family remained silent and without comment. Bertha and Jesse made their position on their brother's murder very clear in the published statement of September 24, 1937. But in spring 1938, the brother and sister heard a rumor that Henry Denhardt's overcoat and revolver were on display as trophies at the Henry County Courthouse. They turned to John Berry for help. Berry always believed Henry Denhardt was innocent of Verna's murder, and he continued to stand by him after his death. The trial and violent death of Denhardt left its mark on Berry, and he avoided capital murder cases for the rest of his legal career. When Jesse Denhardt wrote to him on May 11, 1938, expressing concern over his brother's possessions, Berry assured him that what he had heard was merely a rumor. "The information that these articles are being kept and displayed by the clerk as trophies is erroneous. Some busybody is misrepresenting Mr. Turner and of course hurting you and the family. I think you should not pay any attention to such reports because I am sure Mr. Turner has too strong a sense of propriety to use evidence in his possession in any way to embarrass, or humiliate the members of an accused person's family."

John Berry ended his letter: "I often think of you and Miss Bertha and still General Denhardt's trouble and his tragic death are an obsession which I seem to be unable to rid my mind of. My daily hope is that by some way, some time, every member of the public that condemned him will be convinced as I am of his innocence."[661]

Many decades have passed since John Berry wrote those haunting words about a murdered client he believed was innocent. Since that time, there has been no new evidence, and no one has stepped forward with information that would exonerate the general. The circumstantial evidence remains overwhelming that Denhardt was involved in the death of Verna Garr Taylor. But the extent to which he was involved, and whether he was the man who actually shot Verna is one of the mysteries within the mystery of her death. Shortly after Denhardt's murder, the *Louisville Courier-Journal* lamented that the death of General Denhardt before his second trial effectively ended the search for the truth of what really happened on November 6, 1936. The writer commented: "The question of 'Did General Denhardt kill Mrs. Taylor?' seems destined to remain forever unanswered."[662]

If the general had lived to be tried a second time, we probably would still not know the answer to that question. Denhardt was a clever witness, and Kinsolving struggled during cross-examination. But his testimony in the second trial may have provided more details about the relationship between Verna and Woolfolk. Denhardt could always claim that he nobly perjured himself to protect the reputation of the woman he loved. In 1937, a jury composed entirely of men may have bought into his sentiments. While Kinsolving and Verna's family believed the general would be convicted the second time, they missed their best chance in April. Denhardt may have been acquitted.

Today, the freight trains still rumble noisily through the heart of LaGrange, and their whistles echo across the countryside as they pass the lonely place on Highway 146 where Verna was murdered. The tragic tale of her death, as mournful as the sound of the train's whistle on a cold November night, remains a story of layered secrets and mysteries within mysteries. In his "Ballad of Soldier Henry," Doc Hendon wrote:

> Little did the general fear
> As he sipped his glass of beer
> With lawyer Otte brought from Louisville
> That before an hour had fled

He'd be layin' cold and dead
With Verna's secret locked within him still.

Verna's secret seems destined to lie buried and locked within Verna in her grave at the Valley of Rest Cemetery and the general in his grave in Bowling Green.

EPILOGUE

By the time the gunfire ended in Shelbyville, the murder case against General Denhardt had evaporated into the autumn night with the smoke from Roy and Doc Garr's pistols. The key to what happened to Verna Garr Taylor and possibly Patricia Wilson lay dead, sprawled in the doorway of the Armstrong Hotel. Most people who had followed the case believed that the general's shooting was a fitting end and well-deserved death. A debt had been paid in blood to the Garr and Taylor families, evil had received its just deserts, and it was time to move forward. Public attention quickly refocused on the popular efforts to free the Garr brothers, and the unanswered questions surrounding Verna's death remained unresolved. Many decades later, we are still at the same juncture as the New Castle jury in 1937. Suicide or murder?

The only evidence of Verna's depression and suicide was General Denhardt's version of events, and he could never get his story straight. On the night Verna died, he blamed her daughters. In March 1937, he claimed the pressures of living a double life with Woolfolk caused her suicide. Finally, his version at the murder trial placed the blame squarely on Woolfolk's professed love.

Denhardt's attorneys did their best to argue that a contact shot caused the discoloration around the rim of the gunshot wound. It was a reach, but they worked hard to establish reasonable doubt and give the jury anything that might support their client's story. But much more evidence indicated that Verna's death was not a suicide. This includes her positive state of mind on November 5 and 6; the fact the she was making improvements to a successful business; the size, length, and weight of the alleged weapon that she would have to handle with one hand because her left still clutched a glove; and the strange angle or trajectory of the wound. These all dispelled the defense theory of suicide. I asked a physician friend to look at the autopsy report without giving him any details of the case. His first question after reading it was, "Who killed this woman?" I believe it is a safe assumption that Verna was murdered.

This leaves us with Kinsolving's unlikely theory of Verna's murder—Denhardt chased Verna up the highway, shot her, pulled her body into the ditch, and ran back to the car. He shot his fountain pen pistol to distract Baker.

In researching the case against General Denhardt, one of the most surprising elements was the weakness of the physical evidence against him. The blood drips or stains on Denhardt's coat did not really look like blood spatter, and they did not look like they resulted from pulling a body off the highway. There was no blood on the front of Verna's dress around the wound to indicate Denhardt had grasped her under the shoulders and pulled her upright after she was dead. The lengthy distance Denhardt would have to cover, paired with moving a 145-pound body off the road, would have left him holding his knees and struggling to breathe. But the general was calm and speaking normally when Baker came out of his house a short time after the first loud gunshot. There was no mud on Denhardt's shoes or pants to indicate he had been in the ditch. Finally, there was nothing to indicate that the infamous fountain pen pistol ever left its storage box at Denhardt's farm. So many strange things did not support the theory that Kinsolving gave the jury. They must have struggled as much I did to make sense of it all.

The strongest part of Kinsolving's case was the circumstantial evidence. On the night Verna died, it was obvious that Denhardt was finished with her; his emotional detachment and callousness was damning. Of all the things that Denhardt did or failed to do, it seems unbelievably heartless that he walked away and left Verna's body alone and unguarded in the darkness. If he wanted to return to the car, he could have asked Cuba Shaver to wait with her body. It is hard to imagine that anyone could be so indifferent to the death of someone they claimed to love.

It was also apparent that he knew Verna was dead, and he knew the approximate location of her body. Denhardt told Hundley and Shaver to drive east to the crossroads and back. He never asked them to explore the highway west of Baker's driveway when Verna could have just as easily walked in that direction.

The overwhelming circumstantial evidence added up to murder. Kinsolving knew he had his man, but he could never give the jury a reasonable account of how Denhardt killed Verna. It was the fatal flaw in his case. Yet, because it's widely accepted that Denhardt was the murderer, Kinsolving's version of how Verna died has been viewed as gospel since 1937.

After poring over the trial transcript many times, especially the baffling testimony of the Shepherds, I could never get the puzzle pieces to fit. Even before I found the 1938 article on Doc Garr's fantastic conspiracy theory, I had begun to wonder whether Denhardt had an accomplice. Doc's story was quickly dismissed as the ravings of a madman, but if we accept Verna's death as a homicide, an accomplice theory is no more bizarre than the story Kinsolving told the jury.

The idea is intriguing, and I have attempted to recreate the events of November 6, inserting an accomplice into the story as the shooter. His role would have begun as the couple pulled away from the Sada San Restaurant. It is interesting that one of the stories of the night has the Denhardt car mysteriously shadowed as it leaves Louisville. In the 1985 *Courier-Journal Magazine* article, Rodes Myers insinuated that the driver of the car was Chester

Woolfolk. But Woolfolk was never a suspect, and rightfully so. It was Denhardt who had the motive to murder Verna.

An accomplice would have been instructed to follow and wait for an opportunity. Today, car trouble is usually an unexpected event, and we take it for granted that our vehicles will reach their destination. But in 1936, the cars were unreliable and the roads were rutted and rough, especially the rural roads. Between the car and the condition of the roads, the odds were good that the Denhardt car would encounter a problem along the way.

Earlier in the day, the couple had a flat tire. That evening, the problem was a dead battery. It's possible that the battery died without warning. But it was the stalled car that presented an opportunity to kill Verna, and I've always wondered about that coincidence. It led me to talk with mechanics familiar with vintage cars and explore the possibility that the dead battery was no coincidence.

Kinsolving was never able to account for the lengthy time the couple took to arrive at Browning's Service Station. Denhardt mentions only one short stop along the road that occurred two or three miles from LaGrange. The time that it took to arrive in Henry County indicates there must have been other stops along the way. Those stops would have allowed Denhardt an opportunity to check the car or look under the hood for a problem. In Denhardt's car, a cable connected the generator with the battery, and I've been assured it would not be difficult to sever or loosen.

During the trial, the general was adamant that he knew nothing about cars. But, he also told the jury that he probably cut his finger working on the wire from the battery to his defroster. Denhardt may have known more about cars than he wanted the jury to know. In a car traveling at night using the headlights, a charged battery with a severed or loosened cable would gradually run down. The only question is how far the car would travel first.

The twelve-volt batteries used in modern cars are significantly more effective than the standard six-volt batteries and weaker charging systems of 1930s-era cars. If the battery in Denhardt's Chevrolet was fully charged at the time the cable was severed or loosened, it would travel farther before dying. If the deed was done within several miles of reaching LaGrange, it is quite possible that a six-volt battery would last until the couple reached Browning's Service Station.

In Henry County, the accomplice saw the Denhardt car in front turn left at the intersection by Browning's Service Station. He turned right and parked on the dark road beyond the fields of George Baker's farm. The area was wooded and remote, and provided a secluded spot to park and observe. He watched as the car was pushed to Baker's driveway. He then walked across the fields and followed the old roadbed west to the edge of Baker's yard where he waited in the darkness. Trixie sensed his presence and barked frantically outside at the front corner of the house. Denhardt walked to Baker's side porch with the lame excuse of asking for a telephone, and the accomplice made his move.

The most likely scenario is that he pointed a gun and took Verna by force from the car. The accomplice had been told to use the gun that was in the glovebox and he took it with him. Verna may have had the keys in her hand and in the frantic moment took them with her. The motive could not have been robbery. Verna's purse was left behind in the car and the valuable engagement ring was still on her finger when she was found. It's possible the man scooped up the flashlight along with Denhardt's gun and hurried Verna away from the car.

The Shepherds drove slowly past and saw Denhardt standing next to his car; Verna was nowhere in sight. The accomplice and Verna were walking on the road when the headlights of the Shepherd's car appeared in the distance. The accomplice panicked and ordered Verna to go down the embankment into the ditch. She refused and backed away from the man, leaving her heel prints in the mud beside the road. The flashlight and keys were dropped in the struggle.

The accomplice grabbed Verna and forcibly pushed her into the ditch. She lost one of her shoes as she tumbled down the four-foot embankment. She scrambled backwards away from where she landed at the bottom, trying to escape her assailant. If she screamed for help, it's unlikely that anyone in the Shepherd car would hear over the rumbling noise of the motor. By this point, the two were 689 feet from Baker's driveway.

Once the car passed, the man shot Verna. Verna was probably already on the ground struggling to get up when she was shot and fell backward, dying instantly. There was no bullet hole in her wool coat because it was thrown back off her shoulders in the struggle. It she had been standing and facing her assailant, the shot would have passed through the front of her coat.

A shot fired at Verna on the ground from several feet away could account for the odd trajectory of the wound, approximately two inches higher in the back than in the front. The man was instructed to make the death look like a suicide, but did not do a very good job. He tossed Verna's shoe and it landed in the improbable position between her body and outstretched arm. He fired a second shot as a signal that the job was done. He dropped the gun nearby but left it too far away from Verna's body to look like a suicide. The odd, muffled sound of the second shot may have been caused by a point-blank shot into the mud.

It was after the second signal shot that Denhardt made his odd comment to Baker. "She was the finest woman I ever knew." He already knew she was dead. Later, the death scene was disturbed by Hundley, Shaver, Keightley, Baker, and Ricketts. No one looked for footprints around the body or leading away from the scene.

During his closing arguments, Ballard Clarke said, "If he killed her, he killed her in cold blood." A murder planned by Denhardt and carried out by an accomplice would be even colder than Clarke ever envisioned, but it is not impossible. Denhardt was an angry, powerful man with the money to pay others to do his dirty work, and Verna's relationship with Woolfolk was his motive. Domestic violence, a term common today, but unknown in the 1930s, is at the heart of this tragedy.

The final question for an accomplice theory is who could it have been? It would have to have been a close associate, someone whose loyalty was so unquestioned that he could be relied on to do anything asked of him, or keep a secret if he refused. In my research, few men met the criteria, but there was one who caught and held my attention—a mysterious man with a shadowy background who had been close to Denhardt for many years. It's only conjecture, because there's no real evidence that this man was involved in Verna's murder, or that there even was an accomplice. He will remain nameless here. Curiously, although this man was unqualified, in 1939, he landed a plum position in Kentucky state government. The newly elected lieutenant governor was Rodes Myers.

ACKNOWLEDGMENTS

The journey in writing this book has been memorable and filled with wonderful people. Kentuckians have a reputation for being helpful and friendly, and I have found that to be true in researching and writing this book. I remember calling the offices of *Shelby County Life*, the Kentucky Historical Society, and the Oldham County Deed Room for documents. They often told me that they would mail me the information or articles right away and I could send a check in the mail.

I remember my frustrating search for the old Pendleton Schoolhouse and the place where Verna Garr Taylor died. I knew I was close, but the landmarks no longer exist. One day, I stopped for gas at a service plaza near a crossroads and walked inside. I asked the lady behind the counter if she knew where the schoolhouse used to be located. She looked puzzled, but a heavyset man stuck his head around a door and declared, "You're standing in it!" The Pendleton Schoolhouse was once located on the same site as the busy service plaza. "Tug" Hawkins and I drove the short distance to where Verna's body was found. He lived across the road from the site and his mother had pointed out the spot many times.

My search for an editor was another one of those Kentucky moments when a stranger is willing to help. A telephone conversation with judge, attorney, and author Sid Easley led me to Susan E. Lindsey of Savvy Communication LLC in Louisville. Susan has devoted many painstaking hours to editing the manuscript and helping to make this book a reality. I am very grateful for her fine, meticulous work. I am also thankful that she never threw up her hands and tossed it back at me!

Amazingly, the long-lost Denhardt trial folders were found at the Henry County Courthouse during the time I was writing this book. Circuit Court Clerk Gina Lyle gave me a quiet opportunity to review the files at the courthouse. It was a moment I will never forget when I found Verna's letters to Denhardt tucked inside the pages in one of the old expandable files. I knew they existed and had been searching for them for years. I would especially like to thank Gina for her help with the files and for providing a fascinating insider's tour of the Henry County Courthouse.

So many people helped in providing information and taking time out of their busy lives. I would especially like to thank Dr. William Ellis who generously allowed me to borrow his research files. In 1986, Dr. Ellis wrote the best article I have found on the Taylor-Denhardt tragedy for the *Register of the Kentucky Historical Society*. His files were invaluable, especially the letters between Denhardt and his attorneys that are now part of the John M. Berry Papers at the Filson Historical Society. Dr. Ellis's taped interview from 1980 with *Louisville Courier-Journal* reporter John Herchenroeder described the 1930s' practice of staging scenes for dramatic newspaper photographs.

Jim Holmberg of the Filson Historical Society took time to meet with me, for which I am grateful. I truly appreciate his permission to quote materials from collections at the Filson.

Earl T. "Hammer" Smith and his wife, June, located a copy of the Denhardt trial transcript. Finding that transcript was like striking gold. It gave me added insight into the events and the personalities of the witnesses, and included details that newspaper accounts of the trial failed to mention.

Bill Bright of the Kentucky Military History Museum graciously responded to my unusual request to see and handle a gun identical to the one allegedly used in the crime. Brandon

Slone of the Kentucky Department of Military Affairs located Denhardt's military records for my review.

The employees of the Kentucky Historical Society in Frankfort were gracious in ordering articles and newspapers. Jonathan Jeffrey and Sandy Staebell of the Kentucky Museum at Western Kentucky University in Bowling Green located Denhardt's files as well as some of his personal effects in storage. Jennifer Frazier, the State Law Librarian in Frankfort, was an excellent source in locating background material on the attorneys involved in the Denhardt case. I also appreciate the help provided by employees of the Berry Center in New Castle, and the Filson Historical Society in Louisville.

Donna Shifflette, an old friend and confirmed Texan, traveled to Kentucky and spent several days taking photographs. A special thanks to Donna for taking time out of her busy schedule and putting her gift with a camera to use on my behalf. The current owners of General Denhardt's Oldham County farm graciously allowed us to visit and take photographs. Thanks to Steve Greenwell who helped make the visit possible.

Louisville photographer Vivian Knox-Thompson photographed the highway and death scene on Friday, November 6, 2015, seventy-nine years to the day that Verna died. Vivian and I arrived at dusk and parked in the Bakers' driveway where she set up her equipment. That night proved to me that the lens of a camera can capture images the human eye cannot see. On several of the numerous photographs Vivian took that night, there is the outline of a tall, shadowy figure in the distance. Most chilling to me is that the location of the figure is on the side of the highway above the ditch where Verna's body was found. There is no reasonable explanation why this same figure appears in several separate photographs. One of these photos appears on the cover of this book.

I would also like to thank Dr. Dotty Heady who is the current owner of Verna's home in LaGrange. Dotty answered her door to a curious stranger one Saturday morning and within a short time became my friend. Seeing the inside of her house was invaluable because many of the events in this book occurred there. Dotty also arranged for a tour of the one-time McCarty-Ricketts funeral home, and by the end, I had seen the original embalming room in the basement where Verna's autopsy was conducted. I appreciate Dotty's suggestions with my manuscript, and her support of this project.

It has also been helpful to bounce theories off friends, and Ann Stansel and Margaret Plattner both encouraged me and offered suggestions. Margaret's hands appear in the photograph with the revolver. I appreciate her taking the time from a busy day to help illustrate the size of the gun in a woman's hands. Over the past years, Ann has patiently dealt with my obsession of possibilities and theories, and with her keen insight offered some of her own. From the beginning, she has also faithfully read drafts of chapters, and helped with computer technicalities. My daughter, Linton, has faithfully followed me to museums, cemeteries, and historical societies in my quest. I don't believe she has enjoyed the journey nearly as much as I have, but like most teenagers, she is a whiz at technical issues.

Diana and Andrew Plattner kindly offered invaluable suggestions, especially encouraging me to pare down the trial chapters which the reader of this book will appreciate. Everything the witnesses had to say was of paramount importance to me as an attorney, but not necessarily to a reader without a legal background. I remember Diana encouraging me to "cut through the kudzu" and remember my readers. Dr. Elissa May Plattner loves Kentucky history and offered encouragement over the years. She never doubted that I could write this book. For her help and belief in this project, I have chosen to dedicate the book to her.

I owe a debt to Mildred Connell Lewis, the daughter of Verna's good friend Mildred Connell. She has been one of my bridges to the past, and my conversations with her have not only been enlightening, they have been fascinating. Her ability to recount details such as the color of Verna's burial dress was amazing. I would also like to thank members of the Denhardt family, and descendants of the Garr and Taylor families for speaking with me and discussing details that were sometimes painful. With those conversations, the historical events of this book became a tragic reality.

Retired Kentucky Supreme Court Justice John Palmore graciously shared his memories of the day he attended the Garr brothers' trial with his law school class. Tom Ballard of LaGrange is an expert at recalling and telling tall tales in true Kentucky fashion. His recollections of Chester Woolfolk and stories of the Garr brothers were both entertaining and helpful. Mike Howard of Frankfort patiently answered all of my questions about vintage cars and I appreciate his help.

Finally, I would like to thank the senior citizens of LaGrange who graciously shared their recollections of 1936 and 1937. If I survive to be ninety, I can only hope that my mind functions nearly as well.

BIBLIOGRAPHY

NEWSPAPERS

Local, national, and international newspapers, including those listed below, covered the murders of Verna Garr Taylor and General Henry Denhardt and the ensuing trials. These news accounts were vital to the telling of this story. Specific articles are cited in the notes.

Bowling Green (KY) *Times-Journal*
Chicago American
Chicago Daily Times
Chicago Sunday Times
Chicago Tribune
Hammond (IN) *Times*
Henry County (KY) *Local*
Ironwood (MI) *Daily Globe*
Lima (OH) *News*
London Daily Herald
Louisville (KY) *Courier-Journal*
Louisville (KY) *Times*
New York Times
Oldham (KY) *Era*
Park City (Bowling Green, KY) *Daily News*
Reno Evening Gazette
Shelby (KY) *Sentinel*

Twin City News
Zanesville (OH) *Signal*

OTHER SOURCES

American Jurisprudence Proof of Facts 3rd Series, Attorneys Illustrated Medical Dictionary. St. Paul, MN: West Group, 2002.

Baldwin, William Edward, ed. *Carroll's Eighth Edition, Kentucky Statutes Annotated.* Cleveland, OH: Banks-Baldwin, 1936.

Bell, Rick. *The Great Flood of 1937.* Louisville, KY: Butler Books, 2007.

Brown, Dave. "Detective Hunts Blue Stains Instead of Bloody Fingerprints." *Louisville Courier-Journal Magazine*, December 6, 1936.

John Marshall Berry Papers, 1936–2005, Filson Historical Society, Louisville, KY.

Bomb Yearbook. Lexington, VA: Virginia Military Institute, 1911.

Childress, Morton O. *Louisville Division of Police: History and Personnel.* Nashville, TN: Turner Publishing, 2005.

Commonwealth of Kentucky vs. Henry H. Denhardt, examining trial transcript, Berry Center, New Castle, KY.

Commonwealth of Kentucky vs. Henry H. Denhardt, trial transcript and related exhibits, Kentucky Department for Libraries and Archives, Frankfort, KY: location A1998-077, box 14A, case 1224.

Commonwealth of Kentucky vs. E. S. Garr, Roy Garr, and Jack Garr, examining trial transcript, Shelby County Circuit Court, Kentucky Department for Libraries and Archives, Frankfort, KY: location B10J8, boxes 36 and 37.

Connelly, William E. and E. M. Coulter. *History of Kentucky.* Chicago: American Historical Society, 1922.

Henry H. Denhardt Papers, 1907–1931, Filson Historical Society, Louisville, KY.

"Denhardt: Prosecution Tries to Spell Death with Pen Pistol." *Newsweek*, May 1, 1937.

"Denhardt, Three Angry Brothers Close a Famous Case." *Life*, October 4, 1937.

William Ellis Collection, private collection, Richmond, KY.

Ellis, William E. "'The Harvest Moon Was Shinin' on the Streets of Shelbyville': Southern Honor and the Death of General Henry H. Denhardt, 1937." *Register of the Kentucky Historical Society* 84, no. 4 (Autumn 1986).

Estate of James A. Wallace to H. H. Denhardt, July 17, 1935. Oldham County Clerk, Land Records, Book 55, 138–40.

Estate of Patricia Wilson vs. Henry H. Denhardt, Jefferson County Circuit Court, Common Pleas Branch, case 252166, Louisville, KY.

Forgy, M. L. "The Truth about General Denhardt, Kentucky's Bizarre Love Drama." *True Detective*, January 1938.

Hamilton, Bernard. "Three Brothers and the General's Fiancée." *Actual Detective Stories of Women in Crime*, December 1937.

Henry County Circuit Court Records, Kentucky Department for Libraries and Archives, Frankfort, KY.

Kavanaugh, Frank K. *Kentucky Directory for the Use of Courts, State and County Officials, and General Assembly of the State of Kentucky*, 1934.

Kentucky Bureau of Vital Statistics, Frankfort, Kentucky.

Kentucky Department for Libraries and Archives, Frankfort, Kentucky.

Kentucky National Guard, Frankfort, Kentucky.

Campbell, Peter, *Kentucky State Federation of Labor Bulletin*, no. 41 (July 12, 1923).

"Lieutenant Col. Denhardt," news release, November 23, 1918 (source of the release is unknown).

"Life on the American Newsfront: The Strange Case of the Kentucky General," *Time*, October 4, 1937.

Matthews, William E. "Murder in a Small Town." *Shelby County Life*, September 2007.

Mayer, Elsie Frank. "Kentucky's Bloody Denhardt Feud." *Front Page Detective*, December 1938.

Milward, Burton, Jr. *Louisville's Legendary Lawyer: Frank Haddad.* Bloomington, IN: AuthorHouse, 2008.

Murray, Robert K. and Roger W. Brucker. *Trapped!* New York: G. P. Putnam's Sons, 1979.

Oglesby, Joseph Woodsen. "The Murder Suspect." In *Dinner with D. W. Griffith and Other Memories.* Holicong, PA: Borgo Press, 2005.

Oldham County Clerk Land Records, Book 55, LaGrange, Kentucky.

Pearce, John Ed. "Murder Most Mysterious." *Louisville Courier-Journal Magazine.* December 8, 1985.

Proceedings of the Eighth Annual Meeting of the Kentucky State Bar Association. Louisville, KY: Standard Printing, 1942.

Rule, Leslie. *Ghost in the Mirror: Real Cases of Spirit Encounters.* Kansas City, MO: Andrews McMeel, 2008.

Shakespeare, William. "The Tragedy of Julius Caesar." In *The Complete Oxford Shakespeare.* Vol. 3. Edited by Stanley Wells and Gary Taylor. Oxford, England: Oxford University Press, 1987.

Southard, Mary Young and Ernest C. Miller, eds. "Rodes Myers" in *Who's Who In Kentucky, A Biographical Assembly of Notable Kentuckians.* Louisville, KY: Standard Printing, 1936.

Trowbridge, John M. "Searching for Pancho: The Kentucky National Guard Mexican Border Service 1916–1917," Kentucky National Guard website, www.kynghistory.ky.gov.

NOTES

1   "Denhardt: Prosecution Tries to Spell Death with Pen Pistol," *Newsweek*, May 1, 1937.

2   William Shakespeare, *Julius Caesar*, act 3, scene 2.

3   John Herchenroeder, "Crowd Cheers as Garrs Freed on Bond," *Louisville Courier-Journal*, September 25, 1937.

4   Angela Struck, "LaGrange: First a Crossroad, Then a County Seat," *Louisville Courier-Journal*, February 16, 2007.

5   Commonwealth of Kentucky v. Henry H. Denhardt, trial transcript at 176.

6   Ibid., 227–28.

7   Ibid., 226–27.

8   Ibid.

9   Ibid., 237.

10 Ibid., 285–86.

11 Ibid., 187.

12 Commonwealth of Kentucky vs. Henry H. Denhardt, trial transcript at 618.

13 Ibid.

14 Ibid.

15 Commonwealth of Kentucky vs. Henry H. Denhardt, defense exhibit #2, excerpt from letter dated July 4, 1936.

16 Ibid., defense exhibit #1, excerpt from letter dated June 26, 1936.

17 Ibid., unmarked defense exhibit, closing from letter to Denhardt dated August 4, 1936. Verna's letters to Denhardt are written on heavy paper in blue fountain pen ink that has faded with age. They are in pristine condition as though they were opened carefully to preserve both the letter and the envelope. Their condition so many years later is perhaps a testament to Denhardt's value of the letters when he received them.

18 Ibid., 623.

19 Ibid., 48.

20 John Herchenroeder, "Roy Garr is Termed Temporarily Insane," *Louisville Courier-Journal*, October 22, 1937.

21 Commonwealth of Kentucky vs. Henry H. Denhardt, trial transcript at 48.

22 Mildred Connell Lewis (Mildred Connell's daughter), interview with author, November 10, 2012. Lewis is certain that her mother's conversation with Verna took place in October after her family moved back to LaGrange. Lewis, sixteen at the time Verna died, has a letter from her transferring high schools dated October 20, 1936, which would have placed them back in LaGrange in mid to late October. Birdie Bennett's story of the argument she overheard from the Taylor kitchen is from the same period: mid to late October. The argument overheard by Verna's daughter occurred in late October.

23 Commonwealth of Kentucky vs. Henry H. Denhardt, trial transcript at 62.

24 Ibid., Denhardt at 627–28; also see Dave Brown, "Denhardt in Denial Says Fiancée Told Him of Woolfolk's Jealousy," *Louisville Courier-Journal*, April 30, 1937.

25 Commonwealth of Kentucky vs. Henry H. Denhardt, trial transcript at 629.

26 Executors of estate of James A. Wallace to H. H. Denhardt, July 17, 1935, Oldham County Clerk, Land Records, Book 55, 138-40.

27 Ironically, General Denhardt's farm was originally owned by a branch of the Taylor family. Verna Garr Taylor was related by marriage to the ancestral Taylors who built Denhardt's oversized home. The long-dead members of the Taylor family were buried in a cemetery within sight of his house.

28 William E. Connelly and E. M. Coulter, *History of Kentucky* (Chicago: American Historical Society, 1922), 4:635.

29 "Brother, Sister of General Denhardt Issue Statement Condemning Press of Kentucky; Not to Aid Prosecution," *Park City Daily News*, September 24, 1937; Commonwealth of Kentucky vs. Henry H. Denhardt, trial transcript at 613–16.

30 "Lieutenant Col. Denhardt," news release, November 23, 1918, military file of H. H. Denhardt, Kentucky National Guard, Frankfort, KY.

31   "Bowling Green Plans Welcome Home for Distinguished Son,"
      Bowling Green Times-Journal, February 15, 1918; see also the brief
      official biographical review of Denhardt in Frank K. Kavanaugh's
      *Kentucky Directory for the Use of Courts, State and County Officials,
      and General Assembly of the State of Kentucky* (1934), 186.

32   Affidavits and statements, A D393, folder 170, Henry H.
      Denhardt Papers, Filson Historical Society, Louisville, KY.

33   Campbell County speech, 1923, A D393, folder 19, Henry H.
      Denhardt Papers, Filson Historical Society, Louisville, KY.

34   Peter Campbell, *Kentucky State Federation of Labor Bulletin,* no.
      41 (July 12, 1923), 1–2, A D393, folder 156, Henry H. Denhardt
      Papers, Filson Historical Society, Louisville, KY.

35   Robert K. Murray and Roger W. Brucker, *Trapped!* (New York: G.
      P. Putnam's Sons, 1979), 130.

36   Ellerbe Carter and several other military associates would
      eventually testify at the 1937 trial of the Garr brothers.

37   "Denhardt is Shot in Back in Vote Row," *Louisville Courier-
      Journal,* November 6, 1931.

38   Ruth Denhardt, telephone interview with author, December 9,
      2012.

39   "Denhardt Conditions Offer to Surrender," *Louisville Courier-
      Journal,* August 22, 1935.

40   "Wooten to Aid Chandler in Run-Off," *Louisville Courier-Journal,*
      August 21, 1935.

41   "Denhardt Conditions Offer to Surrender," *Louisville Courier-
      Journal,* August 22, 1935.

42   Commonwealth of Kentucky vs. Henry H. Denhardt, trial
      transcript at 291.

43   Ibid., 219.

44   Ibid., 560.

45   Dave Brown, "Denhardt Prosecutors Silent on Woolfolk Role in
      Murder Trial," *Louisville Courier-Journal,* April 26, 1937.

46   Morton O. Childress, *Louisville Division of Police: History and
      Personnel* (Nashville, TN: Turner Publishing, 2005), 77.

47   "State Woman Found Dead of Gun Shot," *Louisville Courier-
      Journal,* November 8, 1936.

48   Commonwealth of Kentucky vs. Henry H. Denhardt, trial
      transcript at 304.

49 "State Woman Found Dead of Gun Shot," *Louisville Courier-Journal*, November 8, 1936.

50 Ibid.

51 Mildred Connell Lewis, interview with author, November 10, 2012. Seventy-six years after Verna's death, Lewis remembered that Verna wore a pink, sharkskin dress. She recalled that Verna wore it to one of her many church functions earlier in 1936. Sharkskin fabric in the 1930s did not have the shimmering appearance the name implies today. Rather, it had a two-toned woven appearance from using a twill weave.

52 Commonwealth of Kentucky vs. Henry H. Denhardt, trial transcript at 473.

53 Ibid., 476–77; see also Dave Brown, "Detective Hunts Blue Stains Instead of Bloody Fingerprints," *Louisville Courier-Journal Magazine*, December 6, 1936, 4–5.

54 Commonwealth of Kentucky vs. Henry H. Denhardt, trial transcript at 479, 495.

55 Obituary of Verna Garr Taylor, *Oldham Era*, November 13, 1936.

56 "Denhardt Faces Further Inquiry," *Louisville Times*, November 8, 1936.

57 "Roy Garr Saved Denhardt from Mob Threat, Claim," *Louisville Courier-Journal*, September 25, 1937.

58 "Tells of Fiancée's Killing," *New York Times*, November 8, 1936.

59 Jane Dixon, "Denhardt Fills Role of Polite Listener," *Louisville Times*, April 21, 1937.

60 Commonwealth of Kentucky vs. Henry H. Denhardt, trial transcript at 305.

61 Ibid., 657.

62 Ibid., 274.

63 Ibid.

64 Ibid., 275.

65 Ibid.

66 Ibid., 239–40.

67 Ibid., 481.

68 "Kentucky: General & Widow," *Time*.

69 "Taylor Inquest is Deferred," *Henry County Local*, November 13, 1936.

70 Commonwealth of Kentucky vs. Henry H. Denhardt, trial transcript at 313–14.

71 Ibid., 329–30.

72 "Infant of Local Physician Dies," *Oldham Era*, January 31, 1936.

73 Report of Examination of Mrs. Verna Taylor of LaGrange, Kentucky, November 13, 1936 at 8:30 p.m., Kentucky Department for Libraries and Archives, Frankfort, KY.

74 "Kentucky Slaying Traced to One Shot," *New York Times*, November 15, 1936.

75 "General is Charged with Killing Woman," *New York Times*, November 13, 1936.

76 "New Autopsy Considered in Death Inquiry," *Lima* (OH*) News*, November 16, 1936.

77 Bob Hill, "Profile of Frank Haddad," *Louisville Courier-Journal*, October 31, 1992.

78 Burton Milward, Jr., *Louisville's Legendary Lawyer: Frank Haddad* (Bloomington, IN: AuthorHouse, 2008), 30.

79 Connelley and Coulter, *History of Kentucky*, 3:522–25; "Rodes Myers," in *Who's Who In Kentucky, A Biographical Assembly of Notable Kentuckians*, edited by Mary Young Southard and Ernest C. Miller (Louisville, KY: Standard Printing, 1936), 297.

80 *Proceedings of the Eighth Annual Meeting of the Kentucky State Bar Association* (Louisville, KY: Standard Printing, 1942), 146.

81 "Denhardt is Sued for Fee," *Oldham Era*, April 2, 1937.

82 *Eighth Annual Meeting of the Kentucky State Bar Association*, 146.

83 *Bomb Yearbook* (Lexington, VA: Virginia Military Institute, 1911); found on www.e-yearbook.com.

84 John M. Trowbridge, "Searching for Pancho: The Kentucky National Guard Mexican Border Service 1916–1917," Kentucky National Guard website, www.kynghistory.ky.gov.

85 "Judge Marshall, Noted Jurist, Dies," *Shelby Sentinel*, November 12, 1943.

86 Dave Brown, "Denhardt Is Indicted in Mrs. Taylor's Death, To Be Arraigned Today," *Louisville Courier-Journal*, January 20, 1937; Hammer Smith, telephone interview with author, November 2013.

87 Commonwealth of Kentucky vs. Henry H. Denhardt, trial transcript at 753.

88   Wayne Thomas, "Paraffin Tests Veto Suicide in Beauty's Death,"
      Chicago Tribune, November 17, 1936.

89   Ibid.

90   Ibid.

91   Ibid.

92   Ibid.

93   Motion, Commonwealth of Kentucky vs. Henry H. Denhardt.

94   "State to Resist Bond for General Denhardt at His Hearing
      Today," *Louisville Courier-Journal,* November 20, 1936.

95   Hazel MacDonald, "General's Aides Appeal in Effort to Halt
      Widow-Slaying Hearing," *Chicago American,* November 18, 1936;
      "Denhardt is Sent to Jail," *Oldham Era,* November 27, 1936.

96   "Commonwealth's Witnesses First," *Shelby Sentinel,* November
      20, 1936.

97   "State to Resist Bond for General Denhardt at His Hearing
      Today," *Louisville Courier-Journal,* November 20, 1936; description
      of use of paraldehyde: *American Jurisprudence Proof of Facts 3rd
      Series, Attorneys Illustrated Medical Dictionary* (St. Paul, MN: West
      Group, 2002).

98   "State to Resist Bond for General Denhardt at His Hearing
      Today," *Louisville Courier-Journal,* November 20, 1936.

99   "Denhardt is Sent to Jail," *Oldham Era,* November 27, 1936.

100   Commonwealth of Kentucky vs. Henry Denhardt, examining
      trial transcript, Browning at 5.

101   Ibid., 6.

102   In a recorded interview with Dr. William Ellis on October 16,
      1980, *Louisville Courier-Journal* reporter John Herchenroeder said
      that it was common for newspapers of the time to recreate scenes
      for staged photographs by using a model.

103   Commonwealth of Kentucky vs. Henry Denhardt, examining
      trial transcript at 14–15.

104   Ibid., 14–15.

105   Ibid, 15.

106   Ibid, 19.

107   Ibid.

108   "Denhardt, Held to Grand Jury without Bond in Taylor Case, Put
      in Jefferson County Jail," *Louisville Courier-Journal,* November 21,
      1936.

109 Ibid.

110 Commonwealth of Kentucky vs. Henry Denhardt, examining trial transcript, George Baker at 22.

111 Ibid.

112 Ibid.

113 Ibid., 24.

114 Ibid., 35.

115 Ibid., 26.

116 Ibid., 28.

117 Ibid.

118 Ibid., 33.

119 Ibid., 41

120 Commonwealth of Kentucky vs. Henry H. Denhardt, trial transcript at 172.

121 Ibid., 42.

122 "Denhardt, Held to Grand Jury without Bond in Taylor Case, Put in Jefferson County Jail," *Louisville Courier-Journal*, November 21, 1936.

123 Commonwealth of Kentucky vs. Henry Denhardt, examining trial transcript at 44.

124 Denhardt, Held to Grand Jury without Bond in Taylor Case, Put in Jefferson County Jail," *Louisville Courier-Journal*, November 21, 1936.

125 Ibid.

126 Ibid., and Commonwealth of Kentucky vs. Henry Denhardt, examining trial transcript.

127 Ibid.; see also "Denhardt is Sent to Jail," *Oldham Era*, November 27, 1936.

128 Denhardt, Held to Grand Jury without Bond in Taylor Case, Put in Jefferson County Jail," *Louisville Courier-Journal*, November 21, 1936.

129 Ibid.

130 Ibid.

131 Ibid.

132 The complete version of Myers's and Thomas's closing arguments can be found in the examining trial transcript, at the Berry Center, pages 62–79. The author has summarized the lengthy arguments based on the transcript and the events detailed in "Denhardt, Held

to Grand Jury Without Bond in Taylor Case, Put in Jefferson County Jail," *Louisville Courier-Journal*, November 21, 1936.

133   Denhardt, Held to Grand Jury without Bond in Taylor Case, Put in Jefferson County Jail," *Louisville Courier-Journal*, November 21, 1936.

134   "Denhardt, in Jail, Asserts Innocence," *New York Times*, November 22, 1936.

135   "Gen. Denhardt Denies Guilt," *Oldham Era*, November 27, 1936.

136   Ibid.

137   Ibid.

138   Ibid.

139   Denhardt, Held to Grand Jury without Bond in Taylor Case, Put in Jefferson County Jail," *Louisville Courier-Journal*, November 21, 1936; "Denhardt Asserts Innocence," *New York Times*.

140   "Gen. Denhardt Denies Guilt," *Oldham Era*, November 27, 1936.

141   John Berry to Rodes Myers, November 25, 1936, folder 1, John Marshall Berry Papers, Filson Historical Society, Louisville, KY.

142   "Mrs. Taylor's Daughter Is Bride," *New York Times*, November 22, 1936; see also "Friend of Family Tells of Wedding," *Zanesville Signal*, November 22, 1936; "Denhardt Still in County Jail," *Ironwood Daily Globe*, November 23, 1936.

143   Writ of Habeas Corpus in Kentucky, Ky. Const., Bill of Rights, § 16: "Bail Allowed; Habeas Corpus; "All prisoners shall be bailable by sufficient securities, unless for capital offense when the proof is evident or the presumption great; and the privilege of the writ of habeas corpus shall not be suspended unless when, in case of rebellion or invasion, the public safety may require it." Denhardt's Petition for Writ of Habeas Corpus is part of the original Henry County Circuit Court record, filed November 30, 1936, and retained in the Kentucky Department for Libraries and Archives, Frankfort, KY.

144   Commonwealth of Kentucky vs. Henry H. Denhardt, trial transcript at 153 and 203.

145   John Herchenroeder, "Roy Garr is Termed Temporarily Insane," *Louisville Courier-Journal*, October 22, 1937.

146   Commonwealth of Kentucky vs. Henry H. Denhardt, trial transcript at 551.

147   Ibid., 540–41.

148 "Accused Killer Granted Bail," *Reno Evening Gazette,* December 9, 1936.

149 "Denhardt is Free on Bond," *Oldham Era,* December 11, 1936.

150 Ibid.

151 Ibid.

152 John Berry to Rodes Myers, December 18, 1936, A B534a, folder 1, John Marshall Berry Papers, Filson Historical Society, Louisville, KY.

153 William Wight to Henry Denhardt, December 17, 1936, A B534a, folder 1, John Marshall Berry Papers, Filson Historical Society, Louisville, KY.

154 William Wight to John Berry, December 18, 1936, A B534a, folder 1, John Marshall Berry Papers, Filson Historical Society, Louisville, KY.

155 Rodes Myers to Henry Denhardt, December 19, 1936, folder 2, John Marshall Berry Papers, Filson Historical Society, Louisville, KY.

156 Rick Bell, *The Great Flood of 1937* (Louisville, KY: Butler Books, 2007), 12, 23.

157 Dave Brown, "Indictment of Denhardt Today Seen," *Louisville Courier-Journal,* January 19, 1937.

158 "Garr Brothers Now on Trial," *Oldham Era,* October 22, 1937. The debate over African American jurors in this country has a lengthy history in dispute as late as the 1980s. Most legal challenges addressed the issue of the make-up of the jury pool, in particular, the use of an all-white jury for an African American defendant. This common practice was eventually ruled unconstitutional. Marshall's patronizing ban on women was even more problematic because he publicly expressed a personal opinion against women as jurors. It is interesting to speculate whether the outcome of the trial would have been different with several female jurors.

159 Dave Brown, "Indictment of Denhardt Today Seen," *Louisville Courier-Journal,* January 19, 1937.

160 Ibid.

161 Ibid.

162 Ibid.

163 Ibid.

164 Dave Brown, "Denhardt is Indicted in Mrs. Taylor's Death, To Be Arraigned Today," *Louisville Courier-Journal*, January 20, 1937.

165 Ibid.

166 Ibid.

167 Dave Brown, "Denhardt's Trial is Set for Next Monday," *Louisville Courier-Journal*, January 21, 1937.

168 Beckham Overstreet to Henry Denhardt, February 15, 2937, folder 2, John Marshall Berry Papers, Filson Historical Society, Louisville, KY.

169 Beckham Overstreet to John Berry, February 24, 1937, folder 2, John Marshall Berry Papers, Filson Historical Society, Louisville, KY.

170 Memorandum to defense file, March 31, 1937, folder 2, John Marshall Berry Papers, Filson Historical Society, Louisville, KY.

171 Memorandum of Henry Denhardt to his attorneys, April 9, 1937, folder 3, John Marshall Berry Papers, Filson Historical Society, Louisville, KY.

172 Commonwealth of Kentucky vs. Henry H. Denhardt, trial transcript at 42.

173 Ibid., 66.

174 Ibid., 73.

175 Ibid. In a November 10, 2012, interview with the author, Mildred Connell Lewis recalled that Verna also asked her mother if she wanted to ride to Louisville with them that day, but she declined.

176 Commonwealth of Kentucky vs. Henry H. Denhardt, trial transcript at 41.

177 Ibid., 140–142.

178 Ibid., 75.

179 Ibid., 546.

180 Ibid., 83.

181 Ibid.

182 Ibid., 80.

183 Ibid.

184 Ibid., 669.

185 Ibid., 81.

186 Ibid., 67.

187 Commonwealth of Kentucky vs. E. S. Garr, Roy Garr, and Jack Garr, examining trial transcript at 66.

188 Denhardt Memorandum, March, 23, 1937, 17, A B534a, folder 8, John Marshall Berry Papers, Filson Historical Society, Louisville, KY, 17, 31.

189 Ibid., 1.

190 Ibid., 6.

191 Ibid., 7.

192 Ibid., 31.

193 Ibid., 7–8.

194 Ibid., 9.

195 Ibid.

196 Ibid., 10.

197 Ibid., 23.

198 Ibid., 12.

199 Ibid., 12–13.

200 Ibid., 13.

201 Ibid., 8.

202 Ibid., 13.

203 Ibid., 14.

204 Ibid., 23.

205 Ibid., 5.

206 Ibid., 23.

207 Ibid., 14.

208 Ibid., 17.

209 Ibid., 23.

210 Ibid., 10.

211 Ibid., 4.

212 Ibid.

213 Ibid., 15.

214 Ibid., 22.

215 Ibid., 15.

216 Ibid.

217 Ibid., 16.

218 Ibid., 32.

219 Ibid., 16.

220 Ibid., 17.

221 Ibid., 16.

222 Ibid., 18.

223 Ibid.

224 Ibid.
225 Ibid., 25.
226 Ibid., 27.
227 Ibid.
228 Ibid., 28.
229 Ibid., 30.
230 Ibid., 29.
231 Ibid., 33.
232 Ibid., 19.
233 Ibid., 8.
234 Commonwealth of Kentucky vs. Henry H. Denhardt, trial transcript at 458.
235 Henry Denhardt to John Berry, March 20, 1937, John Marshall Berry Papers, Filson Historical Society, Louisville, KY.
236 "General Denhardt on Trial for Murder in Henry County," *Oldham Era*, April 23, 1937.
237 Petition and Motion for Change of Venue, April 20, 1937, Henry County Circuit Court file, Kentucky Department for Libraries and Archives, Frankfort, KY.
238 Affidavit of McClure James, April 16, 1937, Henry County Circuit Court file, Kentucky Department for Libraries and Archives, Frankfort, KY.
239 Response to Defendant's Petition and Motion for Change of Venue, April 17, 1937, Henry County Circuit Court file, Kentucky Department for Libraries and Archives, Frankfort, KY.
240 Affidavit of Judge A. S. Morgan, April 16, 1937, Henry County Circuit Court file, Kentucky Department for Libraries and Archives, Frankfort, KY.
241 "General Denhardt to Face Jury," *Oldham Era*, April 16, 1937.
242 "General Henry H. Denhardt's Will," *Shelbyville Sentinel*, November 5, 1937.
243 Henry Denhardt to John Berry, April 15, 1937, folder 3, John Marshall Berry Papers, Filson Historical Society, Louisville, KY.
244 Henry Denhardt to John Berry, May 22, 1937, folder 3, John Marshall Berry Papers, Filson Historical Society, Louisville, KY.
245 John Berry to Henry Denhardt, January 5, 1937, A-B534a, folder 2, John Marshall Berry Papers, Filson Historical Society, Louisville, KY.

246 Baldwin, William Edward, ed., *Carroll's Eighth Edition, Kentucky Statutes Annotated* (Cleveland, OH: Banks-Baldwin, 1936).

247 "Judge Marshall, Noted Jurist, Dies," *Shelby Sentinel*, November 12, 1943.

248 Dave Brown, "Not Guilty Plea Made by Denhardt as Jury Is Sworn for Trial," *Louisville Courier-Journal*, April 23, 1937.

249 "General Denhardt on Trial for Murder in Henry County," *Oldham Era*, April 23, 1937.

250 "General Jury Expected by Nightfall," *Henry County Local*, April 23, 1937.

251 W. O. Carver, Jr., "4 Witnesses Are Quizzed by Defense," *Louisville Times*, April 21, 1937.

252 Dave Brown, "Named after Venue Shift is Refused," *Louisville Courier-Journal*, April 21, 1937.

253 Carver, "4 Witnesses Quizzed," *Louisville Times*.

254 Ibid.

255 "General Denhardt on Trial for Murder in Henry County," *Oldham Era*, April 23, 1937.

256 Ibid.

257 Dave Brown, "Not Guilty Plea Made by Denhardt as Jury Is Sworn for Trial," *Louisville Courier-Journal*, April 23, 1937.

258 Ibid.

259 Ibid.

260 Ibid.

261 Jerry Rodgers, interview with author, June 20, 2011.

262 Dave Brown, "Not Guilty Plea Made by Denhardt as Jury Is Sworn for Trial," *Louisville Courier-Journal*, April 23, 1937.

263 Dave Brown, "'Denhardt Couldn't Have Done It,' Jury is Told By Witness," *Louisville Courier-Journal*, April 24, 1937.

264 William E. Ellis, "'The Harvest Moon Was Shinin' on the Streets of Shelbyville': Southern Honor and the Death of General Henry H. Denhardt, 1937," *Register of the Kentucky Historical Society* 84, no. 4 (Autumn 1986): 378.

265 Commonwealth of Kentucky vs. Henry H. Denhardt, trial transcript at 24.

266 Ibid., 31.

267 Ibid., 35.

268 Ibid., 37–38.

269   Ibid., 42.

270   Ibid., 47.

271   Ibid.

272   Ibid., 48.

273   Dave Brown, "'Denhardt Couldn't Have Done It,' Jury is Told By Witness," *Louisville Courier-Journal*, April 24, 1937.

274   Commonwealth of Kentucky vs. Henry H. Denhardt, trial transcript at 52.

275   Ibid., 54.

276   William E. Ellis wrote, "Judge Marshall always allowed women to leave the courtroom several minutes before the men in order to prepare the noonday and evening meals. Such a suggestion today would be unthinkable." Ellis, "Harvest Moon,'" 396.

277   Commonwealth of Kentucky vs. Henry H. Denhardt, trial transcript at 57.

278   Ibid., 58.

279   Ibid. 63.

280   Ibid., 64.

281   Ibid.

282   "Class of 1938 Graduates," *Oldham Era*, May 27, 1938.

283   Commonwealth of Kentucky vs. Henry H. Denhardt, trial transcript at 66.

284   Dave Brown, "'Denhardt Couldn't Have Done It,' Jury is Told By Witness," *Louisville Courier-Journal*, April 24, 1937.

285   Mildred Connell Lewis, interview with author, November 10, 2012. Lewis recalled that Denhardt took Verna, Frances, herself, and another friend to this football game on a Saturday shortly before Verna died. They went to the Louisville Country Club for dinner afterward. While she remembered little about the conversations that day, she believed she would remember it well if Denhardt acted badly.

286   Commonwealth of Kentucky vs. Henry H. Denhardt, trial transcript at 70–71.

287   Ibid., 92.

288   Ibid., 98–99.

289   Ibid., 107.

290   Ibid., 110–11.

291   Ibid., 125.

292 Ibid., 133.

293 Ibid., 143–44.

294 Ibid., 149.

295 Ibid., 150.

296 Ibid., 158.

297 J. B. Hundley to John Berry, March 14, 1937, folder 2, John Marshall Berry Papers, Filson Historical Society, Louisville, KY.

298 J. B. Hundley to John Berry, June 16, 1937, folder 3, John Marshall Berry Papers, Filson Historical Society, Louisville, KY.

299 Commonwealth of Kentucky vs. Henry H. Denhardt, trial transcript at 168.

300 Dave Brown, "'Denhardt Couldn't Have Done It,' Jury is Told By Witness," *Louisville Courier-Journal*, April 24, 1937.

301 Commonwealth of Kentucky vs. Henry H. Denhardt, trial transcript at 176.

302 Ibid.

303 Ibid., 181.

304 Ibid., 185.

305 Ibid., 187.

306 Ibid.

307 Ibid., 188.

308 Ibid.

309 Ibid.

310 Ibid., 188–189.

311 Ibid., 188.

312 Ibid., 189.

313 Dave Brown, "'Denhardt Couldn't Have Done It,' Jury is Told By Witness," *Louisville Courier-Journal*, April 24, 1937.

314 Ibid., 189.

315 Ibid.

316 Dave Brown, "Denhardt Prosecutors Silent on Woolfolk Role in Murder Trial," *Louisville Courier-Journal*, April 26, 1937.

317 "Laundry Truck Driver Now in Forefront of Murder Case," *Zanesville Signal*, April 26, 1937; Brown, "Denhardt Prosecutors Silent," *Courier-Journal*.

318 "Gun Not Near Mrs. Taylor, Physician Says," *Louisville Courier-Journal*, April 25, 1937.

319 "Laundry Truck Driver Now in Forefront of Murder Case," *Zanesville Signal*, April 26, 1937.

320 Commonwealth of Kentucky vs. Henry H. Denhardt, trial transcript at 217.

321 Ibid.

322 Ibid., 218.

323 Ibid., 219.

324 Ibid.

325 Ibid., 235.

326 Ibid.

327 Ibid., 235–236.

328 "Gun Not Near Mrs. Taylor, Physician Says," *Louisville Courier-Journal*, April 25, 1937.

329 Ibid.

330 Commonwealth of Kentucky vs. E. S. Garr, Roy Garr, and Jack Garr, examining trial at 54.

331 Commonwealth of Kentucky vs. Henry H. Denhardt, trial transcript at 276.

332 Ibid., 278.

333 Ibid.

334 Ibid., 288.

335 Ibid., 293–94.

336 Ibid., 306.

337 Ibid., 261–62, 230, 587.

338 Ibid., 314.

339 Defense memorandum, March 31, 1937, folder 2, John Marshall Berry Papers, Filson Historical Society, Louisville, KY.

340 Commonwealth of Kentucky vs. Henry H. Denhardt, trial transcript at 327.

341 Dave Brown, "Denhardt Witness Hits Paraffin Test for Powder Stain," *Louisville Courier-Journal*, April 22, 1937.

342 Dave Brown, "Estimate of Distance of Gun From Mrs. Taylor When Fatal Shot Was Fired Is Forbidden," *Louisville Courier-Journal*, April 27, 1937.

343 Commonwealth of Kentucky vs. Henry H. Denhardt, trial transcript at 334. Walsh testified that the bullet missed rib number seven and passed between the fifth and sixth ribs. His

testimony conflicts with the autopsy report, which notes that both the seventh rib and seventh vertebrae were broken.

344 Dave Brown, "Estimate of Distance of Gun From Mrs. Taylor When Fatal Shot Was Fired Is Forbidden," *Louisville Courier-Journal*, April 27, 1937.

345 Commonwealth of Kentucky vs. Henry H. Denhardt, trial transcript at 408.

346 Ibid., 413.

347 Ibid., 430.

348 Ibid., 332–33.

349 Ibid., 731.

350 Ibid., 369.

351 Ibid., 446.

352 Dave Brown, "Estimate of Distance of Gun From Mrs. Taylor When Fatal Shot Was Fired Is Forbidden," *Louisville Courier-Journal*, April 27, 1937.

353 Henry Denhardt to John Berry, May 22, 1937, A B534a, folder 3, John Marshall Berry Papers, Filson Historical Society, Louisville, KY.

354 Ibid.

355 Commonwealth of Kentucky vs. Henry H. Denhardt, trial transcript at 483, 583–85.

356 Ibid., 461.

357 Dave Brown, "Splotches on Denhardt's Coat Shown by Laboratory Tests to Be Blood, Witnesses Say," *Louisville Courier-Journal*, April 28, 1937.

358 Commonwealth of Kentucky vs. Henry H. Denhardt, trial transcript at 460.

359 Ibid., 476.

360 Ibid.

361 Ibid., 487.

362 Ibid., 494.

363 Ibid., 503.

364 Ibid., 464.

365 Ibid., 560.

366 "Defense Begins Testimony as Commonwealth Rests," *Oldham Era*, April 30, 1937.

367 "General Jury sees Death Site," *Henry County Local*, April 30, 1937.

368 Commonwealth of Kentucky vs. Henry H. Denhardt, trial transcript at 223.

369 Ibid., 259.

370 Ibid., 109.

371 Ibid., 716.

372 John Berry, interview with Dr. William Ellis, June, 3, 1985.

373 Dave Brown, "Denhardt Denies He Killed Mrs. Taylor," *Louisville Courier-Journal*, April 30, 1937.

374 Ibid.

375 Commonwealth of Kentucky vs. Henry H. Denhardt, trial transcript at 626-27.

376 Ibid., 627.

377 Ibid., 625.

378 Ibid., 627.

379 Dave Brown, "Denhardt in Denial Says Fiancée Told Him of Woolfolk's Jealousy," *Louisville Courier-Journal*, April 30, 1937.

380 Ibid., 624.

381 Commonwealth of Kentucky vs. Henry H. Denhardt, trial transcript at 628.

382 Ibid.

383 Ibid.

384 Ibid., 628–29.

385 Commonwealth of Kentucky vs. Henry H. Denhardt, trial transcript at 631.

386 Ibid., 632.

387 Ibid.

388 Ibid., 635. In the general's March memorandum, he doesn't say that Verna removed the pistol from the glove box and "toyed" with it during the day. It is also interesting that his April 9 to-do list directs his attorneys to look for suicides in the Garr family. The reference to a "distant relative" who committed suicide may imply that they uncovered useful information, and Denhardt used it here to further support his allegation of Verna's suicide.

389 Ibid., 633.

390 Ibid., 633. In his March memorandum, Denhardt claimed that he became sick after hearing Verna's confession about Woolfolk. By the time he testified a month later, his "illness" was due to a cold.

391 Ibid., 635.

392 Ibid., 637.

393 Ibid.

394 Ibid.

395 Ibid., 638.

396 Ibid., 639–40.

397 Ibid., 640.

398 Ibid., 641.

399 Ibid.

400 Ibid., 643. In his memorandum, Denhardt's story of the suicide pact occurred on the drive home from Louisville to LaGrange. In his trial testimony, the general shifted this story to the scene in Baker's driveway.

401 Ibid., 644.

402 Ibid.

403 Ibid., 645.

404 Ibid., 647.

405 Ibid.

406 Ibid., 649. The one obvious question Myers did not ask was, "Did you have anything at all to do with her death?"

407 Ibid., 652.

408 Ibid., 654.

409 Ibid., 654–55.

410 Ibid., 655.

411 Ibid., 664.

412 Ibid., 665.

413 Ibid.

414 Jane Dixon, "'Denhardt Didn't Shoot My Sister' Dr. Garr Asserts—I Know Who Did," *Louisville Times*, December 8, 1938.

415 Commonwealth of Kentucky vs. Henry H. Denhardt, trial transcript at 668.

416 Ibid., 670.

417 Ibid., 674.

418 Ibid., 675.

419 Ibid., 676.

420 Ibid., 678.

421 Ibid., 682–83.

422 Ibid., 683.

423 Ibid., 714.

424 Ibid., 727.

425 Ibid., 738.

426 Ibid., 740.

427 Ibid., 741.

428 Ibid., 753.

429 Ibid., 756.

430 Ibid., 758.

431 Ibid., 761.

432 Ibid., 763.

433 Ibid., 764–65.

434 Ibid., 768.

435 Ibid., 768.

436 John Main, "A Midnight Ride in Old Kaintuck," *Chicago Sunday Times*, April 25, 1937; reprinted in the *Henry County Local*, May 21, 1987.

437 "Jury in Denhardt Case Unable to Agree and is Discharged," *Oldham Era*, May 7, 1937.

438 Ibid.

439 Ibid.

440 Ibid.

441 Ibid.

442 Ibid.

443 Dave Brown, "General Denhardt Locked in Cell as Jury Argues His Fate in Death of Mrs. Taylor," *Louisville Courier-Journal*, May 4, 1937.

444 "Jury in Denhardt Case Unable to Agree and is Discharged," *Oldham Era*, May 7, 1937.

445 Dave Brown, "General Denhardt Locked in Cell as Jury Argues His Fate in Death of Mrs. Taylor," *Louisville Courier-Journal*, May 4, 1937.

446 "Jury in Denhardt Case Unable to Agree and is Discharged," *Oldham Era*, May 7, 1937.

447 Ibid.

448 "Crowd is Ignored by Prisoner," Dave Brown, *Louisville Courier Journal*, May 5, 1937.

449 "Jury in Denhardt Case Unable to Agree and is Discharged," *Oldham Era*, May 7, 1937.

450 Ibid., 260 and 176. George Baker estimated that Verna's body was twenty or twenty-five feet from the road; Commonwealth of Kentucky vs. Henry H. Denhardt, trial transcript at 115. Keightley believed she was ten feet away; Ibid., 223. Ricketts estimated the distance at fifteen feet. The shortest estimate was J. B. Hundley's at eight feet from the highway.

451 "Jury in Denhardt Case Unable to Agree and is Discharged," *Oldham Era*, May 7, 1937.

452 Ibid.

453 Ibid.

454 "Denhardt Jury Out, Gives Up For Night," *New York Times*, May 5, 1937.

455 "Jury in Denhardt Case Unable to Agree and is Discharged," *Oldham Era*, May 7, 1937.

456 Dave Brown, "Denhardt Jury Fails to Agree on Verdict," *Louisville Courier-Journal*, May 6, 1937.

457 Ibid.

458 "Jury in Denhardt Case Unable to Agree and is Discharged," *Oldham Era*, May 7, 1937.

459 "General Will be Re-Tried in September," *Bulletin*, Associated Press, New Castle, Kentucky, May 6, 1937.

460 Ibid.

461 Dave Brown, "Denhardt's Trial Set for September as Jury Disagrees," *Louisville Courier-Journal*, May 7, 1937.

462 Ibid.

463 "Denhardt Jury is Hung 7 Favor Acquittal, Said," *Henry County Local*, May 7, 1937.

464 "Jury in Denhardt Case Unable to Agree and is Discharged," *Oldham Era*, May 7, 1937.

465 Ruth Denhardt, telephone interview with author, December 9, 2012.

466 Rodes K. Myers, "Premonition of Death Battled by General," *Louisville Times*, September 21, 1937.

467 Earl Thomas "Hammer" Smith, interview with author, April 6, 2012.

468 Benjamin Reeves to Dr. William Ellis, May 12, 1981; personal collection of Dr. William Ellis.

469 Elizabeth Smiser relayed the anecdote in a telephone interview with author, February 2011. Her words are quoted from William E. Matthews, "Murder in a Small Town," *Shelby County Life*, September 2007. Although the magazine article dates the telephone call as "mid-November 1936," it is more likely that it took place when Denhardt was living in Bowling Green after the end of the trial. The inquest was November 13, and the examining trial was November 20. Indications are that in November the general stayed in seclusion on his Oldham County farm or was out on bail and staying with Dr. McCormack in Louisville.

470 Henry Denhardt to John Berry, May 22, 1937, A B534a, folder 3, John Marshall Berry Papers, Filson Historical Society, Louisville, KY.

471 John Berry to Henry Denhardt, May 24, 1937, A B534a, folder 3, John Marshall Berry Papers, Filson Historical Society, Louisville, KY.

472 Ibid.

473 Henry Denhardt to John Berry, May 27, 1937, A B534a, folder 3, John Marshall Berry Papers, Filson Historical Society, Louisville, KY.

474 Henry Denhardt to John Berry, June 14, 1937, A B534a, folder 3, John Marshall Berry Papers, Filson Historical Society, Louisville, KY.

475 Ibid.

476 Henry Denhardt to John Berry, July 6, 1937, A B534a, folder 4, John Marshall Berry Papers, Filson Historical Society, Louisville, KY.

477 Leslie Rule, *Ghost in the Mirror: Real Cases of Spirit Encounters* (Kansas City, MO: Andrews McMeel, 2008), 91–97.

478 Edward C. Langan, Public Administrator & Guardian of Jefferson County, Kentucky de bonis non of the Estate of Patricia Wilson (Plaintiff) vs. Henry H. Denhardt Bowling Green, Kentucky (Defendant), July 2, 1937, Jefferson Circuit Court, Common Pleas Branch, case no. 252166.

479 "Denhardt Charges 'Plot' in $150,000 Damage Suit Filed Against Two Louisville Men," *Park City Daily News*, July 29, 1937.

480 John Herchenroeder (*Louisville Courier-Journal* reporter), interview with Dr. William Ellis, October 16, 1980.

481 "Malicious Extent to Which the Persecutors of General Denhardt Will Resort is Again Proven," *Bowling Green Times Journal,* July 6, 1937.

482 "Denhardt Charges 'Plot' in $150,000 Damage Suit Filed Against Two Louisville Men," *Park City Daily News*, July 29, 1937.

483 Henry Denhardt to John Berry, July 27, 1937, A B534a, folder 4, John Marshall Berry Papers, Filson Historical Society, Louisville, KY.

484 Henry Denhardt to Governor "Happy" Chandler, June 24, 1937, military file of H. H. Denhardt, Kentucky National Guard, Frankfort, KY.

485 Ibid.

486 John Berry to Rodes Myers, August 11, 1937, A B534a, folder 4, John Marshall Berry Papers, Filson Historical Society, Louisville, KY.

487 "Denhardt Gets Command: Kentucky General, Tried for His Fiancée's Murder, Restored," *New York Times*, August 11, 1937.

488 John Berry to Rodes Myers, September 4, 1937, A B534a, folder 4, John Marshall Berry Papers, Filson Historical Society, Louisville, KY.

489 Henry Denhardt to John Berry, September 11, 1937, A B534a, Folder 4, John Marshall Berry Papers, Filson Historical Society, Louisville, KY.

490 Ibid.

491 Commonwealth of Kentucky vs. E. S. Garr, Roy Garr, and Jack Garr, examining trial transcript at 55.

492 Ibid.

493 Ibid., 117.

494 Ibid., 57.

495 Oddly, the news coverage of the trial never mentioned the rented room. It was buried in the trial transcript with Denhardt's testimony, but never revealed by the press. This is strange considering the fact that reporters were quick to jump on the

titillating possibility of a relationship between Verna and Woolfolk.

496 John Herchenroeder, "Roy Garr is Termed Temporarily Insane," *Louisville Courier-Journal*, October 22, 1937.

497 John Herchenroeder, "Roy Garr Testifies He Thought Life in Peril," *Louisville Courier-Journal*, October 21, 1937.

498 John Herchenroeder, "Crowd Cheers as Garrs Freed on Bond," *Louisville Courier-Journal*, September 25, 1937.

499 Letter of Dr. Charles W. Karrakel, folder 4, John Marshall Berry Papers, Filson Historical Society, Louisville, KY.

500 Commonwealth of Kentucky vs. E. S. Garr, Roy Garr, and Jack Garr, examining trial transcript at 60.

501 Rodes K. Myers, "Premonition of Death Battled by General," *Louisville Times*, September 21, 1937.

502 Commonwealth of Kentucky vs. E. S. Garr, Roy Garr, and Jack Garr, examining trial transcript at 6. It is interesting that Myers describes his movements as a "slow run." Denhardt was afraid and running for his life, but was evidently capable of only a lumbering run. On the night of November 6, he would have had to move quickly to murder Verna and return to the car.

503 Ibid., 84.

504 Ibid., 62.

505 Ibid., 118.

506 Ibid., 94–95.

507 Ibid., 12. It was while he was begging for his life that Myers supposedly said the words that Kentucky attorneys would remember: "Don't shoot me; I'm just the lawyer." The author lived in Bowling Green in the 1980s and recalls an attorney in town who had on his office wall a plaque with Myers's words on it.

508 Ibid., 63.

509 Ibid., 47.

510 Ibid., 64.

511 Bruce Tracy, Jeptha Tracy's thirteen-year-old son, was a witness to the shooting. He was on his way home from the pool hall, trailing behind Denhardt and Myers on the sidewalk. When the shooting started, Bruce ran for home and dived under his bed. Mike Tracy, interview with the author, November 2013.

512 W. O. Carver, Jr., "Denhardt, Temper Untamed 'Damned' Enemies at Knox," *Louisville Times*, September 21, 1937.

513 Ibid.

514 Ibid.

515 Commonwealth of Kentucky vs. E. S. Garr, Roy Garr, and Jack Garr, examining trial transcript at 25.

516 Certificate of death, H. H. Denhardt, Kentucky Bureau of Vital Statistics, Frankfort, KY.

517 "Attorney's Life Threatened in Letters," *Park City Daily News*, September 23, 1937.

518 "Sensational Trial Ended by Shelbyville Killing," *Henry County Local*, September 24, 1937.

519 "Body of General Denhardt is Brought Here; Murder Warrant is Issued against Accused," *Park City Daily News*, September 21, 1937.

520 "General Denhardt is Killed by Garr Brothers," *Oldham Era*, September 24, 1937.

521 "Life on the American Newsfront: The Strange Case of the Kentucky General," *Time*, October 4, 1937; "Denhardt: Three Angry Brothers Close a Famous Case," *Life*, October 4, 1937.

522 John Herchenroeder, "Bitter Legal Feud Brews in Denhardt Case," *Louisville Courier-Journal*, September 22, 1937.

523 Ibid.

524 "Judge Cannot Get Jury For Honour Slaying Trial," *London Daily Herald*, October 19, 1937.

525 Molly Clowes, "3 Volleys Over Grave End Denhardt Rites," *Louisville Courier-Journal*, September 24, 1937.

526 Ibid.

527 Ibid.

528 "Remains W. J. Denhardt Will Arrive at 10:18 Tonight," *Bowling Green Times-Journal*, September 20, 1921.

529 Molly Clowes, "3 Volleys Over Grave End Denhardt Rites," *Louisville Courier-Journal*, September 24, 1937.

530 John Main, "Bury Denhardt as Lawyer Gets Death Threats," *Chicago Daily Times*, September 23, 1937.

531 "Brother, Sister of General Denhardt Issue Statement Condemning Press of Kentucky; Not to Aid Prosecution," *Park City Daily News*, September 24, 1937.

532 Ibid.

533 Ibid.

534 Ibid.

535 Ibid.

536 Ibid.

537 Ibid.

538 Letter of Joseph M. Kelly, Major, Calvary, Ky. N.G. Acting, the Adjutant General, September 29, 1937; from the files of the Kentucky National Guard, Frankfort, KY.

539 John Main, "Bury Denhardt as Lawyer Gets Death Threats," *Chicago Daily Times*, September 23, 1937.

540 John Herchenroeder, "Garrs to Tell Their Story of Slaying Denhardt on Witness Stand Today," *Louisville Courier-Journal*, September 24, 1937.

541 Ibid.

542 "General Denhardt is Killed by Garr Brothers," *Oldham Era*, September 24, 1937.

543 John Herchenroeder, "Garrs to Tell Their Story of Slaying Denhardt on Witness Stand Today," *Louisville Courier-Journal*, September 24, 1937.

544 Ibid.

545 Ibid.

546 Ibid.

547 Ibid.

548 Ibid.

549 Commonwealth of Kentucky vs. E. S. Garr, Roy Garr, and Jack Garr, examining trial transcript at 11.

550 Ibid.

551 Ibid., 38.

552 Ibid., 49.

553 Ibid.

554 "Roy Garr Says He Feared Denhardt," *Park City Daily News*, September 24, 1937.

555 Jane Dixon, "Denhardt Fills Role of Polite Listener," *Louisville Times*, April 21, 1937.

556 Commonwealth of Kentucky vs. E. S. Garr, Roy Garr, and Jack Garr, examining trial transcript at 56.

557 Ibid., 57

558 Ibid., 61.

559 Ibid., 63.

560 Ibid., 64.

561 Ibid.

562 Ibid., 67.

563 Ibid., 68–69.

564 Ibid., 76.

565 Ibid.

566 Ibid.

567 Ibid., 81.

568 Ibid., 88.

569 Ibid., 94.

570 Ibid., 100, 102.

571 Ibid., 104.

572 Ibid., 108.

573 Ibid., 118.

574 Ibid., 119.

575 Ibid., 120.

576 Ibid., 122–23.

577 Ibid., 126.

578 Ibid., 128.

579 Ibid.

580 Ibid., 130.

581 Ibid.

582 Ibid.

583 John Herchenroeder, "Crowd Cheers as Garrs Freed on Bond," *Louisville Courier-Journal*, September 25, 1937.

584 Ibid.

585 Ibid.

586 Ibid.

587 Ibid.

588 Ibid.

589 Ibid.

590 Ibid.

591 Ibid.

592 Ibid.

593 One of the youngest men present was a twenty-two-year-old farmer, Robert Coleman "R. C." Haley of Simpsonville, Kentucky.

Haley was experiencing the most eventful year of his quiet, rural life. In January, he aided in the rescue efforts during the Great Flood, and in October his name was called as a grand juror for the case against the Garr brothers. He would later serve in World War II, and eventually became the author's maternal uncle.

594 John Herchenroeder, "Cop is First Witness in Grand Jury Probe of Denhardt Slaying," *Louisville Courier-Journal*, October 5, 1937.

595 Ibid.

596 John Herchenroeder, "Jurors Fail to Take Action in Garr Case," *Louisville Courier-Journal*, October 6, 1937.

597 "Garr Brothers Are Indicted," *Oldham Era*, October 8, 1937.

598 John Herchenroeder, "3 Garrs Indicted After Defense Asks Action," *Louisville Courier-Journal*, October 7, 1937.

599 Ibid.

600 John Herchenroeder, "2 of Garrs to be Tried October 18," *Louisville Courier-Journal*, October 8, 1937.

601 Ibid.

602 "Trial is Set for Monday," *Oldham Era*, October 15, 1937.

603 John Herchenroeder, "7 Selected Tentatively for Garr Jury," *Louisville Courier-Journal*, October 19, 1937.

604 "Garr Brothers Now on Trial," *Oldham Era*, October 22, 1937.

605 John Herchenroeder, "7 Selected Tentatively for Garr Jury," *Louisville Courier-Journal*, October 19, 1937.

606 Ibid.

607 John Herchenroeder, "Handkerchief in Denhardt's Hand," *Louisville Courier-Journal*, October 19, 1937.

608 Ibid.

609 "Garr Bros., Attorneys Smile Their Satisfaction," *Shelbyville Sentinel*, October 22, 1937.

610 John Herchenroeder, "Handkerchief in Denhardt's Hand," *Louisville Courier-Journal*, October 19, 1937.

611 Ibid.

612 Ibid.

613 "Garr Bros., Attorneys Smile Their Satisfaction," *Shelbyville Sentinel*, October 22, 1937.

614 Ibid.

615 John Herchenroeder, "Roy Garr Testifies He Thought Life in Peril," *Louisville Courier-Journal*, October 21, 1937.

616 "Garr Bros., Attorneys Smile Their Satisfaction," *Shelbyville Sentinel*, October 22, 1937.

617 Ibid.

618 John Herchenroeder, "Roy Garr Testifies He Thought Life in Peril," *Louisville Courier-Journal*, October 21, 1937.

619 "Garr Bros., Attorneys Smile Their Satisfaction," *Shelbyville Sentinel*, October 22, 1937.

620 John Herchenroeder, "Roy Garr is Termed Temporarily Insane," *Louisville Courier-Journal*, October 22, 1937.

621 Ibid.

622 Ibid.

623 Ibid.

624 Ibid.

625 Ibid.

626 Ibid.

627 "The vacancy must be filled and those in the know here at Frankfort believe that Major Joseph M. Kelly, Assistant Adjutant General, a Hopkinsville boy and a crack soldier will be named to succeed General Denhardt . . . Kelly has the refusal of the post . . . whether he takes it or not is up to him" in "Moments From the Capitol," *Oldham Era*, October 22, 1937.

628 John Herchenroeder, "Roy Garr is Termed Temporarily Insane," *Louisville Courier-Journal*, October 22, 1937.

629 Ibid.

630 The account of the testimony of Birdie Bennett, Gussie Brawner, and Denhardt's military associates was also related in "Denhardt Assailed by Guard Officers," *New York Times*, October 22, 1937.

631 John Herchenroeder, "Roy Garr is Termed Temporarily Insane," *Louisville Courier-Journal*, October 22, 1937.

632 Mrs. Ralph Gilbert quickly drew the attention of the reporters, but in the group was a young man destined for great things in Kentucky courtrooms. John Palmore, known to his classmates as "Jack," would become an attorney, author, and chief justice of the Kentucky Supreme Court. Seventy-four years later, Justice Palmore still remembered his law school classmates and the day he attended the Garr brothers' trial. He recalled the large crowds in Shelbyville and the packed courthouse. He also remembered the entry of D. W. Griffith and his wife, and recalls with humor

how his male classmates were more impressed by the beautiful Mrs. Griffith than by her famous husband. Retired Chief Justice John Palmore, interview with the author, June 27, 2012.

633 John Herchenroeder, "Roy Garr Acquitted in Slaying of Denhardt," *Louisville Courier-Journal*, October 23, 1937.

634 Ibid.

635 Ibid.

636 Ibid.

637 Ibid.

638 Ibid.

639 Reporters from New York and Chicago who heard the rebel yell were amazed and said they'd never heard anything like it; John Herchenroeder (*Louisville Courier-Journal* reporter), recorded interview with Dr. William Ellis, October 16, 1980. Herchenroeder also wryly commented in the interview that a troop of Marines could not have forced the jury to convict Roy Garr.

640 "Roy Garr is Acquitted," *Oldham Era*, October 29, 1937.

641 Ibid.

642 "Will Drop Charge against Dr. Garr," *New York Times*, October 24, 1937.

643 John Herchenroeder, "Roy Garr Acquitted in Slaying of Denhardt," *Louisville Courier-Journal*, October 23, 1937.

644 "Garrs Turn Down Invitation to Dine," *Twin City News* and *Hammond Times*, October 21, 1937.

645 Jerry Rodgers, telephone interview with author, June 20, 2011.

646 Elsie Frank Mayer, "Kentucky's Bloody Denhardt Feud," *Front Page Detective*, December 1938; M. L. Forgy, "The Truth about General Denhardt, Kentucky's Bizarre Love Drama," *True Detective*, January 1938.

647 Bennett Roach, "Denhardt Case Told in Story, Song," *Shelbyville Sentinel*, November 7, 1984.

648 "Dr. Garr is Dismissed," *Oldham Era*, February 11, 1938.

649 Jane Dixon, "'Denhardt Didn't Shoot My Sister' Dr. Garr Asserts—I Know Who Did," *Louisville Times*, December 8, 1938.

650 Ibid.

651 "Tragic Case is Revived," *Oldham Era*, December 16, 1938.

652 Ibid.

653 Jane Dixon, "'Denhardt Didn't Shoot My Sister' Dr. Garr Asserts—I Know Who Did," *Louisville Times,* December 8, 1938.

654 Tom Ballard, telephone interview with the author, 2011.

655 Arthur McCormack to John Berry, November 15, 1937, folder 5, John Marshall Berry Papers, Filson Historical Society, Louisville, KY.

656 Joseph Woodsen Oglesby, "The Murder Suspect" in *Dinner with D. W. Griffith and Other Memories* (Holicong, PA: Borgo Press, 2005), 85–92.

657 John Ed Pearce, "Murder Most Mysterious," *Louisville Courier-Journal Magazine,* December 8, 1985.

658 Bernard Hamilton, "Three Brothers and the General's Fiancée," *Actual Detective Stories of Women in Crime,* December 1937.

659 Oglesby, *Dinner with D. W. Griffith and Other Memories,* 85–92.

660 Cole family grandson, telephone interview with author, November 23, 2014.

661 John Berry to Jesse Denhardt, May 18, 1938, folder 6, John Marshall Berry Papers, Filson Historical Society, Louisville, KY.

662 "Taylor Killing, Denhardt Trial Set Nation to Arguing," *Louisville Courier-Journal,* September 21, 1937.

ABOUT THE AUTHOR

Ann DAngelo is a licensed Kentucky attorney with an undergraduate degree in history from the University of Louisville and a juris doctor degree from Salmon P. Chase College of Law. Twenty years as an attorney, combined with a lifelong passion for history, have served her well in researching and writing the tragic story of Brigadier General Henry Denhardt and Verna Garr Taylor.